AGENT OF THE IRON CROSS

The Race to Capture German Saboteur-Assassin Lothar Witzke during World War I

Bill Mills

ROWMAN & LITTLEFIELD
Lanham • Boulder • New York • London

Published by Rowman & Littlefield
An imprint of The Rowman & Littlefield Publishing Group, Inc.
4501 Forbes Boulevard, Suite 200, Lanham, Maryland 20706
www.rowman.com

86-90 Paul Street, London EC2A 4NE

British Library Cataloguing in Publication Information Available

Library of Congress Cataloging-in-Publication Data

Names: Mills, William B., 1958– author.
Title: Agent of the Iron Cross : the race to capture German saboteur-assassin Lothar
  Witzke during World War I / Bill Mills.
Other titles: Race to capture German saboteur-assassin Lothar Witzke during World
  War I
Description: Lanham : Rowman & Littlefield, [2024] | Includes bibliographical
  references and index.
Identifiers: LCCN 2023016439 (print) | LCCN 2023016440 (ebook) | ISBN
  9781538182086 (cloth) | ISBN 9781538182079 (epub)
Subjects: LCSH: Witzke, Lothar, 1895–1962 | Jahnke, Kurt, 1882–1945? | Espionage,
  German—United States—History—20th century. | Germans—United States—
  History—20th century. | World War, 1914–1918—Secret service—Germany. |
  Subversive activities—United States—History—20th century. | World War, 1914–
  1918—United States. | Spies—Germany—History—20th century.
Classification: LCC D639.S8 W58 2024 (print) | LCC D639.S8 (ebook) | DDC
  940.48743092 [B]—dc23/eng/20230509
LC record available at https://lccn.loc.gov/2023016439
LC ebook record available at https://lccn.loc.gov/2023016440

♾️™ The paper used in this publication meets the minimum requirements of
American National Standard for Information Sciences—Permanence of Paper
for Printed Library Materials, ANSI/NISO Z39.48-1992.

For Butcher, Altendorf, and Gleaves

Contents

Acknowledgments   ix

1   Escape from Valparaiso   1

2   The Most Deadly Sabotage Team in History   15

3   "You Will Have to Kill Him First. He's in Our Way."   43

4   "I Am Mr. Butcher's Man!"   61

5   "Get Down and Hang On!"   81

6   Placed Together, the Two Scraps of Paper Read: "NOVIA"   93

7   Crossing the Line   107

8   Breaking the Code   125

9   The Court-Martial of Lothar Witzke   141

10   The Jailbreak of Lothar Witzke   157

11   "Every Activity Is to Be Suspended . . ."   165

Notes   189

Bibliography   239

Index   243

Acknowledgments

The "Witzke Affair," Germany's attempt to launch a campaign of sabotage and insurrection across the United States in 1918 is one of the least-known episodes of the First World War. Fortunately, it is also one of the best documented. I first became aware of Witzke's daring mission after reading a brief overview of the operation contained in Captain Henry Landau's classic 1937 work on World War I espionage, *The Enemy Within*. Like many of the German schemes intended to exploit the sociopolitical weaknesses of her enemies, the Witzke mission was the intelligence game played at its highest level, with a plan for destruction on a massive scale, violent insurrection, assassination, master spies and double agents, diabolical sabotage devices, secret codes, and invisible ink.

It is the stuff of legend, and in recent years I began collecting information on this fascinating adventure for a possible book project. The chance discovery of an original set of bound volumes of the "Mixed Claims Commission, United States and Germany, Claimants Exhibits" published by the Lehigh Valley Railroad Company at a used book shop (with the complete trial record of the Lothar Witzke court-martial) provided a giant leap forward. Further months of detective work and additional source material generously supplied by the researchers and archivists noted below allowed me to begin writing the manuscript that developed into *Agent of the Iron Cross*.

Many talented individuals assisted in gathering the information for this book. Dr. John A. Arnold (NICOM Inc.) did an outstanding job combing through records and retrieving documents on the Witzke mission held at the National Archives at College Park, Maryland. Melissa Davis, director of library and archives at the George C. Marshall Foundation Library, Lexington, Virginia, was extremely helpful in locating an original dissertation and notes on the solution of the Waberski cipher written by John Matthews Manly in the library's William F. Friedman Collection. Adriana Luchian Soares provided a translation of Albert Pagel's autobiography, *Mein Leben*, describing his involvement with SMS *Dresden* in 1915. Jane Parr, archivist for acquisitions at the Howard Gottlieb Archival Research Center, Boston University, located information on Kurt Jahnke and German intelligence. Alexa Tulk, public services supervisor at the Hanna Holborn Gray Special Collections Research Center, University of Chicago Library, gave generously of her time in searching the John Matthews Manly Papers for documents related to the Waberski cipher. Michael Pinder employed his incredible digital graphics talents to restore many of the aged, timeworn photographs that were uncovered. Matt De Waelsche, archivist/librarian at the Texana Genealogy Department, San Antonio Public Library, provided postwar information on Byron Butcher.

I am also very thankful for the support and guidance of my exceptional agent Anne Devlin, and for the enthusiasm and professional skill of the editorial and production staff at Rowman & Littlefield, especially Ashley Dodge, Laney Ackley, and Jehanne Schweitzer.

For the assistance provided by all of these individuals, I remain deeply grateful.

I

Escape from Valparaiso

The hurricane was building in intensity when Pagels sailed out of Punta Arenas harbor and turned south into the storm. His twenty-six foot fishing boat, *Elfriede*, equipped with a tired one-cylinder engine and rigged with a small sail, seemed a doubtful proposition for the voyage. Even in good weather, the waters of the lower Chilean coast from the Magellan Straits to Cape Horn were among the most dangerous in the world. Poorly charted and strewn with submerged rocks, the channels and waterways were swept with choppy swells, strong currents, and williwaws—sudden, violent blasts of wind that appeared out of nowhere. Lashed by a rain-driven squall and heavy waves, Pagels steered the small craft toward a passage that only he knew about, Pedro Sound, a mere dotted line on the English nautical maps. He glanced at Schindlich's face and saw the same look of uncertainty and determination as on his own. They would have to endure another 130 miles of these torturous conditions before reaching their destination, an obscure cove at the mouth of Barbara Channel called Hewett Bay. But there was no question of turning back. If they failed in their mission, the lives of two thousand men would be lost.

Albert Pagels was a thirty-six-year-old seaman with a bright red beard and a hardy disposition, originally from the German island of Rügen on the Baltic Sea. As a youth, Pagels had enlisted in the Kaiserliche Marine, eventually rising to the rank of bosun's mate, and in 1900 saw active service in

China during the Boxer Rebellion. While participating in a ground assault on the Taku forts guarding the city of Taijin, Pagel's left hand was nearly blown off when the service rifle that he was carrying burst upon firing. His naval career over, the adventurous mariner emigrated to Punta Arenas, where he found work as a miner, fisherman, and seal trapper, in time earning enough money to buy the *Elfriede*. Pagels became so knowledgeable about the remote mountainous Patagonian region of southern Chile, and the labyrinth of channels and fjords along its coast, that he was hired as a guide by a succession of scientific expeditions that came to the area, including an exploration led by the renowned botanist Carl Skottsberg.

On the stormy afternoon of December 6, 1914, Pagels was at home nursing his wounded hand, which grew sore in wet weather, when he was surprised to hear pounding at the door. He was greeted by a group of prominent officials that included the German consul of Punta Arenas, Rudolph Stubenrauch; Oberleutnant Carl zur Helle of the German navy; shipping agent Walter Curtze of the Kosmos Line; and the first officer of the freighter *Amasis*. The men wasted no time in announcing the reason for their visit. Admiral von Spee's East Asia Cruiser Squadron was in imminent danger of being destroyed!

The East Asia Squadron, Kreuzergeschwader Ostasien, was a naval force created to safeguard the German colonies of Asia and project the kaiser's power into the Pacific Ocean. Four months earlier when the world war began, the seven cruisers of the squadron had been scattered across the Pacific, from Tsingtao in China to the western coast of Mexico. The warships were quickly assembled into a battle group, and after a few changes in the formation—the cruiser *Emden* was dispatched on a lone raiding mission to the Indian Ocean—the squadron set course for South America, where it was expected that enemy merchantmen would be vulnerable and an ample supply of coal could be obtained. The far-ranging cruisers had a voracious appetite for coal, with bunker capacities ranging from 850 to 2,000 tons; to travel just one mile at high speed, a heavy steamship consumed a ton of coal. German naval strategy in Pacific and South American waters would be heavily influenced by access to this critical commodity.

The Kreuzergeschwader was led by aristocratic Vice Admiral Maximilian Graf von Spee, a confident and aggressive naval commander. On November 1, von Spee had engaged a squadron of British warships off Coronel and in less than two hours sank two enemy cruisers against a loss of three German sailors wounded. It was the Royal Navy's first defeat in over one hundred years, and when von Spee's armada arrived at the Chilean port of Valparaiso for coal and supplies, the men of the *geschwader* were hailed as heroes by the local German community. Informed that strong Allied naval forces were now forming in the Pacific, and with future sources of coal uncertain, von Spee decided to cruise around Cape Horn into the Atlantic and attack the British wireless and coaling station at Port Stanley in the Falkland Islands, then follow a northward route back to Germany.

At Punta Arenas on December 6, Consul Stubenrauch received an urgent message from Montevideo that two powerful British battle cruisers, the *Invincible* and the *Inflexible*, along with an escort of smaller ships had been seen departing the Uruguayan harbor and were now converging on Port Stanley. Stubenrauch didn't know the current whereabouts of von Spee's cruisers but assumed that they were also steaming toward the Falklands—to the very location where the powerful British warships waited. With their heavy long-range guns and superior speed, the British battle cruisers would be sure to overtake and annihilate the German squadron.

Stubenrauch and the three marine officials raced to Pagels's house and outlined the desperate situation to the veteran sailor. The only means to warn von Spee that he was sailing into a trap was to get a message to the wireless station on board the German freighter *Amasis*, anchored 130 miles away at Hewett Bay.

"My dear Pagels, can you go out to sea this evening with an important telegram to warn the Count Spee squadron?" Stubenrauch anxiously inquired. "If you agree, you must leave your sailor [deckhand] here, and in exchange, we will give you a man from the *Amasis*, one who was once your comrade in the war in China."

Pagels response was immediate: "I jumped out of bed with both legs at the same time and immediately agreed to undertake the risky mission."

At the German consulate, Pagels was reunited with an old friend from the Boxer Rebellion, Karl Schindlich, and the two men were sworn in as soldiers of the German army on active duty. Daylight was fast receding as they hastily prepared the *Elfriede* for the demanding journey. It would be a race against the clock to reach the *Amasis* in time to warn von Spee before his squadron arrived at the Falklands.

Within hours, the small craft left the sheltered waters of the harbor and entered the Strait of Magellan into the brunt of the hurricane. Struggling against heavy wind and towering waves, the fishing boat traveled at a snail's pace, while the men hunched inside, "soaked and shivering, like a pair of climbing mice" (slang for "drowning rats"). They would be fortunate to escape with their lives. More than once, the rush of incoming waves nearly swamped the *Elfriede*, forcing her exhausted crew to land the boat and bail out water before proceeding.

As they approached the Cockburn Channel on the second day of their odyssey, Pagels spotted a distant cruiser passing through the channel at high speed. From the ship's silhouette, he immediately recognized it as a German capital ship—the *Dresden*. Pagels turned the *Elfriede* toward the warship, and Schindlich waved a half-stick German flag, but the *Dresden* showed no interest in their little craft and steamed quickly past without stopping.

On December 9, after seventy-two hours spent battling through the hurricane, they reached the *Amasis* and boarded the freighter in total darkness, "more dead than alive." Pagels's head was pounding from lack of sleep and the pain of his injured hand as he turned over the crucial message. There was a flurry of excitement, and the men rushed to the *Amasis*'s Telefunken room, where Pagels and Schindlich joined the ship's officers gathering around the wireless set. The room grew quiet as the radio operator began tapping the Morse key: "Von Spee—von Spee—von Spee—*Amasis* calling—*Amasis* calling . . ."

The men glanced at one another expectantly, waiting for the admiral's response. Hearing only silence in return, the radio operator began transmitting once again. "Von Spee—von Spee—von Spee—*Amasis* calling . . ."

The signal was repeated again and again for twenty minutes without any response, and then the room grew still as a terrible realization dawned upon them. There would be no earthly answer to the radio call—the East Asia Squadron had ceased to exist. Vice Admiral von Spee, the two thousand men of his command, and four German cruisers were now resting in the cold darkness five thousand feet below on the floor of the Atlantic Ocean.

The morning before Pagels's fishing boat reached the *Amasis*, von Spee's squadron had arrived at the Falkland Islands. According to a prearranged plan, the armored cruiser *Gneisenau* and light cruiser *Nürnberg* detached from the Kreuzergeschwader formation and cautiously advanced into Port Stanley harbor on reconnaissance. It was a clear, sunny day, and their lookouts soon spotted pillars of black coal smoke rising in the distance. Assuming that the British were destroying their coal reserve to prevent it from falling into German hands, they moved closer and were startled to see that the smoke came from the funnels of British capital ships moored in the harbor—a total of six enemy cruisers in all. As if to underscore the imminent danger, a salvo of twelve-inch shells from a grounded British battleship flashed across the water at the two invaders. The heavy projectiles passed overhead without causing any damage, but the message was clear and the German cruisers quickly withdrew from the harbor to rejoin the squadron.

The British warships fired up their boilers, and soon the chase was on. British Vice Admiral Frederick Sturdee steamed out of Port Stanley in command of a squadron that included two heavily-armed battle cruisers, two armored cruisers, and two light cruisers, the British battle cruisers racing through the water at their top speed of twenty-five knots. The pursuit lasted four hours, and then Sturdee's force closed in on the German warships. Following an intense cannonade, the *Scharnhorst* was the first to sink, her superstructure a shambles of smoking, twisted steel. The *Gneisenau* went down next; straddled by British shells and turning out of control, her crew set off explosive charges and opened the torpedo tubes to scuttle the ship rather than surrender. Overwhelmed by a barrage of cannon fire from three of Sturdee's cruisers, the *Leipzig* was completely ablaze when she rolled over and sank. The *Nürnberg* was the last German cruiser to go down; her boilers having burst under the stress of the chase and the bridge a mass of flames, the warship slowly rolled onto her side and disappeared beneath the waves.

The only ships of the Kreuzergeschwader that escaped destruction that day were the *Seydlitz*, a former liner–turned–hospital ship that sailed into internment at San Antonio Oeste, Argentina, and the light cruiser *Dresden*, the same warship that Pagels had seen steaming through the Cockburn Channel at high speed.

Downhearted at having arrived too late to warn von Spee, Pagels returned to Punta Arenas only to discover that he was still on active duty—with a new assignment from Consul Stubenrauch. During his absence, the *Dresden* had paid a brief visit to the port in search of fuel. After requisitioning a small supply of coal briquettes, the fugitive cruiser departed for Hewett Bay, forty miles to the east. A few hours later, the Royal Navy armored cruiser HMS *Kent* appeared and, learning that they had just missed their elusive opponent, alerted London that the *Dresden* was in Chilean waters. The British Admiralty immediately assigned four cruisers—the *Kent*, *Glasgow*, *Bristol*, and *Carnarvon*—to patrol the fjords and channels around Tierra del Fuego in search of the German warship. Pagels's new mission was to find the *Dresden*'s hiding place without the British becoming aware, and then render all possible assistance.

The indefatigable seal trapper loaded the *Elfriede* with provisions and set sail for Hewett Bay, where he quickly located the hidden cruiser in a sheltered inlet. Over the next twelve days, the red-bearded war veteran made three trips to the *Dresden*, delivering supplies and updating her crew with the latest information on the British navy's efforts to find them.

On his last visit to the stranded warship, Pagels was informed by Fregattenkapitän Lüdecke, the *Dresden*'s commander, that a motorboat called the *Galilee* had passed by with a Frenchman and Russian on board scouting grazing land for their sheep. Instantly suspicious that the interlopers were working for the British, Pagels advised Lüdecke to raise anchor at once and sail for Christmas Bay, an inlet that appeared on nautical charts as unexplored dry land, but which was in fact a sheltered waterway.

"This time I was not forty-eight hours late, but twenty-four hours early!" he would later recall.

After leading the *Dresden* to its new hideaway, Pagels returned to Punta Arenas to keep watch over enemy activity in the port. Although the British warships had departed, a commotion around one of the boats aroused his curiosity. A local tug, the *Eduardo*, chartered by a trio of miners was being readied for a prospecting expedition. Pagels was an experienced pitman, having worked the mines of lower Patagonia, and the "miners'" unusual behavior made it obvious that they were in reality Royal Navy spotters "prospecting" for the *Dresden*. When the *Eduardo* departed the harbor, Pagels shadowed the tug from a discreet distance in the *Elfriede* and was relieved to see the suspect vessel turn south toward Cape Horn, away from the *Dresden*'s remote sanctuary. But his own movements had not gone unnoticed along the waterfront. Within days, a stranger appeared at the landing and offered him £5,000 "to remain neutral"—or else. Pagels declined the man's proposition, but from that point forward he never left the town, or even went to sleep, without a Winchester rifle tucked safely beneath his arm.

On his return voyage to Punta Arenas, Pagels had noticed the *Elfriede*'s engine running roughly. When he removed the cylinder head and checked inside the motor, he was horrified to discover two holes in the cylinder wall. An attempt to repair the damage using iron putty proved unsuccessful, so Pagels consulted an engineer from the interned steamer *Tucuman*, who compressed hard rubber into the holes. Soon the boat's engine was running like new, and thereafter the *Elfriede* became known as the "rubber steamer" throughout Tierra del Fuego.

Safe in its remote hideaway at Christmas Bay, the *Dresden* was out of danger for the moment, but her future was far from certain. The warship's coal bunkers were almost empty and her provisions nearly exhausted; the cruiser could neither escape into the Pacific nor return to Germany, while a powerful squadron of British warships prowled the surrounding waters trying to locate and destroy the renegade vessel.

The First Lord of the Admiralty, Winston Churchill, had said that the ships of the East Asia Squadron sailing without certain access to coal were like "a cut flower in a vase, fair to see yet sure to die." Unless the *Dresden*'s coal supply was replenished soon, Churchill's prophecy was sure to come true for the German sailors stranded at Christmas Bay.

In late December the outlook for their survival brightened when an un-expected visitor arrived in Chilean waters. The North German Lloyd pas-senger liner *Sierra Cordoba* steamed into the Magellan Straits laden with a cargo of 1,500 tons of coal and a rich stock of supplies. Heinrich Schaeffer, the captain of the enormous vessel, had never visited the canals of Tierra del Fuego before and was unaware that they were now under the watch of Royal Navy cruisers. Schaeffer's ignorance of the straits would be the key to his success when he decided to enter the port by the most dangerous route imaginable: across the Orange Bank. The nautical charts of the day were covered with warning notes about the Orange Bank, but no depth readings were listed. Schaeffer had no way of knowing that the water level in the passage was so shallow and variable at three to fifteen fathoms that printed depth readings would have been superfluous, or that the bank was being ignored by British navy spotters for the same reason; no one in their right mind would ever attempt to cross it. Against all odds, Schaeffer brought the huge liner in at high tide, maneuvered through the narrows, and surged straight over the Orange Bank, skirting the coast of Tierra del Fuego, and into the harbor. Then the proud captain steamed majestically into port, serenely unaware that he had just performed a miracle.

The *Sierra Cordoba* was met at her mooring by Consul Stubenrauch who provided Schaeffer with the *Dresden*'s present location, and the pas-senger liner immediately departed for Christmas Bay under a full head of steam. Two hours later, HMS *Kent* arrived in Punta Arenas and, learning that a German liner had just left, raced off in pursuit. A few miles beyond Cape Froward, the British armored cruiser intercepted the *Sierra Cordoba* but was prevented from capturing the supply ship by the timely arrival of a Chilean destroyer which demanded that the *Kent* vacate the neutral wa-ters. Not wanting to cause an international incident, the Royal Navy cruiser withdrew, and the *Sierra Cordoba* proceeded to the Martinez Inlet, an isolated bay enclosed by steep cliffs where she could remain safely hidden, but still one hundred miles away from the stranded *Dresden*.

With the *Elfriede*'s engine repaired and the small boat operable once again, Pagels departed on a new mission for Stubenrauch. His orders were to deliver a set of replacement codebooks to the *Sierra Cordoba*, whose crew had ditched their own codebooks when the *Kent* had been sighted.

Pagels departed Punta Arenas on a chilly December night, cruising slowly past snow-covered mountains into the darkened channel. At two o'clock in the morning, the fog over the water lifted, and he spotted six plumes of smoke dead ahead—the British cruisers *Kent* and *Carnavon*.

The seal trapper said of the tense moment:

I was caught in a bad trap. The English must have seen me. If I turned away they would certainly have hunted me, and that I was a liaison to the *Dresden* "all the sparrows whistled from the roofs" in Punta Arenas.

Pagels decided his only chance to avoid arrest would be to play innocent. He sailed between the two cruisers and dropped anchor, then cast his fishing nets and waited. A few hours later the enemy warships steamed off, one to the north and the other to the south.

Deciding that it was too dangerous to visit the *Sierra Cordoba* with British cruisers in the area, Pagels changed plans and set course for the *Dresden* instead. He had not traveled far into the Magellan Straits when he was spotted by yet another British cruiser, the HMS *Glasgow*, which raced toward the *Elfriede* at high speed. The seal trapper turned away and disappeared into a maze of nearby channels, losing the *Glasgow* in the darkness with the help of a muffler that he had invented—a perforated kerosene canister wrapped in canvas that reduced the sound of the boat's exhaust to a light chirp.

Once the coast was clear, Pagels resumed his journey and reached the *Dresden* at eleven o'clock in the morning. The prospects for the stranded cruiser did not appear promising; the *Dresden* was out of fuel and unable to escape, while its only source of coal, the *Sierra Cordoba*, remained idle in an isolated inlet one hundred miles away, trapped by a squadron of British cruisers patrolling the waters. With few alternatives remaining, Lüdecke handed the seal trapper a sealed envelope to deliver to Captain Schaeffer on the *Sierra Cordoba* containing written instructions to clear the ship's engines the following evening at eight o'clock and proceed to Christmas Bay under Pagels's command.

The voyage to the liner's hideaway at Martinez Inlet nearly proved to be Pagels's undoing. The Cockburn Channel was wracked by a heavy storm, and he had to steer the *Elfriede* directly into its fury. Only by hugging the extreme east side of the channel was he able to avoid three British cruisers that had taken up station at Sholl Bay. When he handed the instructions from Lüdecke to the liner's captain, "Schaeffer was shocked at Lüdecke's order to turn over command of his precious ship to the disreputable-looking ruffian [Pagels]." But a local German pilot sent by Consul Stubenrauch had balked at the idea of leading the *Sierra Cordoba* through the British blockade, and Schaeffer was left with no other option.

The *Elfriede* was hauled aboard the huge liner, and her funnel was wrapped with wire mesh to prevent airborne sparks from betraying them.

At precisely eight o'clock on the night of January 4, 1915, with boiler pressure at the maximum, the anchor was raised, and the *Sierra Cordoba* got underway. For the first ten miles of the journey the supply ship was concealed from view by mountains, and then they turned into Keats Sound where the British cruisers waited. Here fate played a hand once again when a blizzard magically appeared, driven by heavy winds from the snow-capped mountains. The snowfall reduced visibility to less than one hundred meters on the pitch-black night, and they passed the British warships unseen. The liner continued eastward, and with Captain Schaeffer standing beside him nervously grinding his teeth, Pagels guided the *Sierra Cordoba* through a treacherous path of rocky reefs and small islets.

The most difficult obstacle would be the last—threading the 1,500-ton liner through the Christmas Bay channel, a meandering passage that was only one hundred yards wide and riddled with sharp cliffs. Crossing the waterway would have been dangerous for a ship half the size of the *Sierra Cordoba*, but once again their luck held. The heavy liner twisted through at high tide and, with a raging current augmenting its twin screws, entered the bay without running aground. A roar of cheers broke out from the men of both ships as the *Sierra Cordoba* dropped anchor four hundred yards from the German cruiser.

The *Dresden*'s coal bunkers were filled to capacity, and on February 4, Lüdecke departed Christmas Bay for an uncharted fjord on the Isla Santa Ines that offered a discreet entrance to the Pacific Ocean. With a heavy heart, Pagels bade the cruiser farewell for the last time. The seal trapper returned to Punta Arenas and continued to sail the *Elfriede* through the channels and inlets of Tierra del Fuego on spurious voyages to make the British believe the *Dresden* was still hiding there.

In recognition of the perilous missions he had undertaken to safeguard the warships of the Kreuzergeschwader, the German government awarded Albert Pagels the Iron Cross, First and Second Class.

On February 14, 1915, Captain Lüdecke took the *Dresden* into the Pacific and set a westerly course to intercept the merchant shipping lane that ran three hundred nautical miles from the Chilean coast. But the opportunities to capture a prize proved slim. In two weeks of sailing, the only vessel the cruiser came upon was the English sailing bark *Conway Castle* en route to Queensland, Australia, with a cargo of 2,400 tons of barley. After the crew had been safely transferred to the *Dresden*, the outdated windjammer was sent to the bottom.

On March 8, the *Dresden* was en route for a rendezvous with the German collier *Gotha* to replenish her coal stocks when she was sighted by the

HMS *Kent*. The British armored cruiser raced toward the commerce raider at maximum speed—but it was not enough; the lighter *Dresden* turned to the west and disappeared over the horizon. This time her destination would be Isla Más a Tierra, a remote island 360 miles from the Chilean mainland where Lüdecke hoped to repair the cruiser's failing engines.

At this point the luck that had favored the *Dresden* since the Falklands battle passed to the British. A German wireless message was intercepted revealing her position, and HMS *Kent*, HMS *Glasgow*, and the armed merchant cruiser *Orama* cornered their elusive prey at Cumberland Bay on the northeast coast of the island. Although the *Dresden* was anchored in neutral Chilean waters, she was not interned, and her battle flag was still flying. Lüdecke faced a vastly superior enemy force in a cruiser with leaking pipelines, several boilers out of commission, and only eighty tons of coal remaining.

But he still refused to surrender.

The British cruisers opened fire at a range of 8,500 yards. Flames instantly broke out in the *Dresden*'s rear magazine, and succeeding blasts knocked out the raider's guns one by one. Within minutes the German colors were lowered, and a white ensign was raised. Eight *Dresden* sailors had been killed and twenty-nine wounded during the brief engagement. The remaining crewmembers abandoned ship, either taking to the lifeboats or jumping over the side and swimming to the neutral shore, while belowdecks a scuttling party set to work opening the sea cocks and preparing explosive charges for demolition.

Lüdecke dispatched his adjutant, Oberleutnant Wilhelm Canaris, in a steam launch to negotiate with the British squadron commander. Canaris protested that the cruiser was now in neutral waters and that continued aggression was illegal under international law. But his complaint fell on deaf ears. Royal Navy captain John Luce responded that he would accept nothing but unconditional surrender. Canaris steamed back to the derelict cruiser. The German battle ensign was immediately raised and the scuttling charges fired. There was a violent explosion, and the *Dresden* sank by the bow in two hundred feet of water.

The injured survivors from the *Dresden* were transported on the British warship *Orama* to hospitals in Valparaiso, while the rest of the ship's company was interned, first on the North German Lloyd liner *Yorck*, and then on Quiriquina Island near Concepción. Although the men were warned by their superiors against trying to escape, days of boredom in captivity and a desire to return to duty led many of the *Dresden*'s former crewmembers to take flight. As one boilerman said, "The officers used to rant and rave about not escaping, but Chilean fishermen would take you to the mainland for 20 pesos and all the shouting in the world couldn't combat that."

Among the first to depart was Oberleutnant Canaris, who escaped from the internment camp on Quiriquina Island disguised as a peasant. He journeyed 270 miles north to Osorno and crossed the Cordillera de los Andes range on horseback to Neuquén, the largest city in Argentine Patagonia. From there, Canaris made his way by train one thousand miles to Buenos Aires, where an agent at the German embassy obtained a passport for him in the name of Reed Rosa, a fictitious Chilean businessman. He booked passage on a Dutch steamer to Rotterdam and then crossed the Netherlands border into Germany, arriving three months after leaving Chile. (Wilhelm Canaris would engage in secret operations for Germany into the 1930s. He was chosen to lead the Abwehr, the army military intelligence organization, in 1935. Ten years later, suspected of conspiring against Adolf Hitler, Canaris was executed at Flossenbürg concentration camp.)

An even more daring escape by *Dresden* crewmen was made aboard the sailing ship *Tinto*. The 460-ton bark was badly in disrepair when it was purchased by a wealthy German-Chilean businessman to repatriate German sailors exiled in Chile. The sixty-four-year-old coastal trading vessel was secretly renovated and, with a crew consisting of nine escaped seamen from the *Dresden*, sixteen midshipmen from the interned German training ship *Herzogin Cecilie*, and four sailors from the steamer *Göttingen*, set sail from the Chilean island of Chiloé for Cape Horn. The *Tinto* rounded the Horn and by avoiding the main shipping routes managed to disappear into a lonely expanse of the Atlantic. After 126 days at sea on a voyage that traversed twelve thousand miles of open ocean, the escape ship reached Trondheim, Norway, where the fugitive sailors obtained safe passage to Germany.

One of the youngest members of the *Dresden* crew to escape from Chile was naval cadet Lothar Witzke, but his return from internment would have the greatest impact on Germany's fortunes during the war.

Lothar Witzke was born in Kreis Koschmin in the province of Posen, Prussia, on May 15, 1895. Following three years of primary schooling and nine years of secondary education, Witzke attended the prestigious Royal Academy of Posen for a year before entering the German naval academy Marineschule Mürwick, located in the northern coastal city of Flensburg. At the age of nineteen, the mechanically inclined *kadett* was posted to the *Dresden* as a midshipman and journeyed across the Pacific on the cruiser's far-ranging voyages. He would recall:

The war automatically transferred all of the cadets, like myself, to the Navy. We soon saw active duty, for the southern coasts of South America assumed vital importance as a theater of conflict.

Witzke survived the Falklands Islands battle and was a party to the elusive cat-and-mouse struggle with the British navy in the waters of Tierra del Fuego. During the *Dresden*'s final engagement at Isla Más a Tierra, the young midshipman received a shrapnel wound that tore into his left leg and fractured his patella (kneecap). For the rest of his life, Witzke would walk with a delayed stride, described as "a slight crippling effect." Captured after the battle, he was taken aboard the *Orama* with the other seriously wounded sailors and transported to a hospital in Valparaiso.

Lothar Witzke was a "well-built, athletic young fellow, good looking, with keen blue eyes, fair hair, and ruddy complexion." Highly sociable, with his blond hair brushed straight back and a disarming smile, Witzke became the proverbial sailor with a girlfriend in every port. One observer called him "a very likeable boy and an outstanding example of the Prussian military training on an idealistic temperament. . . . He has a very persuasive manner of talking which has every tendency to carry conviction."

Witzke's engaging manner, combined with a serious leg wound, likely caused those watching him to lower their guard during his weeks of convalescence, and one day when their eyes were looking elsewhere, he simply got out of bed and walked away. For his captors to have considered Witzke in a weakened state was a mistake; he was formidable, athletic, and capable of withstanding great pain. His file at the British secret intelligence service MI6 would describe him as "Broad shouldered and strong. Powerful." Once free of hospital confinement, Witzke was able to obtain a berth as a seaman on a steamship headed north:

> Our usefulness in Chile thus ended, I sought action elsewhere. I stowed away on the SS *Colusa*, a Grace Line boat under the British flag. When I was discovered aboard I posed as a Dane, claiming that I was born in Copenhagen and that I had lost my seaman's papers. I was so youthful-looking and resembled a Dane so closely that my story was accepted and I was signed on at Arica.

Witzke arrived in San Francisco during the early summer of 1915. The fugitive naval cadet would need money and travel documents to continue his journey home, so he called at the German consulate on Sansome Street, a ten-story brick building located a few blocks from the waterfront. There he met Consul General Franz Bopp, a heavyset diplomat with a walrus mustache and pince-nez glasses who ran the consulate with the support of two assistants, Vice Consul E. H. von Schack and military attaché Lieutenant Wilhelm von Brincken.

Since the outbreak of war, the consulate had been besieged by German reservists seeking help in returning home from neutral America, but most routes to the Fatherland had been closed by the British naval blockade. For a time, operatives working for the German embassy in Washington were able to purchase neutral passports that they doctored to enable reservists to pass through Allied checkpoints, but the scheme was exposed in January 1915 and the embassy's hirelings arrested. Now there was little that German consular officials could do to assist servicemen hoping to circumvent the blockade.

Bopp proposed an alternative to the injured veteran. Since Witzke was a sworn officer of the German navy and could be trusted with matters of utmost secrecy, would he work for the consulate as a courier delivering confidential messages? With no other options, Witzke accepted the consul's offer, and in the months that followed he crossed the country hand delivering secret letters and documents from Bopp to German officials. But after the thrill of wartime action aboard the *Dresden* and the exhilaration of life on the run following his escape from Chile, Witzke soon grew weary of being a consulate letter carrier: "I was getting tired of working where I was a messenger. I was crippled and could not do much work [but wanted more]."

Consul Bopp sympathized with the youth's plight and put him in touch with a man handling special tasks for the consulate—a man who could provide work more to his liking.

2

The Most Deadly Sabotage Team in History

Kurt Jahnke was a frequent visitor to the German consulate in San Francisco in 1915, where he could often be seen in private conversation with Consul Bopp. Those who knew Jahnke at the time would recall his common, everyman appearance: six feet tall and slim, light brown hair, small brown mustache, and thin face with a long thin nose. He wore decent clothes "but could not wear them well." His most distinguishing characteristic was his upper front teeth, made of solid gold. But Jahnke preferred to maintain a low profile. His unremarkable looks and ability to disappear in a crowd would become a significant asset in his future pursuits, for in the shadowy world of espionage, Kurt Jahnke was a self-made American success story.

Born on February 17, 1882, to a Junker family living on a municipal estate in Gnesen, in the Prussian province of Posen (less than twenty-five miles from where Witzke was raised), Kurt Albert Jahnke emigrated to the United States at the age of seventeen and became a naturalized U.S. citizen.

Little is known of his early life in America. In March 1909, Jahnke enlisted in the U.S. Marine Corps at the recruiting office in Detroit, Michigan, and to improve his chances of being accepted, he shaved six years off the birth date that he entered on the enlistment papers. Even then, twenty-seven was considered a late age to enlist as a private in the Marine Corps. The new recruit received basic training at the Marine Barracks on Mare Island, a major U.S. naval base and shipyard located twenty-five miles northeast of San Francisco in Vallejo, California. He was briefly posted to the Marine Corps base on Pearl Harbor in the territory of Hawaii before being transferred to Company C, 1st Regiment, at Cavite on the Philippine Islands. While on duty in the Pacific, Jahnke contracted malaria and was shipped back to Mare Island to recover. He separated from the Marine Corps on a medical discharge in February 1910 after only eleven months of active duty.

Following his service with the Marines, Jahnke joined the U.S. Customs Service, where the knowledge that he gained in the methods used to prevent smuggling would prove highly lucrative in his next occupation: professional smuggler.

While living in San Francisco, Jahnke had made many friends among the Asian residents of the city's Chinatown. At the time, it was desperately important to Chinese living in America that their deceased relatives be buried with their ancestors in the land of their birth, but for sanitary reasons, U.S. authorities prohibited the export of dead bodies to China. Jahnke conceived a brilliant, if highly unusual, scheme to profit from the situation. He arranged for zinc boxes to be manufactured that could be soldered shut to act as airtight containers for wooden coffins. These he could ship to Shanghai and Hong Kong, and for every corpse he sent to China, Jahnke received a fee of $1,000. Soon he was a very rich man. "So grateful were the Chinese that with the most solemn rites they made him a member of the family of the great Sun Yat-sen. This, of course, provided Jahnke with the best possible contacts in China. The later Madame Chiang Kai-shek, for instance, was a member of this family." While profiting from illegal body export, Jahnke made even more money in the reverse direction, smuggling opium and contraband cigars *into* the United States.

When Lothar Witzke met Jahnke in San Francisco, the former Marine was working as a patrolman for the Morse Patrol. The Harry N. Morse Patrol System and Detective Service was a West Coast competitor of its more widely known rival, the Pinkerton National Detective Agency. Founded by Henry Nicholson "Harry" Morse, a sheriff who had gained fame in the nineteenth century by capturing stagecoach robbers and other western desperados, the Morse Patrol was a security service that guarded private estates and commercial property throughout the Bay Area. If his employer had been aware of Jahnke's history, it would have seemed odd that an individual so wealthy had taken a job as a night watchman at a rate of twenty-five cents an hour. But a position with the Morse Patrol conferred an image of integrity; many Morse patrolmen were former San Francisco police officers, and it was an excellent cover for illegal activities. Guarding commercial buildings also provided Jahnke with fine training for a new field that he entered with the outbreak of the world war: freelance saboteur for the German consulate.

When the Great War began in July 1914, German strategy was based on achieving a fast and decisive victory by invading France through neutral Belgium to seize Paris. When Generaloberst von Moltke's drive was repulsed at the Marne River, the German army and the Allied armies of Britain and France attempted to outflank one another in a race to the sea, moving steadily northward, and soon faced one another across 475 miles of unbroken trench lines that extended from Switzerland to the North Sea. What had been envisioned as a war of speed and mobility descended into a remorseless stalemate, with millions of men held immobile within layered trench works ringed with barbed wire and machine guns. The "no man's land" between the lines became a wasteland dominated by artillery fire. The bombardment was devastating and relentless; during major engagements the opposing armies would literally fire millions of artillery rounds within a single day. It has been estimated that artillery shells were responsible for two-thirds of all deaths and injuries on the western front during the First World War.

The munitions factories of Europe were unprepared for the insatiable demand for artillery ammunition resulting from trench warfare and turned to manufacturers in the neutral United States to make up the shortfall. Although U.S. companies were prepared to accept orders for munitions from either side in the conflict, the British naval blockade of war supplies to the Central Powers meant that in reality shipments could only be sent to the Allies. During the fall of 1914, purchasing agents from Britain, France, and Russia descended on the United States and negotiated huge contracts with American manufacturers for artillery projectiles, fuzes, gunpowder, and a wide range of other military goods. Overnight, the business outlook in America changed from a deep recession to a boom economy, with companies making artillery shells posting huge gains. The earnings of the U.S. Steel Corporation quickly rose to the highest level in the corporation's history.

For the German General Staff now at war on two fronts, the Allies' access to a near limitless supply of munitions was nothing short of catastrophic. As one officer noted, "it was a spectre, an intangible phantom, against which strategy, tactics, and all the courage of the German soldier was helpless. These shipments of American munitions were the ghost which haunted the corridors of the Army Command in Charleville." When German diplomatic overtures to the U.S. government failed to stem the flow of arms and ammunition to Britain, France, and Russia, the country's military leaders adopted a more direct approach to end the shipments.

On January 15, 1915, German army councilor Dr. E. Fischer dispatched a communiqué addressed "From the General Staff to Military Attaches and all Agents in the United States" advising:

In all branch establishments of German banking houses in Sweden, Norway, Switzerland, China and the United States, special military accounts have been opened for special war necessities. Main headquarters authorizes you to use these credits to an unlimited extent for the purpose of destroying factories, workshops, camps, and the most important centers of military and civil supply belonging to the enemy. In addition to the incitement of labor troubles, measures must be taken for the damaging of engines and machinery plants, the destruction of vessels carrying war materials to enemy countries, the burning of stocks of raw materials and finished goods, and the depriving of large industrial centers of electric power, fuel, and food. Special agents who will be placed at your disposal, will supply you with the necessary means for effecting explosions and fires, as well as with a list of people in the country under your supervision who are willing to undertake the act of destruction.

On November 28, 1914, a circular issued by the Intelligence Bureau of the General Staff of the High Seas Fleet to naval authorities stated:

You are ordered to mobilize immediately all destructive agents and observers in those commercial and military ports where munitions are being loaded on ships going to England, France, Canada, and the United States of North America, and Russia where there are storehouses of such munitions, and where fighting units are stationed. It is necessary to hire through third parties who stand in no relation to the official representatives of Germany agents for arranging explosions on ships bound for enemy countries and for arranging delays, embroilments, and difficulties during the loading, dispatching, and unloading of ships. . . . Funds required for the hiring and bribing of persons necessary for the designated purpose will be placed at your disposal at your request.

The importance of these directives was not lost on the officials at the German embassy in Washington, where activity to disrupt the shipment of Allied war supplies from America had been underway for months. The ambassador, Count Johann von Bernstorff, a career diplomat with a lifetime of foreign service experience, used his charm and social skills to maintain friendly relations with the United States and ensure American neutrality, while keeping silent watch over the covert operations being organized to disrupt the Allied war effort. German consular officials across the United States, like Franz Bopp in San Francisco, were under his direct order to support sabotage efforts within their regions. The commercial attaché at the embassy, Dr. Heinrich Albert, received over a million dollars from the Imperial War Department to fund sabotage, and raised even more from the sale of German war bonds to American investors. Through Albert, embassy officials would have access to secret bank accounts around the country for bankrolling sabotage missions. Military attaché Franz von Papen, a dueling-scarred cavalry officer, was the prime instigator of German sabotage operations in the United States from 1914 to 1915. Von Papen's schemes ran the gamut from employing Hindu laborers in Vancouver to dynamite the Canadian Pacific Railway to organizing an attack on the International Bridge in Vanceboro, Maine; he would foster an army of saboteurs and agents throughout the United States and Canada. Naval attaché Karl Boy-Ed arranged for the clandestine resupply of German warships by employing freighters dispatched from U.S. ports with false manifests, and recruited informants from among the German merchant seamen stranded by the war to obtain information about ships and cargoes to be targeted for destruction. In the spring of 1915, von Papen and Boy-Ed were joined by Captain Franz von Rintelen, a naval officer sent to America by the German Admiralty with orders to "prevent or delay the exportation of materials of war, especially of munitions, by all means."

One of the "destructive agents" that von Papen recruited to conduct sabotage on the U.S. East Coast was Paul Koenig, the massively built superintendent of detectives for the Atlas Line, a subsidiary of the Hamburg-American Steamship Line. Koenig "had arms like an ape, and the bodily strength of one. . . . His powerful frame and lurid vocabulary made him a figure to avoid or respect. . . . Waterfront society did both—and hated him as well." During the years he spent investigating criminal activity for the steamship company, Koenig had come in contact with dockworkers, tugboat captains, seamen, and a variety of miscreants that would now be employed on sabotage missions for the German government.

In 1914 there had been few fires or explosions at U.S. powder mills and manufacturing plants, and most of those could be attributed to carelessness or to accidents caused by the increased production of hazardous materials. But during the first six months of 1915, the number of "accidents" at munitions plants increased at an alarming pace as saboteurs in the pay of German officials took to the field. The agents typically operated at night or on weekends to reduce the chance of innocent workers being killed or injured, and often utilized common factory materials as a source of ignition, with the munitions stored at the plant being used to trigger an explosion or conflagration. The lack of physical evidence or ready suspects meant that the mysterious fires and explosions at most of the defense plants would never be solved.

Sinking merchant ships loaded with munitions presented a far more difficult problem for the saboteurs. Setting off an explosion on a munitions ship docked at a pier could devastate a harbor, killing thousands of innocent civilians in the process, and risk America entering the war if traced to German agents. Yet attempting to plant a bulky time bomb aboard a freighter to cause an explosion at sea would greatly increase the chance of the perpetrator being caught.

For a solution to destroying Allied munitions ships, von Papen turned to Germany's only prewar spy in the United States, Dr. Walter T. Scheele. Born in Cologne in 1865, Scheele was a graduate of the University of Bonn and received a doctorate in chemistry from the University of Freiburg. As a young lieutenant of artillery in 1893, Scheele had been dispatched on a brief visit to the United States to report on new discoveries in the fields of explosives and military chemistry. His intelligence reports on U.S. chemical developments and the parallel research he conducted in his own laboratory proved to be so valuable that his stay was extended for another twenty-one years. Scheele was made a consultant chemist for the Scientific Department of the German army at a salary of $1,500 per year and was eventually promoted to the rank of major.

The solution that Dr. Scheele devised for attacking cargo ships was a marvel of simplicity and ingenuity. It consisted of an inch-wide lead tube that was partitioned into two halves by a copper disk at the center. One side of the tube was filled with a yellowish powder mixture of one-third urotropin and two-thirds peroxide of soda and then sealed with a pressed-in plug at the end. The other side of the tube was filled with sulfuric acid and closed with a screw cap. After a set time period had elapsed, the acid would eat through the copper divider and reach the powder mixture. An intense, white-hot flame would then shoot out the side of the tube. Varying the thickness of the copper disk would alter the time delay before the incendiary ignited, from four hours to up to eight days after the device was loaded. The incendiaries were made in three tube lengths—four inches, six inches, and eight inches—each yielding a different flame duration. Captain von Rintelen arranged for Dr. Scheele's invention to be manufactured in volume in the machine shop of the German liner *Kaiser Friedrich der Grosse* interned at Hoboken, New Jersey. To make the devices less conspicuous when placed in the hold of a ship carrying ammunition, a later version was developed that included a hollow aluminum nose cone, which gave the appearance of a small artillery shell. In addition to ship sabotage, the incendiaries could also be used to destroy factories and warehouses.

Dr. Scheele's "cigars" provided German agents with a deadly tool for attacking supply ships and munitions plants that could be carried safely and placed inconspicuously. Altogether, approximately 500 to 1,400 of the incendiary "cigars" were manufactured on the interned liner, although it was later estimated that only 25 percent were actually planted aboard merchant ships, the rest being tossed overboard by the nervous dockworkers bribed to place them. The "cigars" that *were* planted caused millions of dollars in damage to the Allied war effort and were utilized in many of the sabotage incidents that occurred across the United States during the first six months of 1915:

- January 1, 1915—incendiary fire at the John A. Roebling plant, Trenton, NJ
- January 3, 1915—explosion on the SS *Orton*, Erie basin
- February 28, 1915—mysterious fire on board the SS *Carlton*
- March 5, 1915—explosion at the DuPont factory at Haskell, NJ
- April 1, 1915—explosion at the Equitable Powder plant at Alton, IL
- April 29, 1915—the SS *Cressington Court* catches fire at sea
- April 31, 1915—bomb found in the hold of the SS *Devon City*
- May 3, 1915—explosion at the Anderson Chemical Company at Wallington, NJ
- May 8, 1915—two bombs found in the hold of the SS *Bankdale*
- May 10, 1915—explosion at the DuPont plant at Carney's Point, NJ
- May 13, 1915—the SS *Samland* catches fire at sea
- May 25, 1915—explosions at the DuPont plant at Carney's Point, NJ
- May 30, 1915—explosion of a dynamite barge in Seattle harbor
- May 31, 1915—bombs discovered aboard the SS *Kirkoswald* at Marseille
- June 4, 1915—bomb explodes aboard the SS *Minnehaha* while at sea
- June 26, 1915—incendiary fire at the Aetna powder factory in Pittsburgh
- July 7, 1915—explosion in the DuPont factory at Pompton Lakes, NJ
- July 13, 1915—the SS *Touraine* catches fire at sea
- July 16, 1915—incendiary fire at the Aetna plant at Sinnemahoning, PA
- July 19, 1915—incendiary explosion at the DuPont plant at Wilmington, DE

The port at Marseille was one of the busiest in Europe in 1915 when the freighter SS *Kirkoswald* arrived for unloading. The 4,211-ton steamship, owned by a company in Liverpool, had departed the Fabre Pier in Brooklyn on May 2 with a cargo of sugar loaded on board by the immigrant Swedish, Danish, and German stevedores who worked the New York waterfront. Upon arrival in Marseille, a work gang of *débaudeurs* began to offload the heavy sugar bags under the warm Mediterranean sun, when one of the bags slipped and burst open on the deck. In the pile of spilled sugar, the men were startled to see six sealed lead tubes—clearly bombs of some sort. The authorities were called, and a search of the cargo uncovered three more of the unusual devices.

After analyzing the bomb casings, the French government contacted Washington about the unusual development, and since the shipment originated in Brooklyn, New York City police commissioner Arthur Woods was notified. Woods sent a cable to Marseille asking to be sent one of the incendiaries for examination. A sample "cigar" was dutifully shipped to the United States, where it was ceremoniously presented by the French ambassador to the State Department and then forwarded to New York.

The incendiary device landed on the desk of Inspector Thomas J. Tunney of the New York Police Department's bomb squad. A tough former street cop, Tunney was a nineteen-year veteran of the force who had led city detective bureaus in Brooklyn and Manhattan before taking charge of the bomb squad in 1914. Among their early victories, Tunney's squad had solved a series of anarchist and Black Hand "dynamite outrages" plaguing the city. The detectives were already investigating the mysterious fires that had broken out on freighters carrying munitions bound for Europe, but until the *Kirkoswald* incident, any failed "cigars" that were discovered had been hastily thrown overboard after being found. Now their luck had changed.

"Our study disclosed that it [the incendiary] was of a new type," Tunney recalled, "a metal tube ten inches long, divided into two compartments by a thin disk. The acid had been expected to eat through the disk and explosion was to have followed, but for some reason it had failed. The metals were of good quality and the workmanship was thorough. Here was our first clue on the case."

Since the incendiaries had been discovered within bags of highly flammable sugar in several of the ship fire incidents, the investigators thought that it might be a good idea to follow the path the sugar had taken from being refined to lightering and stowage aboard ship. But after weeks spent following sugar shipments from refining plant to pier, this line of investigation had led nowhere. Watching the activities of lightermen and stevedores at the waterfront and attempting to trace the chemicals used in the tube bombs had similarly proven fruitless.

"Just about the time when the bomb case was growing dull and the ship fires which were constantly occurring had almost found us calloused, the French government, with traditional courtesy, helped us again," the inspector noted.

Captain Martyn, the French military attaché in New York, contacted Tunney to say that he had received word about a man who wanted to purchase twenty-five pounds of TNT from a munitions exporter named Wettig for use in "experiments." Detectives from the bomb squad paid Wettig a visit and formulated a plan to follow the path of the explosives to the suspicious buyer. After passing through the hands of several unwitting intermediaries, the package of TNT was delivered to a boarding house in Weehawken, New Jersey, where it was picked up by a German army lieutenant named Robert Fay. When Fay and two accomplices went to a secluded wood to test the explosives, they were arrested. A search of Fay's room and rented garage uncovered twenty-five sticks of dynamite, an assortment of dangerous chemicals, and bomb parts. The German officer was working to develop a mechanical bomb for sinking munitions ships that would be triggered by movement of the ship's rudder. But Fay had no connection to Dr. Scheele, and his arrest brought the bomb squad no closer to apprehending the individuals behind the incendiary "cigars."

It was time for a change in strategy.

Tunney directed three of his German-speaking investigators, Detectives Barth, Correll, and Senff, to visit saloons, restaurants, and hotels in Hoboken posing as secret agents to see what information they could pick up. The detectives circulated throughout the district making vague references to being engaged in undercover work for the Fatherland to any German émigrés that they came across. In due course, Barth was introduced to a man who quietly told him that he knew someone else doing secret work for the German government, Captain Charles von Kleist. Barth obtained von Kleist's address and paid him a visit, saying that he had been sent by Wolf von Igel, aide to military attaché Franz von Papen. Von Kleist was a "funny little old man" with a goatee and mustache, a chemist and former officer in the kaiser's army. Barth invited him to lunch at a local restaurant, Hahn's on Park Row, and during the conversation that followed, von Kleist mentioned that he had a grudge against another member of the secret service—Dr. Walter Scheele.

"I was his superintendent for a long time," the gray-haired chemist confided, "and he owes me several hundred dollars, but he does not pay me. I think von Igel ought to know about it, and perhaps Captain von Papen himself."

"So do I," said Barth. "I'll see that it gets to him. What was it you were doing over there?"

Grateful for the chance to speak with a senior member of the secret service, von Kleist gave the detective a complete overview of the bomb-making operation, from the work at Dr. Scheele's laboratory in Hoboken to manufacturing the incendiary "cigars" on the interned liner *Kaiser Friedrich der Grosse*, and their delivery to stevedores in the dockyard for placement on munitions ships. Having played a key part in the success of the scheme, von Kleist was highly indignant that he had not been paid for his services.

"Just you wait," Barth told von Kleist. "I'll get you fixed up. I know a man who is close to von Igel and I'll have him meet you. If what you say is true, you certainly have something coming to you."

A few days later, von Kleist again met Barth at Hahn's Restaurant, this time finding him seated at a table with "Herr Deane," bomb squad detective Barnitz. Anxious to prove the truth of his story to the two secret service men, von Kleist led them to the backyard of his house where he dug up an empty "cigar" tube that was an exact duplicate of the *Kirkoswald* incendiary.

"So that no money might be paid to the wrong parties," the detectives suggested that the chemist write a complete statement of his illegal activities. Von Kleist happily complied and signed the document when finished.

After pocketing the evidence, Barth announced that it was time to "go up and see the chief."

At police headquarters, the now-enlightened von Kleist implicated a score of participants in the incendiaries plot, including pier superintendents Eno Bode of the Hamburg-American Steamship Line and Otto Wolpert of the Atlas Steamship Line, who had distributed the tube bombs to stevedores; the chief engineer of the *Kaiser Friedrich der Grosse*; and four of his assistants who had manufactured the bombs, as well as Dr. Scheele himself. All of the men were tried and sent to prison, except Dr. Scheele, who fled to Havana where he was apprehended by Bureau of Investigation agents two years later.

The unexplained fires and explosions at U.S. munitions plants and aboard ships carrying war supplies continued unabated during the last six months of 1915, even as a progression of German agents and diplomats were being arrested or deported.

In October 1915, Lewis J. Smith, a former explosives mixer at the Hercules Powder plant in Pinole, California, appeared at the office of the U.S. attorney in Detroit to relate an extraordinary tale of German intrigue.

Smith informed the attorney that he had been recruited to identify targets for sabotage and to plant bombs on ships by a former railroad detective named Charles Crowley who was employed by military attaché Wilhelm von Brincken. One of the vessels they destroyed was a barge in Seattle carrying tons of smokeless powder that had rocked the city when it exploded. Smith confessed to helping Crowley plant bombs on munitions ships bound for Vladivostok, sabotage gunpowder plants in California, and lay plans for dynamiting military trains as they passed through Ontario. Now, fearful that the knowledge he held might cost him his life, Smith wanted to turn state's evidence.

For months the Justice Department had been monitoring the activities of the German consular officials in San Francisco—Bopp, von Brincken, and von Schack—collecting evidence of their involvement in "violations of the Federal Criminal Statutes in connection with conspiracies to interfere with the transportation of munitions of war." Unlike the diplomats at the German embassy in Washington, the consular officials were not protected by diplomatic immunity. With the support of Lewis Smith's testimony, evidence was presented to a grand jury that resulted in the three officials being tried and convicted of conspiring to destroy ammunition plants and ships.

In New York, Tunney's bomb squad arrested Paul Koenig, the hulking superintendent of detectives for the Atlas Steamship Line who had organized sabotage for military attaché Franz von Papen. During raids on Koenig's home and office, investigators seized papers and a diary detailing the many missions of destruction that he had arranged for the embassy official. On December 10, von Papen and naval attaché Boy-Ed were recalled to Germany at the insistence of the U.S. government, which found the two representatives "unacceptable" due to "their connection with the illegal and questionable acts of certain persons within the United States."

But the two men responsible for the most devastating sabotage in prewar America, Consul General Bopp's principal agents, Kurt Jahnke and Lothar Witzke, continued to slip through the net. In fact, government investigators were unaware that they even existed.

By 1915, Jahnke had graduated from working as a freelance saboteur to carrying out assignments at the direction of Nachrichtenabteilung N, German naval intelligence, headed by Fregattenkapitän Walter Isendahl. The young naval cadet that Consul Bopp sent to assist him, Lothar Witzke, became the ex-marine's faithful lieutenant.

"My youthful appearance, my merchant marine training, and natural talents convinced the 'chief' that I might be of far greater service to Germany as a spy than as a naval officer," Witzke would recall.

Jahnke refined the process of sabotage into an art form. Every operation was meticulously planned, with alibis established well in advance and red herrings planted after each mission to send investigators in the wrong direction. To further avert suspicion, Jahnke became a naturalized U.S. citizen and encouraged Witzke to take out his "first papers" toward naturalization. Both of the agents adopted an alias. Jahnke became "Kort Borden," the name under which he was employed as a night watchman with the Morse Patrol, and Witzke became Pablo (sometimes "Harry") Waberski. Jahnke even went so far as to list "Kort Borden" in the San Francisco city directory at the same address where he resided under his own name, 669 Clay Street, probably the first time in history that a secret agent and his alias were listed in a public directory as living in the same household. Richly paid as a confidential adviser to Consul General Bopp, the wealthy Jahnke earned even more in cash bonuses for successful sabotage and could well afford to pay Witzke's weekly salary. Although his position as a security guard with the Morse Patrol only generated twenty-five cents an hour, it yielded a handsome dividend, in that company records did not disclose *who* performed work on a given date, Jahnke or a confederate, providing a ready alibi when the need for one arose. The patrol service also issued Jahnke a "Morse Patrol" badge that was available for display to anyone curious about "what he was up to" while carrying out a covert assignment.

A full roster of the sabotage missions conducted by the Jahnke-Witzke team will never be known. Because of their flawless execution, most of the planned disasters were written off as "accidents" or left investigators without leads or suspects. In one known incident (a rare case of false targeting), Jahnke arranged an explosion at a small factory that the Bopp organization had identified as producing munitions, but which was actually manufacturing window sash weights. The consul initially refused to pay Jahnke the $1,000 promised for the job, but eventually relented and settled with a payment of $500 after the agent argued that he had not been responsible for selecting the target, only for destroying it. "In addition to their work on the west coast, they [Jahnke and Witzke] made frequent trips east on sabotage missions. After Consul Bopp's arrest they gradually shifted their theatre of operations to the industrial areas of the eastern seaboard."

In an unguarded moment, Witzke would later confess that the team had executed three of the most devastating sabotage operations ever performed: wrecking the boilers of the SS *Minnesota*, destroying the munitions depot on Black Tom Island, and igniting the gunpowder explosion at Mare Island Naval Station. The magnitude of the losses inflicted by the pair explains why British spymaster Captain Henry Landau would call Kurt Jahnke and Lothar Witzke "the most deadly sabotage team in history."

The SS *Minnesota* was the largest ocean liner ever built at an American shipyard when she was launched in 1903. Considered an engineering marvel in its day, the ship was over 600 feet long with a beam 73.5 feet wide and boasted a cargo capacity of twenty-eight thousand tons—equal to one hundred trains with twenty-five freight cars each. For a decade the *Minnesota* plied the oriental trade, steaming between Seattle and Yokohama, remaining competitive with Japanese carriers by engaging an all-Chinese crew. That cost advantage was lost in October 1915 when the Seaman's Act was passed, a measure intended to increase employment of U.S. merchant seamen by mandating that 75 percent of the seamen aboard a vessel must understand the language spoken by its officers.

To remain profitable with a higher-paid English-speaking crew, the Great Northern Steamship Company, owner of the *Minnesota*, was forced to quit the Asian trade and transfer the liner to the Atlantic. West Coast newspapers announced that the SS *Minnesota*, the largest cargo carrier in the world, would sail between East Coast ports and Liverpool to supply grains, fish, and other necessities. Not mentioned in the press accounts was the enhanced capability that the vessel would provide for transporting another valued commodity to Britain—artillery ammunition.

In order to raise a crew that complied with the requirements of the Seaman's Act, the steamship company was obliged to recruit sailors from the Sailors' Union, a labor collective whose members could be employed on U.S. flag vessels. The *Minnesota* required a crew of 190 seamen to operate, including ninety firemen and coal passers, eleven engineers, six water tenders, fifteen oilers, three electricians, and three ice men. Despite the diligence taken in hiring its new employees, after the ship's roster had been filled a company official cautioned, "It is apparent that there is no trouble for undesirable or dangerous men to get employment on a boat through the Sailor's Union officials."

One of the new recruits was an athletic twenty-year-old with blond hair and a ready smile. The young man was well mannered and spoke with a European accent (most likely one of the twelve Norwegians that came on board) and clearly knew his way around the engine room of a ship. Witzke would later recall:

At San Pedro I [had] joined the Sailors and Fisherman's Union of the Pacific. I think it was called. A short trip on a coastwise vessel then gave me my first "discharge paper," which endowed me with a definite status as a sailor with experience.

On November 14, 1915, the SS *Minnesota* steamed out of Seattle on its first voyage to Liverpool where the liner was to be placed under English registry, carrying a sixteen-thousand-ton cargo of wheat, barley, lumber, and frozen fish. The ship traversed Puget Sound without difficulty, steamed past San Francisco a day or two later, and headed out onto the open ocean.

Four days later the Balfour-Guthrie Company, which owned the cargo on board the *Minnesota*, received an alarming call from the British secret service. Information had been received that a water tender aboard the ship named William A. Martin had made out a will and told his wife that "he did not expect to return . . . that they would fix the boat so she would not get to her destination." Balfour-Guthrie immediately notified the Great Northern Steamship Company, which forwarded a warning by wireless to Captain Garlick on the *Minnesota*. Garlick responded that the ship was maintaining a steady speed of twelve knots and there had been no trouble, but he would act accordingly. The water tender, William Martin, was placed under discreet observation, but in the days that followed nothing out of the ordinary was observed.

The following week their troubles began.

The *Minnesota* was equipped with sixteen pipe boilers that fired the liner's two powerful twelve-thousand-horsepower engines. The ship was proceeding routinely along the southern route toward Britain when suddenly, without warning, boiler tubes began to fail one after another. On November 27, the Great Northern received a wireless message from the *Minnesota* that the ship had stopped on the high seas and they were "having trouble with the machinery." A few days later, Captain Garlick sent another message advising that the liner was 1,320 miles south of San Francisco and must return at once. He included a cryptic remark, "More than one Martin aboard," suggesting that a team of destructive agents were at work. On December 2, the steamship company was informed, "Boilers giving out rapidly." Three days later a final wireless message was received which advised that everything possible was being done to keep going, but the liner could only make a speed of three knots. "Now 653 miles from San Francisco, weather favorable, boilers all gave out, boat completely crippled and have fires in the side bunkers." Setting fires in a ship's coal bunkers was a popular tactic used by agitators to cause trouble aboard a steamship.

National wire services picked up the story, and sensational accounts of the *Minnesota*'s troubles appeared in newspapers across the country. On December 6, 1915, the *Victoria Daily Times* reported:

PLOTTERS MAY HAVE USED CHEMICALS
One Theory Advanced to Explain Breakdown
Of S.S. Minnesota's Boilers
SAILOR BOASTED VESSEL WOULD
NOT MAKE VOYAGE

San Francisco, Dec. 6—The crippled freighter Minnesota, wallowing on a heavy sea off the Coronado Islands, more than 600 miles south of San Francisco, was expected to be reached sometime today by the tug Dauntless and the salvage steamer Iaqua, which were sent from here Dec. 3 to find and assist the big vessel.

In addition to trouble with her machinery, the Minnesota is reported to have had trouble with members of the crew, and one man is reported as being in irons on the vessel.

Chemicals put in the water of the Minnesota's boilers may have caused the breakdown, according to information received today by C. W. Wiley, marine superintendent of the Great Northern Steamship Company. All of the sixteen boilers were put out of commission by leaky tubes at various times since the Minnesota left Seattle, Nov. 14 for Liverpool with a cargo of 16,000 tons of freight. Five hundred extra tubes were carried for replacing any of the 500 tubes in the boilers, but the supply has been practically exhausted.

"British agents informed the company," Mr. Wiley said, "that W. A. Martin, a water tender, had boasted to his wife that the vessel would not make the voyage. I sent this information to Captain T. W. Garlick by wireless, but he has made no comment on it."

"I know that the breakdown of so many tubes and all the boilers was not natural. Chemicals placed in the water would have caused this, or ashes might have done it. . . . Every boiler has been repaired, only to give way again so that the vessel makes slow time."

Concerned that the liner might have been sabotaged, J. H. Carroll, an attorney for the Great Northern Steamship Company, sent a letter to the U.S. Department of Justice asking for an investigation into the "suspicious circumstances" that had led to the ship being put out of commission. The director of the Bureau of Investigation, A. Bruce Bielaski, instructed the Bureau's Seattle field office to conduct a thorough investigation of the alleged sabotage before anyone from the *Minnesota* was allowed to land. The federal agents were told to secure a list of all officers and crew, obtain a signed statement from Mrs. Martin, and obtain all information known by the British agent.

With one suspect already identified by the British secret service, physical evidence to be found in the sabotaged boilers, and hundreds of witnesses on board, the Bureau director likely anticipated an efficient, well-ordered investigation.

Special Agent Tom Howick called at the British consulate to interview the secret service agent who contacted the Balfour-Guthrie Company. He was advised by Consul Pelly that "their office possessed no special agent, and that so far as they knew the story referred to came from no British officer." Howick contacted other Bureau offices for assistance and learned from sources in Seattle that in fact there was no "British agent," that a woman named Anderson had misrepresented herself as a British secret service agent to Balfour-Guthrie. The investigator returned to the British consulate and discussed the matter with Pelly who informed him that he "was well aware of the Anderson woman" and that "she visits the German consulate regularly." Howick subsequently discovered that Anderson was said to have received her information about Mrs. Martin "from a friend of the Martin woman who has since left Seattle." Howick reported to Washington that "it now appears that the Anderson woman never saw the wife of W. A. Martin but her story is based on the report of someone who has purported to be a friend of the Martin woman, which informant has since moved from Seattle." The field office began a search for the imposter throughout greater Seattle but was unable to locate "the Anderson woman."

Agent Howick next obtained a complete list of the officers and crew of the SS *Minnesota*. He reviewed the roster with the U.S. shipping commissioner and was told there were no reports of anyone on the list having engaged in suspicious or criminal activity.

Special Agent E. M. Blanford of the Bureau's Los Angeles field office interviewed W. D. Martin, the father of water tender William A. Martin, and learned that the suspect was twenty-two years old and had served continuously on steamships since the age of sixteen. If William Martin was married, it was news to his father. W. D. Martin gave Blanford several letters that he had received from his son. One of the notes was written on the stationery of "The L. Koppel Tailoring Company," which the father stated was where William obtained his clothes. The tailor shop also acted as a mail drop for his son, receiving his correspondence when he was away at sea. Special Agent in Charge Donald Rathbun telephoned Mr. Koppel and was informed by the tailor that he had known William Martin for over a year and that so far as he knew, the young man was "of good habits." Koppel also stated that he had never heard of Martin being married and did not believe that he was married.

On December 14, the *Minnesota* docked in San Francisco, and Agent Rathbun boarded the vessel to question the crew. Captain Garlick told the investigator that he had been "unable to discover anything which would be sufficient basis for an accusation against anyone." Rathbun met with the ship's carpenter and was informed "there was a little 'crew talk' to the effect that there were German spies on board causing trouble with the boilers, but he was unable to hear any definite statement against any man. He stated that one of the engineers had complained that certain valves which should be open were mysteriously closed immediately after he opened them."

Agent Rathbun accompanied several of the ship's engineers be-lowdecks to a location where a quantity of material taken from the boil-ers was exhibited. Rathbun noted that "in the course of time the interior of the larger [boiler] tubes had become coated with some sort of hard material which deposited from the water. In many places this coat had become more than a quarter of an inch thick. When this coating became quite thick the result is that the water is kept from contact with the tube, and when this occurs the fire on the outside overheats the tube with the result that it becomes weakened at that point and bursts. One tube was exhibited which had become entirely filled with a hard deposit." Rathbun then observed the failed tubes being examined by government inspectors to determine whether the coating on the tubes was a man-made occur-rence; the results were inconclusive.

Following weeks of negative publicity, the Great Northern Steamship Company was having second thoughts about what had transpired on the stricken liner. Further public statements suggesting that there had been problems with the crew would be sure to antagonize the Sailors' Union, upon whom the company was reliant for labor, and it was suddenly re-membered that there had been trouble with the *Minnesota*'s boilers on a previous voyage. Company officials informed the federal agents that they now believed "the failure of the ship's boilers off the Mexican coast was caused, not by spies nor mutinous sailors, but by natural mechanical de-fects." On December 29 the crew received their pay and were dismissed from the ship.

With nothing to investigate but a false report from a British agent who was not a British agent, concerning a statement made to a man's wife who was not married, and with no witnesses or clear evidence that an act of sabotage had even occurred, the Bureau of Investigation quietly closed the case titled "Steamer Minnesota: Probable Neutrality Matter."

Throughout 1916, a pivotal year in which battles raged at Verdun, the Somme, and Galicia consuming huge amounts of ammunition, the SS *Minnesota* was laid up in San Francisco undergoing repair. On February 16, 1917, fifteen months after all sixteen of her boilers had mysteriously failed, the largest cargo carrier in the world passed under the Golden Gate Bridge headed for London with a full load of freight.

Martha Held's neighbors were convinced that she was operating a bordello. At all hours of the night, a stream of male callers arrived at her four-story brownstone in Manhattan—sea captains, diplomats, businessmen, military officers—and, intermittently, attractive young ladies, all discretely entering through the basement door beneath the steps at 123 West 15th Street. Her neighbors' concerns would have been alleviated, or perhaps heightened, if they had known what was actually going on behind the walls of the shuttered row house.

A former opera star in the old country, the buxom, middle-aged Held operated a safe house and social club for visiting Germans, a place at which they could obtain traditional food and drink, and where confidential matters could be freely discussed. German saboteurs visited her establishment on a regular basis, and the destruction of factories producing munitions for the Allies was an ongoing topic of conversation. "The china and silver would be removed, the candles set back, and great rolls of blueprints and maps and roughly drawn plans and camera snapshots brought in by secret scouts would be unfolded and spread on the table." The agents would then gather round and discuss the most lucrative opportunities and the best way to destroy them.

One of the young women who mingled among the guests at the safe house was Mena Edwards, a popular and vivacious model who frequently appeared in advertising photographs for the Eastman Kodak Company and was widely known as the "Eastman Girl." Unseen and ignored during the sabotage discussions, Mena knew enough German to understand what was being said and, years later when questioned by investigators, would recall the name of the most important site marked for destruction: a munitions depot called "Black Tom."

Named for its tomcat shape, Black Tom is a promontory that protrudes from the New Jersey shore almost a mile into Upper New York Bay near the Statue of Liberty. Originally an island, in the late nineteenth century the site had been joined to the shoreline by a fill of land about 150 yards wide. After the world war began, Black Tom became a major transit point for munitions being shipped to the Allies, and one of the most dangerous locations in the United States. Artillery shells, small arms ammunition, and high explosives arrived at Black Tom by the trainload from factories across America before being offloaded and moved onto ships bound for Europe. To support the transfer operation, the Lehigh Valley Railroad had built a network of railway tracks, ten piers, and a complex of twenty-five storage warehouses for housing the hazardous material.

The facility was protected by a detachment of security guards employed by the railroad, and by a squad of watchmen from the Dougherty Detective Agency hired by the Allied governments. There were only two approaches to the munitions depot—from the surrounding waters of the bay and across the land bridge from the mainland. Although there were no security fences, the complex was believed safe from sabotage due to the constant vigilance of the patrolling guards and detectives. Not until 1928, when records seized from von Papen's hulking agent Paul Koenig were reexamined, would it be learned that several of the Dougherty watchmen were in the pay of the German plotters.

At ten o'clock on the evening of Saturday, July 29, 1916, Black Tom was a "dead yard." Hours earlier, the locomotives had been uncoupled from the freight cars and returned to the mainland. The depot workmen had also departed to prepare for a restful Sunday at home. There was nothing to arouse the interest of the security officers as they made occasional rounds beneath the waning moon. All was still, and a gentle breeze was blowing in from the southwest. Standing at rest in the peaceful yard were eleven railroad cars filled with high explosives, seventeen cars of artillery shells, three cars of nitrocellulose, one car of TNT, and two cars of detonating fuzes. At the northernmost pier, ten barges full of high explosives rocked gently with the tide against their mooring lines. Altogether, 2,368,803 pounds of volatile explosives lay waiting at the terminal, practically unguarded.

In the upper bay, a rowboat bearing Kurt Jahnke and Lothar Witzke drew ever closer to the lonely depot. Witzke was a skilled oarsman from years of rowing boats on the Baltic as a naval cadet, and his powerful frame effortlessly propelled the craft across the dark water. With the dim outline of the Statue of Liberty as a marker, the two saboteurs headed for their objective at the outer edge of the promontory: Pier 7 and the *Johnson 17*. A spy on the island had revealed that Theodore Johnson's barge number 17 was loaded with one hundred thousand pounds of TNT and 417 cases of artillery fuzes—a giant time bomb capable of causing massive damage if detonated. Jahnke scanned the darkened pier while protecting a compact wooden box that held their precious supply of glass "pencils" wrapped in gauze.

Developed by Abteilung III B, the intelligence department of the German General Staff, and manufactured at a small factory in Karlsruhe, the glass pencils were a new type of incendiary that made Dr. Scheele's lead pipe bomb incendiaries look primitive in comparison. The incendiary pencil was a concealable glass tube about the width of a wooden pencil, drawn to a near point at one end and open at the other. The body of the tube was divided into two chambers with a narrow capillary hole at the center. The chamber at the pointed end was filled with sulfuric acid and then closed by melting the glass tip to seal the opening. The chamber on the other end was filled with a mixture of two-thirds potassium chloride and one-third powdered sugar, and closed with a stopper. When it was time for the device to be used, the pointed tip would be snapped off, the stopper removed, and the tube placed upright near flammable material. Gravity would draw the acid through the capillary opening, and it would combine with the powder mixture. Thirty-five minutes later, the glass pencil would burst in a white-hot flame that would destroy the glass tube, leaving no evidence.

Around midnight the saboteurs reached the pier and secured the rowboat. Moving swiftly and silently, they boarded the eighty-foot-long *Johnson 17* and started planting the incendiaries among the piled cases of TNT and detonating fuzes. Few words were spoken as they snapped the tip off one incendiary pencil after another and set them into position. When they were done, the mooring lines that held the barge to the pier were cast into the water, and the *Johnson 17* drifted slowly away from the dock.

Now nothing could prevent the holocaust that was to come.

Somewhere in the darkened yard a third saboteur was at work. Crouched in a freight car packed with explosives, Michael Kristoff, a mentally unstable Austrian immigrant, was also placing incendiaries. The year before, Kristoff had been hired as an errand boy at twenty dollars a week by Frederick Hinsch, a former North German Lloyd steamship captain who turned to organizing sabotage operations after his freighter was interned. Kristoff had since graduated to bigger things. Hinsch offered him a sizable payment to walk across the land passage to Black Tom and plant incendiary pencils in the munitions cars. Kristoff knew Hinsch by his alias "Graentnor" and had limited knowledge of the sabotage plan. If the unstable youth was apprehended while setting fire to one of the freight cars (which was likely), he would be the perfect fall guy, diverting the security guards' attention from the activity underway at Pier 7.

Jahnke and Witzke hurried back to the rowboat. The naval cadet brought the small craft around and began rowing toward the Statue of Liberty at a ferocious pace with strong, heavy strokes. The boat surged forward across the calm water while Jahnke's attention remained focused on the mass of land behind them.

At 12:45 a.m., a Dougherty watchman named Barton Scott spotted a fire burning in one of the freight cars. A fire alarm was sounded, and the security detail fled the depot in terror. On nearby Bedloe's Island, a witness noticed a second fire flare up on a barge near the end of the pier. The two fires grew in intensity for over an hour, and then at 2:08 a.m. the *Johnson 17* exploded with an earthquake-level blast.

Out on the open water, Jahnke and Witzke saw the brilliant flash of the explosion and were instantly struck by the massive shock wave from fifty tons of TNT being detonated. Like the flicker of a silent movie frame, the rowboat heeled to the side and nearly swamped, with bay water rushing over the gunwale. Jahnke was thrown overboard, and Witzke had to move quickly to pull him back into the boat. Both of the agents were rendered almost senseless by the blast. Struggling against the heavy waves that followed the initial shock wave, after hours of rowing they managed to reach landfall before dawn.

The explosion of the *Johnson 17* was felt as far away as Lancaster, Pennsylvania, 158 miles distant. Thousands of plate-glass windows throughout Manhattan and Brooklyn were shattered by the blast, showering the streets and sidewalks with shards of glass. At 2:40 a.m., a second tremendous explosion occurred when the munitions in the burning freight car detonated. The skyline turned red as "car after car and barge after barge ignited." Shells and debris rained in every direction. The Ellis Island immigration station and the Statue of Liberty were bombarded with shrapnel. A thunderous barrage of exploding ammunition continued unabated for eight hours, and wreckage was still burning with shells popping off a day later.

Miraculously only five people were killed in the blast; one of the dead was a ten-week-old baby named Arthur Tossen who was thrown from his crib. The total damages were estimated to be $20 million, which included $5 million worth of ammunition that was destroyed, as well as eighty-five railroad cars, twenty-one storage warehouses, six piers, and four barges. The disruption caused to the Allied war effort was immeasurable.

The smoke had not cleared over the ruins before an investigation began to determine the cause of the Black Tom disaster. It was quickly established that the fire which set off the conflagration began on the *Johnson 17*, but no evidence was found of sabotage. Jahnke and Witzke had disappeared without a trace, and even Michael Kristoff managed to return to the mainland without being spotted. The investigators decided that the combustion had been initiated by natural causes and that the subsequent explosions were the result of barges loaded with high explosives being allowed to remain at the piers overnight in violation of New Jersey state law and city ordinances. Executives of the Lehigh Railroad, the National Storage Warehouse Company, and Johnson Lighterage (which owned the *Johnson 17*) were placed under arrest and charged with manslaughter.

Lawyers working for the owners of the ruined terminal and munitions would hunt for the real culprits behind the disaster for over twenty years. In the late 1920s, when Witzke and Jahnke fell under suspicion, the legal investigators were chagrined to discover that both had ready alibis. Witzke had applied for American citizenship in San Francisco five days before the depot blew up, and the records of the Morse Patrol showed that a man using the name "Jahnke" had worked in San Francisco on July 12, 15, 16, 29, and 30, 1916. Not until 1939 would an intergovernmental war claims commission declare that Black Tom had been sabotaged by German agents.

None of the perpetrators would ever stand trial for the destruction of Black Tom.

By 1916, rumors about Jahnke's opium and cigar smuggling activities and his frequent visits to Mexico City for meetings with the German consul had reached the ears of federal authorities. It therefore came as a considerable surprise when on February 10, 1916, the spymaster arrived unannounced at the Bureau of Investigation field office in San Francisco to offer inside information about a "German spy" at work in the United States. Jahnke had an unusual manner of speaking. He would periodically close his eyes and only open them again to ascertain the reaction of his listeners. With eyes half closed, Jahnke told the federal officers that he had been approached on two occasions by a German agent named Lang, once in October 1915 and a second time in January 1916, to inquire whether he could obtain information about the U.S. Navy shipyard on Mare Island. Flashing a gold-toothed smile, Jahnke proudly confided that he had served in the U.S. Marine Corps and was now employed by a detective agency, showing the men his Morse Patrol badge. The German agent Lang, Jahnke added, had also been involved in the disappearance of a codebook from a U.S. Navy warship. When the officers inquired about Lang's present whereabouts, Jahnke hesitated and then stated that he had no idea where to find the man. The meeting drew to a close, and Jahnke quickly departed the federal building, leaving the investigators to ponder whether the information he had provided on the supposed agent was valid or if there was another motive behind the visit, such as an attempt to divert suspicion from *himself* as a German operative.

Seventeen months after Jahnke's visit to the Bureau of Investigation, a Russian émigré appeared at the U.S. immigration station in Laredo, Texas, seeking permission to enter the United States from Mexico. The friendly twenty-two-year-old youth with tousled blond hair and a disarming smile presented papers identifying himself as "Pablo Waberski" and told the immigration officer that his final destination was Portland, Oregon, where he hoped to reside.

After being granted entry, Lothar Witzke immediately took a train to San Francisco. There were several important tasks that he had to take care of before continuing his journey. On June 6, 1917, Pablo Waberski, alien from Petrikau, Russia, registered for the draft, listing his trade on the registration card as "sailor." Three weeks later, June 27 proved to be a very busy day for Pablo. He visited the Department of Commerce Steamboat Service and obtained a certificate as an "able seaman for service on the high seas and inland waters," then went to the U.S. Coast Guard office where he received a "Certificate of Efficiency as Lifeboat Man" to establish that he was trained in launching lifeboats and using oars. Following the stopover in San Francisco, Witzke traveled twenty-five miles north by rail to Vallejo, California, to complete his assignment. With a draft registration card that affirmed his loyalty to the United States, and government certificates proving his ability as a seaman, the German saboteur had little difficulty signing on as a civilian mechanic at the Mare Island Naval Shipyard.

The first U.S. naval station on the Pacific Ocean, Mare Island was one of the country's most important military bases. The vast installation included a shipyard with two shipbuilding ways, dry docks, a coaling station, and an ammunition depot. Mare Island employed thousands of workers and launched a range of vessels for the Navy each year, from colliers to battleships, and also played a crucial role in supporting the ships of the Pacific Fleet. An ammunition magazine located at the southern end of the island included fifteen large explosives storehouses. When a warship visited the station for service or overhaul, its artillery ammunition would be filled with new explosives from the magazine and loaded aboard the ship. As a key naval base and shipyard, Mare Island was of significant strategic value and was kept under round-the-clock protection.

One quiet night in late June 1917, an unusual occurrence took place on the island. While patrolling a dimly lit area of the base, a Marine on sentry duty spotted an intruder moving through the shadows. He challenged the man to stop and identify himself, but the stranger ignored the order and turned to flee. As the Marine raised his rifle, threatening to shoot, he was struck on the back of the head and fell to the ground unconscious. When he awoke, both intruders were gone, and a search of the area yielded no clue as to their identity. The attack on the sentry was duly noted in the duty officer's log, but with no further developments, the curious incident was soon forgotten.

Monday, July 9, began like any other day for Chief Gunner Allen Mac-Kenzie. He took his usual place at the breakfast table and chatted with two of his daughters, Dorothy, age twelve, and Mildred, age eight, while his wife Melvina cooked their morning meal in the kitchen. Outside, a gardener that MacKenzie had hired, seventy-two-year-old George Stanton, could be heard trimming the lawn of the little duplex bungalow they shared with their neighbor, Gunner James McKenna. The small house was located a quarter mile from the ammunition depot, allowing MacKenzie a very easy commute to work. The topic of their breakfast conversation, as it had been for weeks, was his third daughter, eighteen-year-old Roberta, who had left four days before for Cleveland where she was going to marry Jim Osborne, a former employee of the Mare Island yard. Melvina and the girls would soon begin packing for a rail journey east to take part in the wedding.

The family's routine continued the same as always until 7:54 a.m., when the dining room was lit by a brilliant flash followed by a terrific blast as a storehouse at the ammunition magazine containing 127,660 pounds of black powder exploded. MacKenzie, Dorothy, and Mildred were blown though the walls of the house and killed instantly, their mangled bodies landing on a hillside one hundred yards away. Melvina's remains would later be recovered from the basement of the bungalow, which was reduced to splinters by the force of the explosion. Their neighbor George McKenna, his wife, and their baby were buried under a pile of debris on the other side of the duplex and survived, although McKenna's right arm was nearly severed. The aged gardener, George Stanton, died instantly, his body torn to pieces by flying wreckage. Thirty-two other victims who were in the vicinity of the magazine when the explosion occurred were injured—noncommissioned officers, enlisted men, and civilian workers—with four of the wounded left in critical condition.

The black powder storehouse and an adjoining warehouse were completely destroyed by the blast, while twelve of the remaining explosives storehouses were badly damaged. Fires broke out in the wrecked buildings, and only the desperate efforts of a line of volunteers who raced to the scene prevented an even greater catastrophe. While one group of servicemen frantically fought a blaze that threatened the nitroglycerine storehouse, other sailors and Marines could be seen hand carrying the dangerous explosive to safety. When the conflagration was finally brought under control, four million pounds of explosives had been saved from destruction, and a column of black smoke rose three hundred feet above the smashed installation.

Captain Harry George, the commandant of the Navy yard, immediately sealed the base and posted two hundred Marine sentries to ensure that no one entered or left the island. Unlike previous explosions that had occurred over the magazine's history, there was no doubt that the storehouse blast was the result of sabotage. One of the country's foremost explosives experts, chemist Arthur Crane of the Hercules Powder Company, affirmed that "blackpowder would not blow up from spontaneous combustion, and unless it had been set on fire, would not have exploded."

Investigators from a naval board of inquiry and the U.S. Justice Department descended on Mare Island. Although a number of promising leads were uncovered, none would explain how the sabotage had been carried out or who was behind it.

The naval investigation revealed that there were nine keys at the station that opened the lock on Building No. 40, the black powder storehouse that exploded. Some of the keys were in the constant possession of men who worked at the magazine, while others were issued for temporary use and returned to a keyboard in the foreman's office each night. All of the keys were accounted for except the one belonging to Nils Damstedt, a civilian ordnance employee who was killed in the explosion. To learn whether a duplicate key had been made, federal agents questioned locksmiths throughout the area. A locksmith named King told the investigators that ten days earlier a man visited his shop and asked for a like key to be made, but he was unable to cut a duplicate because he did not have the correct key blank. King could not recall what the man looked like. At another local shop, a locksmith named Madistrini recalled a man requesting a duplicate key two weeks prior, but he also did not have the correct blank and had sent the customer away. He too was unable to provide a description of the man. (The week before the explosion, Damstedt, the ordnanceman who died in the blast, had been "demoted for cause and his pay halved," which might have made him a target for bribery by enemy agents seeking access to the storehouse. Like the Dougherty watchmen at Black Tom, it's possible that Damstedt accepted a payoff to provide entry to Building No. 40; he may also have been an innocent victim, struck down while investigating suspicious activity at the site.)

Miss Julia Daly told the naval board of inquiry that shortly after the blast she saw a man in Vallejo with binoculars looking across the river toward the scene of the explosion, laughing to himself as if pleased by the destruction.

The Vallejo assistant postmaster thought Miss Daly's description bore a resemblance to Otto Hickstein, a local man who subscribed to a German-language newspaper and "had never appeared to read this paper, but always took it and clipped a piece from one of the inside pages." The special agents were unable to locate the suspicious newspaper clipper Hickstein.

Mrs. Schmertman of South Vallejo sent a letter to Commandant George stating that she had seen a man running from the scene of the crime. When interviewed by Special Agent W. G. McMillian, Mrs. Schmertman said that she was standing outside washing clothes before the explosion when she happened to notice someone running along the side of the hill near Building No. 40 toward the base hospital. Just as the man disappeared from view, Mrs. Schmertman was thrown to the ground by the concussion of the blast. The man had been too far away for her to see his face.

McMillian visited the location and reported: "I went on the side of the hill about the spot where the man was seen running on the morning of the explosion and followed the trail. It led into the rear of the Marine Barracks, which is known as the Recruiting Depot. On the right, this trail is hidden by a bunch of trees and a hospital, and on the left by a hill." He was unable to discover any evidence left by the running man.

Investigators found a piece of a clock near the site where Building No. 40 had stood, but it was unclear whether it came from a time bomb or one of the wrecked bungalows in the area. Many hours were spent searching for a man rumored to have visited secondhand clothing stores in Vallejo in search of a U.S. Marine Corps uniform. The suspect was eventually located but turned out to be a crank who had tried to enlist in the Marine Corps and been rejected.

At a time without modern-day investigative tools and techniques—forensic analysis of evidence, crime scene management, fingerprint identification, and centralized crime records—combined with the meticulous planning of the saboteurs, it was almost inevitable that the Mare Island bombing would remain unsolved.

Kurt Jahnke had served on Mare Island as a Marine only eight years before the explosion. The Marine Barracks was where he received basic training; Mare Island was his first and final base assignment as a U.S. Marine. He would have been very familiar with the security measures employed to safeguard the naval station. The saboteurs could have gained access to the island by rowboat, repeating the tactic that was successfully employed at Black Tom, which may explain "Pablo Waberski's" need for a lifeboat certificate—for use in securing the loan of a boat. It is likely that some form of time-delay incendiary was used to ignite the black powder in Building

No. 40. Witzke later claimed that he had "laid the wires" that triggered the explosion, but whether he was speaking figuratively of placing incendiary glass pencils or literally that he had pulled wire to remotely trigger the detonation will never be known. Witzke also stated that his accomplice in destroying the magazine had been agent Gustave Wild. Investigators traced Wild to a large German restaurant in San Francisco but were unable to obtain evidence to support his internment. Months after the Mare Island explosion, Witzke boasted to a companion: "I was lying [in bed] at 5:00 in the morning when I heard it and I laughed. I knew there were women and children in it, but I laughed. I knew that I had done it for the Fatherland."

The MacKenzie family was laid to rest in the Navy cemetery on Mare Island with full military honors. A Marine honor guard fired three volleys over the grave, and a bugler blew taps. Among the floral bouquets lining the gravesite was a large wreath for the two children sent by the Marine Barracks with the inscription: "To Our Playmates." In Washington, the U.S. House of Representatives introduced a resolution to appropriate $50,000 for Roberta Mackenzie Osborne, the surviving daughter of Chief Gunner MacKenzie who had been away preparing for her wedding that day.

On August 26, 1917, six weeks after the fatal explosion, "Special Agent G. C.," an informant with U.S. Army military intelligence, waited for a German spy to appear at a street corner in Corona, California. He had made the acquaintance of Captain von Allstein, an officer from one of the interned ships at La Paz (Mexico), a few days earlier outside a poolroom in downtown Los Angeles. G. C. was certain that von Allstein was an enemy agent, and when he overheard him say that he was going to Corona that afternoon, the informant boarded a jitney to Corona to wait in advance for his arrival. The sea captain would be easy to spot on the city street: von Allstein was about thirty-five years old, stood five feet nine inches tall, and was clean shaven with blond hair. He claimed to possess U.S. citizenship papers. His most distinguishing characteristic was his upper front teeth, which were made of solid gold.

When von Allstein appeared, the informant accompanied him on his travels for much of the day, roaming between Corona and Riverside, while working to gain his confidence. But he had little success. Kurt Jahnke knew that G. C. was a government "stool pigeon" and used the meeting as an opportunity to plant another "red herring" about Mare Island with the Americans. In a confidential tone, "von Allstein" informed his companion that Captain Eberfeld from Culiacán and Captain Waldenburg at Tijuana were responsible for the deadly blast. Their helpers on the job had been "a Russian who was working as a ranch hand near Frisco, and a person who was killed at the explosion while in a room [Nils Damstedt]. This explosion, counting bribes and everything, [had] cost Germany about $10,000."

After acquiring additional fictitious information about German agents and operations, G. C. last saw Jahnke waiting for a train to San Diego at the Corona station. The informant advised his superior, Captain Walter Volkmar, district military intelligence officer, that von Allstein was now planning to leave for Tijuana to meet with Waldenburg: "It is expected that he will not attempt to cross the line until tonight, but will hang around drinking until after dark." Volkmar sent a coded telegram to the district intelligence officer in San Diego directing him to arrest Captain von Allstein "on suspicion."

But Kurt Jahnke was nowhere to be found in San Diego.

3

"You Will Have to Kill Him First. He's in Our Way."

The German agents crossed the border into Mexico according to a prearranged plan. On January 31, 1917, Germany announced a policy of unrestricted submarine warfare against any merchant ships entering the war zone, and three days later President Wilson broke off diplomatic relations. War was in the air, and the exodus soon began. Among the first to leave were Jahnke and Witzke, who took up residence in Mexico City. They were soon followed by most of the other German operatives who had been active in prewar America. Some passed into Mexico none too soon. Frederick Hinsch, pursued by federal investigators armed with a presidential warrant for his arrest, bought a train ticket from Baltimore to San Francisco, then lost his shadows in El Paso by hopping a train to Chihuahua before continuing on to Mexico City.

When Wilson appeared before Congress to ask for a declaration of war against the German Empire, the president stated that war was justified in part by the enemy's sabotage campaign in neutral America:

> Self-governed nations do not fill their neighboring states with spies. . . . One of the things that has served to convince us that the Prussian aristocracy was not and could not be our friend is that from the very outset of the present war it has filled our unsuspecting communities . . . with spies and set criminal intrigues everywhere afoot against our national unity of counsel, our peace within and without our industries, and our commerce. Indeed it is evident that its spies were here even before the war began.

With the United States on a war footing, the "American front" became a more dangerous place for German agents to operate. After years of mysterious fires and explosions, the public was convinced the country was teeming with enemy spies and saboteurs, and many responded by joining "vigilance associations" dedicated to ferreting out foreign spies. The largest of these private watch groups was the American Protective League (APL), an organization of volunteer businessmen that operated under the direction of the Justice Department's Bureau of Investigation. By mid-July, APL divisions had been established in over 900 U.S. cities and towns, with 112,000 members in every significant industry and company on the watch for enemy agents; by the end of 1917, the League had grown to 1,270 local chapters with 250,000 members enrolled. Another private group maintaining domestic surveillance was the American Defense Society (ADS), a national organization with strong financial and political backing that counted Theodore Roosevelt and former attorney general Charles J. Bonaparte on its advisory board. ADS recruitment ads promoted the society as a means to guard against spies and saboteurs: "If you can't go to the trenches, serve at home and stand by the man at the front. Telegraph, write or bring us reports of German activities in your districts." The ADS encouraged prospective members to join the organization by sending in a one-dollar enrollment fee, reasoning: "To win this war we must jail German spies. Will you give a dollar to put them all in jail?"

At the same time that thousands of U.S. citizens were joining vigilance associations to "report on German activities in their districts," Washington was at work toughening the nation's laws against espionage and sabotage. On June 15, Congress passed the Espionage Act of 1917, whose provisions included a statute making communication of defense information to a foreign government in time of war a crime punishable by death or imprisonment for not more than thirty years. Ten months later, the Sabotage Act made it illegal to obstruct the U.S. war effort by destroying material or facilities needed to carry on the war, punishable by a fine of not more than $10,000 or imprisonment for up to thirty years, or both.

The flight of German spies and saboteurs into Mexico was not prompted by fear of being captured and prosecuted. Three months after the U.S. declaration of war, Witzke had effortlessly crossed the Mexican border into the United States to blow up the black powder magazine at Mare Island, and in August "Captain von Allstein" paid a visit to Southern California; both had returned to Mexico City without any interference from the authorities. The withdrawal below the Rio Grande was dictated entirely by the agents' need to maintain contact with their intelligence headquarters overseas.

When diplomatic relations between Washington and Berlin were severed in February 1917, German embassy and consular staff had departed; the responsibility for acting as the clearinghouse for espionage activity in North America passed to Heinrich von Eckhardt, minister to Mexico. Von Eckhardt had access to communication channels for sending coded messages to Berlin and ample funds to finance espionage operations.

The warm relationship between Germany and the government of President Venustiano Carranza helped bolster Mexican support for covert German missions into the United States. The two countries were drawn together by a common enemy—the "Colossus of the North," the United States. In 1914, after an incident in which eight American sailors were briefly detained at the port of Veracruz, the U.S. Navy retaliated by shelling the city, killing 126 Mexicans. Two years later, a raid on the city of Columbus, New Mexico, by Pancho Villa resulted in President Wilson ordering an expeditionary force of 6,600 men into Mexico in pursuit of Villa, which eventually battled Carrancista troops. In contrast, Germany cultivated Mexican favor by providing military and financial support, and fifty German nationals held commissions as officers in the Mexican army. Von Eckhardt was on intimate terms with President Carranza, frequently visiting him in his office at the National Palace without an intermediary. At a special session of the Mexican Congress addressed by Carranza in April 1917, von Eckhardt was greeted with enthusiastic applause, while Henry Fletcher, the new American ambassador, was booed and hissed as he entered the gallery.

German officials viewed the "Yankees'" concern over border security as an opportunity to distract the American military and divert munitions from the European war. Behind a facade of peaceful statecraft, German secret agents and diplomats pursued a variety of schemes and subterfuges to provoke a conflict between the United States and Mexico. Ironically, one of these—the Zimmerman Telegram, a message sent by Foreign Minister Arthur Zimmerman to von Eckhardt for delivery to Carranza which proposed an alliance with Mexico in the event of war with the United States, while promising to help Mexico regain the lost territories of Texas, New Mexico, and Arizona—would contribute to the United States' entering the war against Germany (see chapter 8). With America now in the war, the German government still maintained hope of finding a means to divert U.S. troops to the southern border, while President Carranza continued to regard Germany as a potential ally to counter the strength of the United States.

Once established in Mexico City, Jahnke rose quickly in prominence. He developed as close a bond with Minister von Eckhardt as he had with Vice

Consul Bopp in San Francisco and was rumored to have a private telephone line to the diplomat's home. Jahnke was also on excellent terms with Carranza himself and, in concert with von Eckhardt, attempted to persuade the president that "only through concert with Germany could Mexico be saved from disaster and made wealthy and prosperous." The Austrian ambassador to Mexico reported that "Jahnke was as big a man as von Eckhardt [in Mexico]." No longer just a freelance saboteur earning income from the rewards paid for destroying munitions plants and ships, by December 1917 Jahnke was under the direction of Eugene Wilhelm, chief of the German Naval Intelligence Service at Antwerp, receiving his orders through the military representative at the legation. Four months later he became the service's sole naval confidential agent in Mexico, the *Bevollmächtigter Geheimagent*, head of the espionage system for the American continent.

Already a man of great wealth from smuggling cigars, dead Chinese, and opium, Jahnke enjoyed a lavish lifestyle and used the funds from naval intelligence to form an expansive and formidable espionage system. He directed the network from four offices in Mexico City: his personal residence on Calle Colonia No. 4 secured with a high-voltage electric fence, an office at Calle Liverpool, a room in the German embassy, and an office at the Hotel Juarez on Calle de Cuba. Jahnke's correspondence was delivered to his aliases, Jahuka Jenke or José Iturbe, at PO Box 306, Mexico City. Jahnke built a network of fifteen to twenty secret operatives located across Canada, the United States, Mexico, Central America, and South America and forwarded their reports along with his recommendations to Wilhelm in Antwerp. The spymaster also maintained a press-clipping service, sending articles of political or military interest—especially those published in the United States—to naval intelligence headquarters as well.

The Hotel Juarez was the central gathering place for Jahnke's espionage ring. It was managed by Otto Paglasch, his chief talent scout, who rented the hotel from Señorita Theodora Sanchez, a woman with whom he was said to be "very friendly." Paglasch had little difficulty locating suitable agent material for Jahnke, but less success at spotting double agents. Aside from promising new arrivals at the hotel, Mexico's four-thousand-strong German community was a ready pool to draw from, and Paglasch kept his eyes and ears open for new recruits that might prove useful for secret operations.

Jahnke was wary of working with the other prewar saboteurs who had passed into Mexico at a dusty border crossing, or on a Spanish steamer from Havana, agents like Dr. Anton Dilger, the Virginia-born microbiologist formerly responsible for running a germ warfare program that infected horses and mules bound for the Allies with deadly bacteria, or Frederick Hinsch, the burly sea captain who had organized sabotage missions in the United States with the management style of a waterfront tough. Strong-willed and independent, under the direction of Abteilung III B army intelligence, in the coming months they would challenge Jahnke for leadership of German espionage operations in the Americas. He also had to be on guard for Major Campbell's informants and enemy plants like William Neunhoffer.

Major Robert Madison Campbell, the military attaché at the U.S. embassy, arrived in Mexico City in August 1916. The thirty-seven-year-old Campbell was a graduate of West Point and had been awarded the Silver Star for gallantry in action while serving as a cavalry officer during the recent Punitive Expedition into Mexico. Campbell reported directly to the American ambassador, and with generous funds from Washington he had organized a network of counterespionage agents to monitor the German spy system. From his basement office at the embassy, the former horse soldier kept tabs on Jahnke, Witzke, and a host of other German agents, tracking their activities with his own well-placed spies.

William Neunhoffer, supposedly a "slacker" (draft dodger) from Texas, was a recent arrival in the city. The twenty-eight-year-old, slightly built Neunhoffer claimed to be engaged in business in Tampico but never left the Cosmos Hotel, and although slackers in Mexico were usually destitute, Neunhoffer spent money freely. He spoke German with an American accent and asked questions about the saboteurs' activities—too many questions. The German agents were certain that Neunhoffer was an American spy.

They weren't wrong.

William Neunhoffer was a special agent of the U.S. Justice Department's Bureau of Investigation. Born in Texas to German parents, Neunhoffer had been practicing law when his National Guard unit was mobilized and sent to the Mexican border in 1916. At his new posting, Neunhoffer's ability to speak Spanish and German brought him to the attention of Robert L. Barnes, the special agent in charge of the Bureau field office in San Antonio. He was hired as a federal agent and sent to Mexico City in August 1917 to investigate the activities of German spies and saboteurs in the Mexican capital. Neunhoffer took up residence at the Cosmos Hotel and attempted to infiltrate the German network, but with no training in counterespionage and limited talent in the art of deception, his results were something less than dismal.

Corresponding under the pseudonym "Number 30," Neunhoffer sent weekly status reports on his progress to A. Bruce Bielaski, the director of the Bureau of Investigation. In his first dispatch, dated August 29, he advised the Bureau chief:

> I must report that my efforts to get in touch with the real Germans in this city have so far been virtually a failure, and I have very little hope for future success along those lines. They seem to be almost impossible of approach and are apparently determined to avoid anybody "contaminated" by America.

Two weeks later Neunhoffer reported that the situation had not improved:

> During this period the writer has associated with a number of Germans and also Mexican officers, but without any success, probably owing to the general whispering that I am of the American Secret Service. I feel confident that Ricardo W. Schwierz knows my connection [with the Bureau] while I was in Arizona and has circulated same freely. It has come to my attention from several sources that the Germans are having, to say the least, strong suspicions of me. . . . Major Schwierz is still at this hotel with his associates. I have not made any headway with them, probably due to the reasons mentioned heretofore.

Richard Walter "Ricardo" Schwierz was an agent who worked for both Mexican and German intelligence agencies. In early 1914 he had been sent to Canada by the German secret service to secure maps of the dominion and any other military information he could obtain, but after the war began, he was delegated to Ambassador Bernstorff in Washington who assigned him to obtain shipping information for von Papen and Boy-Ed. The following year Schwierz was dispatched to support the German naval station at Tsingtao, China, but had only reached Tokyo when the port fell. Returning to the United States, he was recruited as an operative by Mexican consul Gonzales in Los Angeles. In July 1916, Schwierz was arrested by federal agents in Nogales for violating U.S. embargo laws, but soon after being apprehended, "he escaped from a deputy marshal across the border into Nogales, Senora [Mexico], where he jumped into a waiting automobile and disappeared."

Once in Mexico, Schwierz established a training camp for German reservists at El Claro in Sonora that eventually grew to a colony of 850 to 1,450 men being prepared for an anticipated German-Mexican invasion of the United States. Commissioned a major in the German army, Schwierz was assisted in this endeavor by Lieutenant Auch, a tough-talking German reservist, and a new agent recruited by Otto Paglasch, an Austrian medical doctor named Paul Bernardo Altendorf.

It soon became clear to both Major Campbell and Neunhoffer that Dr. Altendorf was a highly capable adversary—and someone to be kept under watch. A university-trained physician, Altendorf spoke multiple languages and was very intelligent, with nondescript looks that enabled him to pass as either a native Mexican or a German.

On the evening of September 16, Neunhoffer was introduced to Schwierz, Auch, and Altendorf by an acquaintance at the hotel. During the week that followed, the Justice Department agent spent virtually all of his time in their company.

Neunhoffer shared the information that he learned from Dr. Altendorf in his weekly report to Bielaski:

> In conversation with Dr. Altendorf the latter stated that he had lived in Cuba and more recently had been in Yucatan and other parts of Southern Mexico. This man claims to be an Austrian and I believe Altendorf is not his correct name. It seems he has been in every country in the world, including all of the principal cities in the United States. The doctor is highly educated and speaks English and Spanish well, although with a pronounced German accent. This morning after having had a few drinks together, I showed the doctor an Associated Press article concerning the transmission of news from Mexico to the States by Germans through soiled linens. Altendorf told me that Capt. Heitzshe, who is mentioned in said article, is a personal friend of his and then attempted to point out to me the impracticability of sending information as indicated in the article. He told me that during the English-Boer War he had belonged to the English Intelligence Office and had worked in that connection for a period of fourteen months; that he was later sentenced to be shot by the English and that only his quick-wittedness saved him from execution. He then began telling me about the efficiency of the German spy system and that the Japanese had the next best spy system to the Germans. He pointed out the necessity of education, refinement, dress, self-control, etc., in a spy and especially laid stress upon the point that a spy should be careful of what he says and when he says it. He then ridiculed the crudeness of the American Secret Service, calling my attention to several parties whom he had picked as such officers and pointing out how they revealed their identity by their actions in public. The doctor gave the writer a regular lesson on spying. Doctor Altendorf states that he is 43 years old, but has the appearance of being about 35. He is approximately 5 ft. 8 or 9 in., weighs about 160–170, has black hair streaked with gray, thin on top, gray eyes, black mustache, skin smooth and white, full face, and carries himself very erect. He is a man of handsome appearance and talks rather rapidly.

By this time the German espionage establishment was fully aware of Neunhoffer's identity as an American investigator. Not only had he been unable to discover the true nature of their activities, but the special agent was now being used as a channel of disinformation to the U.S. authorities. In the following discourse with Schwierz reported to the BOI director by Neunhoffer, the German operative decried the munitions plant sabotage that had occurred in the Unites States and reassured his listener that the training camp being organized at El Claro had few men and was solely intended for a campaign against Yaqui Indians:

> During the course of the night Schwierz told the story of his life in the United States; that he had always pointed out to Franz Bopp that the bombing policy of von Papen and Boy-Ed in the United States was the wrong policy to pursue and that he had personally written to Count von Bernstorff and opposed their destructive policy in the States. . . . Schwierz showed me an order from Governor Calles for what money he needed. Schwierz and also his companion Auch told me that they had now 83 Germans in their organization in Santa Anna [near El Claro]; that they were all well-armed and provided with horses and saddles; that he was now procuring sabers, clothing, and helmets for his men; that they would probably go on a campaign against the Yaquis upon their return to Sonora; that he was determined to do what he could against the United States but that he would only strike his blow when the inevitable revolution in the States had started.

On October 3, Major Schwierz, Lieutenant Auch, and Dr. Altendorf departed Mexico City by train for the reservist training camp. Neunhoffer heard little about them for months, and then in early January 1918, Auch and Altendorf returned with startling news: the German colony at El Claro "had gone to pieces." Mexican governor Calles had angrily dismissed Schwierz for corrupt business dealings related to camp finances and demoted the major to *"jefe de policía de la frontera,"* a commander of border police at a remote outpost. The training camp was now a shambles.

With little to show after five months spent trying to penetrate the German espionage network in Mexico, Special Agent Neunhoffer was withdrawn from the Mexican capital by Director Bielaski and assigned to the Bureau of Investigation field office in San Antonio.

Upon his return to Mexico City, Dr. Altendorf went to the Hotel Juarez where he was cordially received by Otto Paglasch. The hotel proprietor contacted von Eckhardt to advise him that Altendorf was back in the city and an appointment was made for the doctor to call on the minister at six o'clock that evening.

At the appointed hour, Paglasch and Altendorf took a cab to the German embassy where von Eckhardt greeted them with dignified courtesy. The minister stood just five feet seven inches tall and was heavily built, with gray hair and a gray mustache turned up at the ends in the style of the kaiser. He asked Paglasch to excuse them for a moment and then led Altendorf into a closed chamber for a private discussion about what had transpired at the El Claro training camp.

"I have been informed about Schwierz, but I should like to have more details," he told the Austrian doctor.

"Your excellency, I left here with every confidence in Schwierz and his good intentions," said Altendorf sadly. "I suspected that something was wrong, but was not sure. . . . I warned him that some of these strangers might fool him, [but] he replied that he knew exactly what he was doing, and ordered me not to interfere in things that did not concern me." Speaking in the manner of a person who with the best of intentions has been involved in a disgraceful affair, Altendorf continued, "I had great suspicion of Schwierz, that he was misleading your excellency and giving secrets to [the] American agents which he was well-acquainted with. In Hermosillo, when I stayed at the Hotel Cohen he was receiving all kinds of correspondence from the border. I was sure that he was an American spy and also telling an American agent by the name of Page everything that was going on in General Calles' office. I have [even] found a letter containing information for the Americans."

"Why did you not send this letter to me?" von Eckhardt demanded.

"I was afraid that Schwierz might find out something and would do some harm to me, but I can tell you what the letter said. Schwierz was asked by an American agent if he had some good news for him from his trip to Mexico, and to write to him immediately as he was very anxious to know what is going on with the Germans."

"Dieser verfluchter hund [This damned dog]!" the minister exclaimed. "How he fooled me after giving him so much money. . . . Doctor you have told me quite enough. I should like to have you make a report on this affair to be sent to Germany."

Altendorf advised von Eckhardt that Schwierz had stolen all of his medical instruments, his clothes—everything that he had in his possession.

"I really am sorry this happened to me," said the doctor, beginning to tremble with nervous excitement. "I am left absolutely a poor man."

Von Eckhardt walked to a safe and removed fifty dollars in American gold coins, which he gave to Altendorf, telling him not to worry, that everything would be replaced.

"Buy yourself a good supper and tomorrow Jahnke will give you some money to buy clothes." (After months at the remote training camp, Altendorf's clothes were in tatters.)

"Make out a written statement and hand it to Jahnke," the minister continued. "He is coming tomorrow, and will arrange to see you. We shall want you to go to the border with Waberski [Witzke]. You remember him do you not?"

"Yes, your excellency," Altendorf replied. "If I am not mistaken I was introduced to him at the same time that I met Jahnke."

"That's right," said von Eckhardt. "He is a very nice man and you can have all confidence in him. Jahnke will explain everything to you. I know you are a great friend of General Calles. He wrote all about what happened at El Claro and spoke very highly of you. The rest you will know from Jahnke tomorrow."

Their private conference concluded, the minister called Paglasch into the room and then dismissed the pair with a warm handshake and an encouraging smile.

The following afternoon Jahnke sent for Altendorf, and they met at his private residence. Jahnke asked the doctor about the troubles he had encountered with Schwierz at Hermosillo. Once again, Altendorf related what he had discovered, that "Major Schwierz was a bad man working with the American agents and giving information to the American Intelligence Department."

Jahnke responded that they would send a wire from Minister von Eckhardt to General Calles to do away with Schwierz in any manner he pleased.

"If he is not dead now, he will be shortly," said Jahnke. "Come and have a drink and a good cigar. Have you got some money?"

"I am broke," Altendorf replied.

Jahnke gave the doctor another fifty dollars. "Enjoy yourself as much as you can. You have done good work to get rid of Schwierz."

The spymaster informed Altendorf that he was going to leave the next day for Veracruz "al mes trese" to meet a Spanish liner of the Transatlántica Line, the Alfonso XIII that would dock on January 10. He needed to deliver some secret correspondence to a courier on the ship and in return would receive important papers and a large sum of money that had been forwarded by submarine to Spain for the circuitous route to Havana and Veracruz.

Jahnke advised the doctor that upon his return he would discuss the details of an extremely important assignment—a trip to the border with Lothar Witzke.

"Yes, the Minister told me I was to go back to Sonora," Altendorf replied, "that there were going to be some operations there. Where is Waberski?"

"He is coming home to go to Nogales," said Jahnke. "He is a good boy. You will have to go back with him. He has a very complete force to work against the United States."

"Yes, I am only too willing to do anything for you that you want," said Altendorf.

Jahnke told the doctor that while he was away, he would require someone trustworthy to watch over his house and maintain his affairs. "You are a very trustful man," Jahnke said assuredly. "I know you can keep things confidential and you can stay in my house here."

Altendorf attempted to decline Jahnke's offer to stay at his residence, politely insisting that he could not impose on his good nature to such an extent, but he eventually relented. Jahnke told him to leave his baggage at the Hotel Juarez to give the impression that he was still living there should anyone be keeping track of his whereabouts, and showed him to the room he would occupy at his house.

The spymaster placed his household staff in the doctor's charge with instructions to allow no one whose identity could not be verified past the electrified fence, and to permit no one into his office except Kettenbach (his personal secretary and a second lieutenant in the German army). The next day Jahnke departed for Veracruz accompanied by Karl Gobel, a stocky, fortyish agent with blond hair and a close-cropped mustache.

Altendorf had only been living at Jahnke's residence a few days when Witzke arrived. The youthful saboteur was surprised to find Altendorf in Jahnke's home.

"Hello, Doctor! Are you here?" asked Witzke, eying Altendorf with suspicion.

Altendorf explained that Jahnke had asked him to keep watch over the household while he was away. He was to greet any visitors that might call and guard the office. When Witzke learned that Altendorf was receiving Jahnke's correspondence and seemed to be aware of many confidential matters, his doubts receded. He informed the doctor that he had just returned from Mazatlán and Manzanillo where he had been making sketches of the harbors, taking snapshots, and measuring the depth of the water for submarines.

"Yes, and I think we shall have a trip together," the doctor replied, advising that he had heard there would soon be an operation against the United States.

"Oh, you know something about it," Witzke responded.

"I am only too glad to be able to help you," said Altendorf.

Glancing about the room, Witzke inquired, "Where is Jahnke?"

"He went to Veracruz to meet a steamer."

"Yes, I knew he had to go there," Witzke responded.

Altendorf took a telegram off Jahnke's desk and handed it to the ex–naval cadet. Sent by Jahnke from Veracruz, it contained a simple two-line message that the doctor found puzzling: "Business bad. I am coming without merchandise."

The youth flashed a smile. "Do you know what that means?" he asked. "It means that everything is all right; we shall leave very soon [for the border]."

On January 14, Jahnke's train pulled into the station at Mexico City where Altendorf and Witzke stood waiting. The spymaster exited the coach incongruously holding a single orchid for a lady friend. He told them that during the journey from Veracruz, rebels had fired on the train and several of the escort had been wounded; he distributed four hundred pesos among the injured Mexican soldiers "to display the sympathy of the Germans." Jahnke's residence was located nearby, and the two agents accompanied him to his home. They were followed by Gobel who carried two heavy leather bags that contained secret documents and a small fortune in currency, partly in gold coin, for financing intelligence operations.

Jahnke was in high spirits, and over a hearty breakfast he briefed them on their assignment.

"Well Witzke," he began, "you and the doctor will leave for the border on the 16th. I have received everything I wanted. I have the plans for the invasion of the United States all complete from Berlin with the funds to finance the preliminaries."

In the discussion that followed, Jahnke revealed details about the coming operation. Witzke was going to enter the United States on a mission that would be the prelude for a German-Mexican invasion of the United States by a combined force of forty-five thousand men, coincident with the German spring offensive in Europe. The young agent was to instigate an insurrection by disaffected blacks in the American South, "who were to massacre the white population," and arrange for the destruction of munitions plants, food stores, "and whatever else was useful to America and her allies, doing what he could personally and the rest through IWW agents." Lastly, Witzke was tasked with the assassination of an American intelligence officer in Arizona who had been interfering with German secret service operations in the United States and Mexico.

Jahnke informed them that the invasion plan had been developed by the German General Staff as a means to keep U.S. troops at home defending the southern border. Even if it achieved only partial success, the consequences would be significant, as shown by the American reaction to Pancho Villa's raid on Columbus, New Mexico, two years before.

In his euphoria over the coming operation, Jahnke harshly criticized the diplomats who had supervised previous actions in the United States. With a golden sneer, he characterized Ambassador von Bernstorff as "das groesterindsfich [a big ass] throwing away money on everyone who came to him with a plausible scheme. He blamed von Bernstorff for allowing the United States to enter the war and said that disaster could have been avoided if Germany had played good politics." Germany was lucky to have a man like von Eckhardt, who gained friends readily and was someone that people could work with.

In his unusual manner of speaking, Jahnke closed his eyes and resumed the briefing. "Doctor, listen very carefully to what I have to say. You will accompany Witzke to Hermosillo where you will introduce him to General Calles and tell him that Witzke is travelling on a Russian passport into the United States, but that he is a German agent. Rademacher, our consul in Guaymas, will know all about this and will have informed General Calles before you get to Hermosillo. You will go and see Carranza tomorrow. Carranza will also advise General Calles fully. Everything has been arranged by Herr von Eckhardt. When you have explained everything to Calles after introducing Witzke I want you to ask Calles to procure a revolver for Witzke. Never mind what it costs. We will pay whatever price is necessary."

At that time, firearms were unobtainable in Mexico City. Assaults and robberies had become such an everyday occurrence that anyone who could buy a pistol carried one for personal protection, and as a result, the shelves were empty in the city's gun shops.

"Why do you want to send me into the United States with a pistol?" asked Witzke. "I have done very important work without carrying a pistol."

The spymaster opened his eyes and looked at the agent.

"They may know you this time," Jahnke replied, "and you must be very careful. Besides you will carry important papers, such as you have never carried before. And you must do away with that special agent Butcher at Nogales. You will have to kill him first. He's in our way.

"There are *two* very important papers that will be in your possession," he continued, displaying the documents. "One is a message from von Eckhardt in the German imperial code to be presented to German consuls when asking for money or assistance. The other is a code which you will use in giving information about the progress of operations in the coming drive. No son-of-a-bitch of an American is to get hold of this code. You know what to do. It's the reason I am giving you a pistol."

"Nothing will happen to the codes," Witzke responded. "Nobody can get me as long as I have a gun in my hand."

The spymaster nodded. "You will send your messages to the doctor and he will forward your communications to me. If everything works out right I shall come with someone else. The first thing for you to do is see the IWW delegates on the border and let the third party who is going with you operate with his own class of people. Give him all the money he wants. He is all right."

Jahnke rose from the table and departed for a conference with von Eckhardt. The look of resignation on Witzke's face left no doubt that the fate of a special agent named Butcher was now a dead certainty.

Three years before Jahnke briefed his subordinates on the historic mission to the border, another meeting of grave importance had taken place not far away.

On the afternoon of September 13, 1914, General Álvaro Obregón was a man in trouble. The senior general of future president Venustiano Carranza, Obregón had been riding a train to Mexico City with a group of Pancho Villa's generals at the height of the Mexican Revolution when Villa was informed about hostile acts that Carranza had taken against his forces. The murderous Villa flew into a rage and ordered his officers to stop Obregón's train and divert it to Chihuahua where he was encamped. It was a foregone conclusion that when they arrived at Villa's location, Obregón would be taken from the train and executed.

As the train approached Chihuahua, Obregón called American journalist Byron Butcher to his compartment and presented him with a suitcase containing thirty thousand pesos ($16,000).

"It is likely that after our arrival at the station, we will not see each other again," said Obregón soberly. "I want to give you this money which does not belong to me—it belongs to the nation. I need you to deliver it to Mr. Francisco S. Elías, commercial agent of my government, so that he can account for it in entirety."

Being handed a suitcase containing a fortune in banknotes for delivery to a distant businessman during the lawless days of the revolution was not something to be accepted lightly; the chances were great that Butcher would be robbed and murdered. That Obregón had delegated the assignment to Butcher was as much a testament to the newsman's toughness as to his integrity. The two men had become close friends. Without hiding his emotion, Butcher uttered a few words of quiet encouragement to the imperiled general, shook his hand, and departed with the suitcase. Days later Obregón had managed to escape execution at the hands of Villa, and the thirty thousand pesos had been delivered to Mr. Elías.

Guarding the cash reserve of a Mexican general was just another passing exploit in the adventurous life of Byron S. Butcher.

Byron Samuel Butcher was born on November 10, 1885, in Burlington Junction, Missouri, just a few years after Jesse James had been killed in St. Louis. Following high school graduation, Butcher attended college for one year—a rare privilege in 1903—before becoming an accountant with the Southern Pacific Railroad in Cochise, Arizona. After seven years of bookkeeping with the railroad, Butcher discovered his true calling—journalism. He moved to northern Mexico and lived in the mining camps of Sonora, sending news from the mines to newspapers in lower Arizona. Life in the mining camps was rough, but Butcher hung on for two years, acquiring a nose that would later be described as "slightly crooked." News that a rich vein had been struck in a Mexican mine or that a site was producing a higher grade of ore was vitally important to mine owners, investors, and mine workers in the "Copper State," and Butcher's reporting was greatly valued. In 1912 he joined the staff of the *Douglas Dispatch* (Arizona) as a reporter. It was an ideal time for a single young man fluent in Spanish, with experience living below the border, to join the newspaper. When the Mexican Revolution began, Butcher was promoted to war correspondent and assigned to cover the escalating conflict with the army of General Álvaro Obregón. Sometimes reporting on events, and at other times an active participant in the fighting, Butcher witnessed the battles of Naco, Nogales, and Agua Prieta and covered Obregón's capture of Mexico City and his drive down the west coast of Mexico that ended in the defeat of Villa at Celaya. After the years spent campaigning together, Butcher was a close friend and confidant of the influential general, able to gain access and personal interviews on any area of interest.

In July 1916, Butcher's experience and connections in Mexico came to the attention of Robert L. Barnes, who had resigned from the Bureau of Investigation to become a major in the U.S. Army military intelligence branch. Butcher was hired as a special agent and assigned to the intelligence office at Nogales, Arizona. As a cover for his counterespionage activities (and a vehicle for exposing German schemes after their discovery), Butcher also became a correspondent for the International News Service, the Hearst organization's news-gathering agency. A press release announcing his new position described the lengths that he would go to gather information: "Mr. Butcher made a trip throughout Mexico for the International Service a couple of years ago, being gone eight months and traversing the entire republic." Butcher ran a number of well-placed agents in Mexico and was not averse to crossing the border himself to get the "inside story" when necessary.

The results of Butcher's efforts soon became clear in a series of articles that appeared in international newspapers exposing German secret operations in Mexico. In the story "German Secret Agent's Trunk Is Seized by U.S.—Captain Schwierz, Who Escaped into Mexico, Now Military Instructor There," Butcher suggested that agent Schwierz had revealed German military secrets during interrogation. "Schwierz, following his arrest for violating embargo laws, escaped to Mexico where he is now. However, before his escape, he made a complete confession of all that he knew in regard to Germany's aims in regard to a German-Mexican alliance and the intent to precipitate a war between Mexico and the United States. Schwierz is now a major instructor on the staff of the Mexican secretary of war. His headquarters are at Mexico City." A report about the Zimmerman Telegram titled "It Failed—But Mexican Plot Was Deep" advised readers: "The Rio Grande frontier has been a hot bed for German intrigue. Wiring from Nogales, Arizona, Byron S. Butcher, staff correspondent of the International News Service, declares that he has learned from unimpeachable authority there that the conquest of Mexico and the making of that country a German empire ruled by one of the Hohenzollerns was Germany's ultimate object in the gigantic plot to stir strife on the American continent." Full details of the Zimmerman plot were disclosed by correspondent Butcher.

The special agent's sensational press releases were not missed by Jahnke's news-clipping service in Mexico City, and the byline "By Byron S. Butcher, Correspondent of the International News Service" left no doubt who was to blame. British intelligence circulated a false rumor that the secret diplomatic telegram had been stolen by an Allied agent in Mexico City. Butcher's sensational account appearing in newspapers only a week after the contents of the Zimmerman note were revealed led Jahnke to believe that the American military intelligence officer was responsible for spoiling the plan—and placed Butcher at the top of the spymaster's death list.

On the morning of Tuesday, January 15, 1918, Jahnke and Witzke visited the German embassy and met with von Eckhardt to discuss the coming operation. They returned with good news for Altendorf. "I have just made an appointment for you to see Carranza this afternoon," Jahnke told the doctor. "I will send you there with my own chauffeur."

At 3 p.m., the spymaster called Altendorf for his appointment with President Venustiano Carranza, self-proclaimed *"Primer Jefe"* (First Chief) of the Constitutionalist rebel forces during the revolution and now the chief executive of Mexico. Following a twelve-minute ride in a closed touring car, Jahnke's chauffeur pulled up in front of the president's stately home. A liveried footman escorted the doctor inside and led him up a staircase to a study where Carranza waited. The president, a man of medium height with a gray beard and mustache, peered imperiously at the new arrival through thick spectacles, without displaying a trace of a smile.

"I am Doctor Altendorf," the agent announced. "I was sent here by von Eckhardt. I have orders to return to Sonora and introduce my friend Witzke to General Calles."

"I have been informed that you were coming and what you were coming for," Carranza responded.

"Your excellency, I would like a letter to General Calles so that I can show that I have been to see you."

"It is not necessary to give you this in writing," Carranza warily responded. "You have been on his staff for some time."

Altendorf frowned. "I think, your excellency, that it would be better if I had a written statement so I can go ahead with the work without delay," the doctor replied.

"It is too dangerous to carry any papers now, especially documents, as rebels attack trains and take everything away from passengers. I shall wire General Calles and explain everything to him. You can work freely and cooperate with him without any delay. This is a very secret mission, therefore I cannot give you any letter. Go to Hermosillo and everything will be arranged by the time you get there. All your code messages will be sent without interference or delay [over the Mexican government telegraph wire]. They are to be sent to Mendez (Carranza's private secretary) and by him delivered to von Eckhardt. This is all the instructions I have to give you."

Altendorf smiled and made a few positive comments about the success of the coming operation, concluding with the statement: "We are going to play hell with the gringos."

"Yes," said Carranza, "they are the cause of all our misfortunes. *Adios Bien viaje!*"

As he exited the official residence, Altendorf never noticed the man watching him from the shadows. The stranger had trailed Jahnke's touring car from Calle Colonia to the president's estate and then kept the building under surveillance while Altendorf was inside. When the visit ended, the man shadowed the automobile on its return to Jahnke's home.

Then he left to prepare a report for Major Campbell.

4

"I Am Mr. Butcher's Man!"

The idea that a few German intelligence agents could trigger a black insurrection in the southern United States or unleash a campaign of destruction to pave the way for a cross-border invasion from Mexico was not a *luftschloss* ("castle in the sky" or fantasy) to those who planned the mission. In addition to engaging saboteurs to blow up munitions plants, set fire to cargo ships, and infect army draft horses with deadly bacteria, German foreign office and military strategists had also organized a series of operations targeting the sociopolitical vulnerabilities of their enemies to divert troops from the battlefronts.

As an imperial power, Britain's strength—and its greatest weakness—was the subjugated peoples within its empire of colonies, mandates, protectorates, and dominions. If a nationalist movement were to rise in one of its valued territorial possessions like India or Ireland, the British government would be forced to dispatch an army to quell the uprising and reestablish control, potentially diverting enough infantrymen to shift the balance of power on the western front toward Germany.

In December 1914, the German foreign office initiated a scheme to smuggle arms and ammunition from the United States to Indian nationalists for a rebellion in the Punjab. Military attaché von Papen directed Captain Hans Tauscher, a New York–based arms merchant, to purchase eight thousand rifles and four million rounds of ammunition, which were shipped by rail to the U.S. West Coast and loaded aboard a chartered schooner, the

Annie Larsen. The plan called for the ship to sail to the South Seas where the arms and ammunition would be transferred to an oil tanker, the *Maverick*, which had been purchased in San Francisco by Frederick Jebsen, a reserve officer in the German navy. The weapons were to be hidden in the *Maverick*'s oil tanks and taken to Karachi for distribution to Hindu revolutionaries. But the tanker's departure was delayed, and the two ships failed to meet at the appointed rendezvous. After months wandering the Pacific, the *Annie Larsen* landed at Hoquiam, Washington, where her cargo was seized by U.S. authorities.

Another German stratagem to incite a revolt against British rule in India called for a holy war to be proclaimed by an Islamic leader that would result in an uprising by the country's seventy million Muslims and cause an invasion of India by Arabs from neighboring Afghanistan. Three weeks after Turkey signed an alliance with Germany, the sultan issued the desired declaration, ordering Muslims everywhere to "rise as one and smite their infidel oppressors wherever they could be found." Thousands of inflammatory leaflets were secretly printed and smuggled into India to spread news of the sultan's fatwa. On December 15, 1914, the Germans dispatched an expedition led by Captain Oskar von Niedermayer to Afghanistan to forge an alliance that would lead to an Arab revolt against Britain. But the hoped-for Muslim uprising never came about, and the emir in Kabul refused to attack British India single-handedly without strong outside military support. In May 1916 the scheme was abandoned, and von Niedermayer's unit withdrew to Germany.

Ireland had been a British colony for over seven hundred years when World War I began, and nationalist sentiment favoring home rule offered excellent prospects for a rebellion. Germany pinned its hopes for an Irish uprising on Sir Roger Casement, a former British consular official and ardent nationalist who traveled to Berlin in 1914 seeking support for Ireland's independence. The German foreign office encouraged Casement to recruit an "Irish Brigade" of volunteers from among Irish prisoners captured on the western front to return and fight for their independence, but few POWs responded to Casement's appeal. When the Germans were informed that a rising by Irish Republicans was planned for Easter 1916, they agreed to arm the rebels and shipped twenty-five thousand captured Russian Mosin-Nagant rifles and one million cartridges on a disguised freighter bound for the coast of Ireland, the *Aud*. Casement departed for Ireland on the German submarine U-19 to meet the shipment, but shortly after landing at County Kerry in southwest Ireland, he was captured by the Royal Irish Constabulary. As the *Aud* approached the Irish coast, it was overtaken by British warships and scuttled by her crew to prevent the arms shipment from being seized. The rebel uprising took place on Easter Sunday as planned, but lasted only six days before being put down by British troops, ending further nationalist activity in Ireland for the duration of the war.

Imperial Russia's Achilles' heel was the undercurrent of discontent spreading across the land. Following a popular rising in March 1917, the tsar had abdicated and been replaced by a provisional government. But the new rulers vowed to continue the war against the Central Powers in spite of horrendous casualties, low morale, and a failing economy, making conditions ripe for a second revolution. When a Russian revolutionary named Parvus approached German minister Brockdorff-Rantzau with a proposal that Germany allow Bolshevik leader Vladimir Lenin to travel from his exile in Switzerland across Germany to Russia, the German foreign office jumped at the opportunity.

"Since it is in our interests that the influence of the radical wing of the Russian revolutionaries should prevail," Foreign Minister Zimmerman wrote to a liaison officer at military headquarters, "it would seem to me advisable to allow transit to the revolutionaries."

In a secret operation, a "sealed train" consisting of a locomotive with a single green carriage was assembled to convey the revolutionaries through German territory to Russia under extraterritorial privileges. On April 9, 1917, Lenin and thirty-one fellow revolutionary exiles departed Switzerland for their homeland, guarded by two handpicked German officers who had been personally briefed for the assignment by Quartermaster General (chief of staff) Erich Ludendorff. Seven months after Lenin's return to Petrograd, the provisional government was overthrown by the Bolsheviks, and on December 15 an armistice was signed between the new Soviet government and the Central Powers. Following the Russian surrender, the German General Staff was able to transfer forty-eight divisions from the eastern front to the trenches in France. The "sealed train" would be one of Germany's most successful clandestine missions of the war—and an exploit that would haunt the world for years to come.

German intelligence hoped to achieve similar results in the United States with the Witzke mission. The suggestion that black Americans could be induced to join an insurrection and murder their white neighbors, or that union members would willingly sabotage the country's defense plants, may seem far-fetched today, but in 1918 it did not appear outside the realm of possibility. Racial tensions in America had never been greater—sixty-four black lynchings were recorded that year, and widespread financial inequity had given rise to a radical form of industrial unionism whose goals would lead to direct conflict with the U.S. government.

Industrial and agricultural production had grown at a staggering pace during the first decades of the twentieth century, with great fortunes being generated for U.S. corporations, holding companies, and trusts. But despite the wealth flowing to these largely unregulated business entities, life had never been worse for the average American worker. "Whether in the grain fields of the Midwest, the mineral mines of the Southwest, the lumber forests of the Northwest, or the textile mills of the East, laborers typically worked ten to twelve hours a day for subsistence wages (or less) in dismal and often dangerous working environments." This economic disparity re-sulted in a major expansion in the size and power of industrial labor unions in the United States.

The most radical labor union of the time, and certainly the most uncom-promising, was the Industrial Workers of the World (the "Wobblies"). Part labor union, part revolutionary movement, the IWW was founded in 1905 to counter the power of big business with the power of "one big union," a labor collaborative that would force decent wages, better working condi-tions, and eventually spearhead the overthrow of capitalism by the working class. In 1917, the IWW numbered over one hundred thousand members, with a broad-based enrollment that included workers from every class, race, and gender.

The tactics that the Wobblies employed in dealing with "capitalist" busi-ness owners were outlined in an IWW treatise, "The IWW—Its History, Structure and Methods," by Vincent St. John, one of the organization's early leaders:

> As a revolutionary the Industrial Workers of the World aims to use any and all tactics that will get the results sought with the least expenditure of time and energy. The tactics used are determined solely by the power of the organiza-tion to make good in their use. The question of "right" and "wrong" does not concern us.
>
> No terms made with an employer are final. All peace so long as the wage system lasts, is but an armed truce. At any favorable opportunity the struggle for more power is renewed.
>
> Where strikes are used, it aims to paralyze all branches of the industry in-volved, when the employers can least afford a cessation of work—during the busy season and when there are rush orders to be filled.
>
> The Industrial Workers of the World maintains that nothing will be con-ceded by the employers except that which we have the power to take and hold

by the strength of our organization. Therefore we seek no agreements with the employers.

Failing to force concessions from the employers by strike, work is resumed and sabotage is used to force the employers to concede to the demands of the workers.

After the outbreak of war in Europe, the IWW General Executive Board issued a resolution stating, "We will resent with all of the power at our command any attempt to compel us—the disinherited—to participate in a war that can only bring in its wake death and untold misery, privation, and suffering to millions of workers, and only further to rivet the chains of slavery on our necks, and still more secure the power of the few to control the destinies of the many." To the Wobblies, the world war was nothing more than a capitalist scheme to control markets, a class struggle that set worker against worker for the enrichment of the factory owners selling munitions to the warring powers.

Despite their opposition to the capitalist-inspired conflict, the Wobblies also saw the war as an opportunity for extracting higher wages and improved working conditions for its members. "During the spring and summer of 1917, IWW Locals throughout the West and Midwest called for strikes in industries vital to the U.S. war effort. Timber strikes against loggers and sawmills soon broke out in the states of Oregon, Washington and Idaho. IWW strikes were called against copper mines and smelters in Arizona and Montana." An IWW strike in Bisbee, Arizona, only ended when 1,300 striking mine workers were (illegally) arrested by Sheriff Harry C. Wheeler and 2,200 members of a citizen posse formed in collusion with a local mining company, Phelps Dodge, and deported on cattle cars to Hermanas, New Mexico, 150 miles west.

The response from government authorities to IWW attempts to curtail war production was equally swift and severe. On September 5, 1917, acting under the direction of Attorney General Thomas W. Gregory, U.S. marshals launched simultaneous raids on the headquarters of forty-eight IWW locals across the country and confiscated a mass of union records, including checkbooks, meeting minutes, correspondence, and membership lists. The evidence that the marshals obtained resulted in 165 IWW leaders being indicted by a grand jury in Chicago and charged with "conspiracy to prevent and hinder the government from executing the prosecution of the war" and violation of the newly enacted Espionage Act.

Hounded by federal investigators, and with its leadership in jail on conspiracy charges and a disgruntled membership situated in critical U.S.

defense industries predisposed to using sabotage as a means to achieve its ends, to German intelligence the IWW appeared ready made to assist Witzke in the planned campaign of destruction. (It is possible that the IWW had already engaged in German-financed sabotage activities. In July 1917, American newspapers reported rumors that the Industrial Workers of the World were working with German agents to cripple mine production, while IWW general secretary "Big Bill" Haywood "branded as absolutely false the rumors that German influence and German money [were] behind the copper mine strikes in the west.")

The growing labor unrest also fueled some of the worst incidents of racial violence ever to take place in American history. A labor shortage in northern cities created by increased war production and white workers leaving to join the armed services drew an influx of black workers from the South seeking better, higher-paying jobs.

One of the cities that experienced an increase in black population was East St. Louis, Illinois, an industrial metropolis that was home to major iron and aluminum companies, stockyards, and meatpacking plants. During the summer of 1916 a strike was called at the Armour, Swift, and Morris meatpacking plants in East St. Louis by 4,500 predominantly white union workers. The meat-processing companies responded by hiring eight hundred black workers as strike breakers. When the labor dispute was settled and the strike ended, the black workers retained their jobs while an equal number of white workers were dismissed. The combination of white union workers struggling for increased wages and better conditions believing that their efforts were being undercut by lower-paid black workers, together with increasing competition for jobs and housing, set the stage for an interracial conflagration. All that was needed was a spark to set it off.

On the afternoon of May 28, 1917, a public meeting was underway at the East St. Louis Town Hall of white workers "protesting the importation of blacks from the south to work in packing houses and munitions factories" when a report was received that "two white men had been held up at gun point and that a white woman had been insulted by a negro." A mob of several thousand whites quickly formed and swept through the downtown area beating every black person in their path. The racial violence continued through the night into the following day, when the police disbanded the crowd, but by that time, three blacks and three whites had already been shot.

East St. Louis was quiet for several days, and then on the night of July 1, a Ford sedan with four white occupants—likely misidentified as vigilantes—was fired on in a black area of the city. Two of the car's passengers were police detectives—Detective Sergeant Sam Coppedge, who was killed instantly, and Detective Frank Wodley, who fell mortally wounded. On July 2, thousands of white rioters stormed into the black quarter of East St. Louis and unleashed an orgy of violence. Homes and businesses owned by black residents were set on fire in five parts of the city, and many of those fleeing the flames were shot as they abandoned the burning districts. According to a period news report, "As three negroes were trying to escape from a burning building a mob spied them. One negro was hanged from a telephone pole and the other two were shot. The three dead bodies were left lying in the street." The crazed mob spiraled further out of control, turning on any black person they came upon—indiscriminately beating, shooting, or lynching the unfortunate victims. "Hundreds of negro women, most of them carrying bundles that held their most precious belongings and leading small children, fled across the [Eads] bridge to shelter and safety with friends on the Missouri side," while a throng of black men, women, and children took shelter in the East St. Louis town hall, which became a haven from the carnage. The rioting finally ended on July 3 when Illinois governor Frank Lowden dispatched the Illinois National Guard into the city to restore order. By that time an estimated 75 to 250 blacks had been killed and 312 homes destroyed, with property losses estimated at $3 million.

The nation was stunned by the magnitude of the racial violence. The Negro League for Afro-American Suffrage called on Governor Lowden "to maintain justice for colored native American citizens," concluding that press reports of the riots "indicate in our judgement, great danger of an uprising of 12,000,000 colored citizens, who will not much longer submit to injustice and outrage by white Americans and the indifference of the national government." In New York City, ten thousand black Americans marched down Fifth Avenue in a silent parade to protest the St. Louis race riot.

Three weeks later, another deadly rampage broke out in Chester, Pennsylvania, once again fueled by the migration of southern blacks into a northern city. In the racially charged tone of the period, the *Washington Post* reported: "The situation in Chester is akin to that in other sections of the country where the shortage of labor has forced the importation of negroes from the South. Chester is believed to have a population of 81,000, and of this number fully 5,000 are negroes. The present influx has augmented the normal [*sic*] negro population by 4,000 to 6,000 according to various estimates. . . . These men were brought here first by the Pennsylvania Railroad to take the place of Italian reservists called home by the war. After their arrival here however, they shifted to the steel plants, the shipyards, and other industrial establishments."

The Chester race riot began on July 24 when a white man named William McKinney got into an argument with four passing blacks that escalated into a fistfight during which McKinney was stabbed and killed. News of the crime spread quickly, and an enraged white mob formed that stormed into the city's "black belt" attacking black residents. The fighting continued for four consecutive days, with large groups of blacks assembling to combat the white throng. In an effort to quell the violence, the city's mayor called in the police, a company of the Chester National Guard, and a posse of deputized volunteers. "Hundreds of men armed with rifles and revolvers patrolled the streets, driving back infuriated mobs of both races who shot up the [black belt] section and clamored for each other's blood." When the rioting subsided on July 30, seven people had been killed and hundreds more injured in the violent episode.

Three weeks passed, and then the country's racial unrest took a disturbing new turn when a mutiny broke out among black troops of the U.S. Army. During the summer of 1917, two battalions of the all-black U.S. 24th Infantry Regiment had been deployed to Houston, Texas, to perform guard duty during the construction of Camp Logan, a training camp for national guardsmen. Houston was a bastion of the Old South, and at their new posting the black soldiers were subjected to constant racial slurs and discrimination.

On the afternoon of August 23, two Houston police officers, Rufus Daniels and Lee Sparks, were called to break up a gambling game underway on San Felipe Street in the black district of the segregated city. Sparks chased one of the participants over a fence near the home of Sara Travers, a black resident. When Travers proved uncooperative in helping him capture the suspect, Sparks placed her under arrest. As the officers were leading Travers to a call box to request a police wagon, a private from the 24th Regiment, Alonzo Edwards, appeared and offered to pay her fine. In response, Sparks pistol-whipped Edwards and placed him under arrest as well. Then a military policeman from the regiment, Corporal Charles Baltimore, arrived and asked the officers what had happened. Sparks pistol-whipped Baltimore and took the bloodied soldier to the police station where he was put in a cell with Private Edwards.

Word of the incident soon reached Camp Logan. After nightfall, 156 of the 24th Regiment's black soldiers mutinied, seized rifles and ammunition from a supply tent, and went on a murderous rampage through the streets of Houston. Among the first to die was a Mexican laborer shot in the backyard of his home. Several passing cars with white occupants were riddled with bullets. In one of the vehicles, a father of six was killed, in another, an army captain from the camp. Three white teenagers who ventured onto their front porch to investigate the commotion were also shot. When the two-hour killing spree ended, seventeen white victims had been killed, including two national guardsmen and four policemen.

The renegade troops were captured and disarmed the next day by soldiers from the Texas National Guard and the U.S. 19th Infantry. Following secret and hurried courts-martial for mutiny in a time of war, nineteen of the black soldiers were executed by hanging, and forty-one others were sentenced to life at hard labor at Leavenworth Penitentiary.

Concerned about the effect that the growing racial unrest was having on the war effort and suspicious that German influence might be behind it, Colonel Ralph Van Deman, director of the U.S. Army Military Intelligence Section, opened a new subject for investigation: "Negro Subversion." To look into the situation, Van Deman hired a "colored agent that we have had employed for some time to keep his eye on Negro agitation," a retired officer from the Philippine Constabulary, Major Walter H. Loving. During the fall of 1917, the ironically named Major Loving opened an office in Washington, DC, engaged a secretary to support the effort, and then toured the country building a network of volunteer black informants to report on conditions in the black community. His subsequent summaries to Van Deman outlined the real cause of unrest among black Americans—uncurbed lynching, discrimination in public transport, and Jim Crow segregation. Due to government indifference with regard to black lynching, Major Loving advised the director of military intelligence in 1918: "Not since the East St. Louis riot have the colored people been so worked up as they are today."

In Mexico City, Jahnke also recruited a former officer of the Philippine Constabulary—not to prevent a racial uprising in the United States, but to help incite one.

William "Guillermo" Gleaves had been born in Montreal in 1870 and raised in Pennsylvania before drifting to Mexico in 1893. Older than many of the other German agents, but still "a man of great physical strength," the gray-haired Gleaves mightily impressed Jahnke when he revealed that he had served in the Philippines as a lieutenant in the constabulary, and the spymaster readily accepted him for the cross-border operation. Gleaves was originally recruited by the Germans in 1917 for possible sabotage work in the Tampico oil fields, whose output supplied the British fleet. The black operative then moved to Mexico City where he worked for Consul General Dr. Friedrich Rieloff, to whom he reported on a daily basis. Recognizing the potential for the Industrial Workers of the World to assist the German war effort, the consul directed Gleaves to enroll as a member of the radical union, and before long Gleaves was attending secret IWW inner council meetings in the Mexican capital.

Consul Rieloff next instructed Gleaves to travel to the U.S. border "and try to work up a revolt" among the American troops stationed there, providing the agent with $1,500 to cover expenses and for use in bribing disaffected soldiers to mutiny. Gleaves departed for Ciudad Juárez in November and from there crossed into El Paso and then circulated throughout the army towns. On his return to Mexico City, he advised the consul that he had made some progress, informing him that he "thought he could accomplish something through some of the American soldiers and sergeants that he had been in touch with, but would need some help on another trip." Rieloff told the agent to await further instructions in Mexico City; there was a man arriving soon from the United States who would accompany him on his next cross-border journey.

While biding his time, Gleaves frequented the Hotel Calle Wiener Vesta and the patio of the Plaza Hotel where German agents often socialized. In due course, he came to the attention of Otto Paglasch, Jahnke's chief recruiter. Paglasch considered Gleaves a valuable man, particularly when he learned that the German agent had penetrated the British embassy and found work as a low-level employee. "The black traitor . . . was able to report to them [the Germans] such information as he gleaned around the British embassy."

Consul Rieloff told Gleaves that he was a member of a "Revolutionary Association" that had been formed in Mexico on behalf of Germany for the purpose of carrying out a revolution in the United States. The association was now going to sponsor Gleaves's return trip to the border to raise a revolt. Details of the operation were to be discussed at a meeting of the revolutionary committee that very evening; a car would be sent to take him to the conference.

At ten o'clock on the night of January 15, 1918, Gleaves was picked up in front of his hotel by a chauffeured automobile. Inside the car were Rieloff and a man Gleaves didn't recognize. Few words were spoken as the car wended its way through the darkened streets of Mexico City. The only passing landmark that Gleaves could identify was a park called the Alameda Central. Known as El Quemadoro, "the Burning Place," the Alameda had been established in 1592 during the Mexican Inquisition as the location where witches and sorcerers convicted by the inquisitor were taken to be publicly burned at the stake. The automobile drew to a stop at a house hidden in the shadows and they went inside.

Five members of the association were waiting to meet them. Gleaves was introduced to the secretary, Jahnke; the treasurer, Gobel; Pablo Waberski, Witzke; and two other unnamed German agents. The Revolutionary Association was a fiction created by Jahnke to lead Gleaves into believing that a committee of private individuals, not the German government, was behind the plan for mounting a campaign of sabotage and insurrection in the United States. This subterfuge would protect Germany from any political fallout if the operation should fail and Gleaves be captured. It would also improve the chances of success if the IWW delegates and renegade U.S. Army soldiers believed they were working for a group of pro-Germans rather than the German government itself. Gleaves was told that although the Mexico City committee of the Revolutionary Association acted as the headquarters for the enterprise, there were also committees in Nogales and Piedras Negras, among other cities in Mexico, and the association was well organized in the United States.

The conversation quickly turned to the impending mission to the border. Gleaves recounted what he had learned from black soldiers at U.S. Army camps on his last crossing, that a secret organization had been formed that linked the black regiments for a planned rebellion. Each regiment had elected officers to coordinate the operation who were ready to seize ammunition and start a general war against the United States. The uprising would be like the recent mutiny of the U.S. 24th Regiment at Camp Logan, but on a *much* bigger scale. "They expect to have the sympathy of lots of white men," Gleaves told the group, providing the names of several white soldiers who would support the rising.

Jahnke nodded approvingly. The spymaster explained that the association's plan was to use the IWW to call strikes and blow up mines, plants, railways, and telegraph facilities in the western states while Gleaves worked to incite a mutiny among the "negro troops" of the U.S. 10th Cavalry at Fort Huachuca. These actions would be the opening blow for an invasion of the United States from Mexico by Germans, Mexicans, South Americans, and others that would force the Americans to redeploy troops headed for Europe to repel the invaders. The men for the offensive were now being assembled, and the arms and ammunition for the effort were stored in Mexico ready to be disbursed. Gleaves and "Pablo" were to leave the next day to set the plan in motion "whereby Hell would break loose in the United States sometime in April or May."

Jahnke asked Gleaves and Witzke to stand up. "Will you know each other when you see each other again?" he asked.

"I think I will know him," Gleaves responded.

"I will know you," Witzke said firmly, staring at Gleaves.

Jahnke asked Gobel for the maps. The "treasurer" left the room and returned with a set of topographical maps that detailed the routes from Mexico into the United States. Flipping through the charts, Witzke explained the roads and crossroads that Gleaves would follow to reach Fort Huachuca, and the routes leading to mining camps in the vicinity of Globe, Arizona, where the IWW would foment strikes.

Gleaves would have an important role to play in the operation. First, he was to meet with delegates from IWW locals in Arizona at a conference in Nogales and introduce them to Waberski. He would then travel to Piedras Negras for a similar conference with IWW delegates from Texas, Oklahoma, and Colorado. On his return, Gleaves was "to go see the colored soldiers and the colored population," explain the purpose of the revolution that was going to be carried out, and distribute propaganda material. He would "go up the line by horseback to Fort Huachuca" and bring mutinous soldiers from the 10th Cavalry to meet with Witzke in Nogales, who would furnish them with money and instructions from Mexico City. When the strikes began in the mining district around Globe, Gleaves was to "take charge of the negro soldiers . . . and see that they did not 'come in' against the strikers."

During the operation, Gleaves would be under the direct order of Witzke and was to obey all instructions given. He was "not to talk to any white men, whatever; [he] was only to talk to negroes unless Pablo gave other instructions." Jahnke handed Gleaves three hundred pesos; when he needed additional money he could obtain it from Pablo who would be carrying sufficient funds.

By the time the meeting drew to a close, Jahnke was confident that Gleaves could be relied on to complete his assignment. The agent was given a ticket for the Southern Pacific train from Mexico City to Guadalajara leaving at 7 a.m. the next morning and was told not to be late.

It had been a beautiful afternoon in Mexico City, but Major Campbell never saw the sun shine. In his basement office in the depths of the American embassy, Campbell was hard at work on the task that had occupied nearly all of his time since being posted to the legation—keeping watch on the German agents of the city, particularly those employed by "Jenke," who Campbell was certain was the chief of the German secret service for the Western Hemisphere. His operatives had kept "Jenke" under observation almost continuously since September, but Campbell found the German spymaster to be "a slippery customer," reporting to Washington that "for two or three times during the past three or four months he [Jahnke] has disappeared and remained absent from five days to two weeks, and he has always succeeded in getting away without my agents knowing when he left and so I am unable to state where he has been." In the fall, a new man had joined "Jenke's" inner circle; his agents reported that they called him "the doctor." They later told him the man's name was "Doctor Altendorf," and Campbell had directed that he also be watched.

As Campbell sat at his desk working on reports, Ambassador Fletcher's private secretary appeared. "There's a man upstairs to see you," the secretary informed him. "He claims to be a U.S. Secret Service agent. Seems excited. Will you speak with him?"

"Bring him down," Campbell responded.

"I wanted to bring him down," the secretary said, "but he's afraid he'll be seen."

Annoyed at the interruption, the military attaché went to the main floor of the embassy and found the visitor waiting for him in a hallway. The stranger was extremely anxious, almost overcome with nervous tension.

"My name is Doctor Altendorf," he said urgently.

Campbell was stunned. Standing before him was the enemy's most dangerous agent—the same individual they had been pursuing for months.

"I am Mr. Butcher's man!" Altendorf declared. "Do you know Mr. Butcher?"

Ordinarily a man of supreme self-confidence and iron nerve, Altendorf was near the breaking point. If word reached Jahnke that he had been spotted in the U.S. embassy, his life expectancy could be measured in minutes.

"Yeah, I know Butcher," said Campbell, trying to maintain his composure following this second shock.

"I am Mr. Butcher's man," Altendorf repeated and handed him one of Byron Butcher's calling cards.

Altendorf hurriedly explained the purpose of his visit to the startled military attaché. He was a spy for the American secret service and was now associated with a ring of German agents. One of them, an operative named Pablo Waberski, had obtained a Russian passport and would be leaving for the United States the next day; Altendorf was to accompany him. He gave Campbell a bundle of documents containing important information and provided instructions on how to mail them so that they would reach Butcher's hands, calling the major's attention to the most valuable items: copies of codes that German spies used to communicate between the United States and Mexico.

Campbell assured the agent that he would dispatch the documents without delay (likely in the embassy's diplomatic pouch). Then as suddenly as he had arrived, Doctor Altendorf bid the major farewell and made a hasty—and discreet—exit from the embassy grounds.

A roving adventurer who could have stepped from the pages of a Dumas novel, Altendorf's personal history and natural abilities would make him a perfect spy, while a remarkable series of chance events enabled him to become one of the greatest double agents of the First World War.

Paul Bernardo Altendorf was born on June 1, 1875, in Cracow, Poland, a city that had been annexed by Austria-Hungary to become the "Grand Duchy of Cracow" decades earlier. His father, banker Joseph Altendorf, and mother, Bertha Castenberg, were of German ancestry, but both had been born and raised in Poland. Although an Austrian subject, Altendorf considered himself a Pole and harbored an intense dislike for both Austria and Germany. As an adolescent, the future spy studied design and foreign language at Cracow's Jaczka College, becoming fluent in English, Spanish, German, French, Yiddish, and Italian, as well as his native Polish. Altendorf then completed coursework in surgical chiropody at the University of Cracow. After receiving his degree, the young doctor "deserted the country to avoid service" in the Austrian army he detested and traveled the world. He lived in Paris in 1894, moved to Egypt in 1896, and four years later participated in the Boer War in South Africa. Altendorf enlisted in a British cavalry unit, Brabant's Horse, which saw significant action against the Boer commandos, and received a field promotion to the rank of corporal. Following his discharge from British service in 1901, Altendorf relocated to South America, where he traversed the continent, making his living as a self-employed physician in Argentina, Brazil, Uruguay, Paraguay, Bolivia, Chile, Peru, Ecuador, and Colombia before sailing to Cuba and finally arriving in Mexico.

When the world war began, Altendorf was in Mérida, the capital of Yucatán, governed by a pro-German Carrancista general named Salvador Alvarado. When Alvarado's officials learned that Altendorf had been making public statements favoring the Allied cause, he was given twenty-four hours to leave Mérida—or face the consequences. To avoid becoming his own patient, the doctor caught a fast boat to the distant city of Frontera, but ran into trouble with Carranza's officials there for not exchanging his savings of gold and silver coins into the worthless local paper currency. To escape arrest, Altendorf was forced to flee in the middle of the night to Puerto México and then set off on a grueling 175-mile train ride to Mexico City. The first forty miles of the journey were completed on a push car or "dump car" used for hauling railroad ties and supplies, Altendorf taking turns at pushing with three Mexican laborers he had hired for the task.

At a station called El Burro, Altendorf managed to obtain a seat on a passenger train headed north. The intrepid doctor carried a Colt .45 revolver for protection and engaged in gun battles with wayward revolutionists and marauding bandits on four separate occasions along the route before safely reaching Mexico City forty-two days after his journey began.

As the train pulled into the station, a hotel runner came aboard soliciting business for a lodging called the Hotel Juarez and gave Altendorf a promotional card.

"Who is the proprietor?" the doctor inquired.

"The proprietor is Mr. Otto Paglasch, a German," the runner responded.

With no other plans, Altendorf registered at the hotel located in the Avenida Cinco de Mayo, the chance encounter on the train landing him at one of the central meeting points for German agents in the city. The highly educated Austrian physician speaking refined German made a strong impression on Paglasch, and days later the hotel keeper introduced him to Jahnke and Witzke, who Paglasch advised the doctor were involved in the secret service.

"We had a little conversation," Altendorf would later recall, "and they asked me about the war, and I told them I could not give them any report, no more than I knew from the newspapers."

After a few days spent sizing him up—Jahnke even visited the physician on a professional basis for treatment of symptoms from the jarring impact of the Black Tom explosion—the spymaster put forth the idea of his becoming an agent.

"Have you ever done any secret service work?" he asked Altendorf.

"No, I'm afraid I am too nervous for that sort of thing," the doctor responded. "Besides, one must have special training for everything."

Having an idea where the discussion was headed, Altendorf's hesitation was intended to throw Jahnke off guard and make the ringleader even more desirous of hiring him. The plan worked.

"I'll tell you what, doctor," Jahnke said. "My friend, Major Schwierz, who is operating in Sonora, is now here in the city recruiting Germans, and Mexicans too, to be drilled as soldiers; for we are getting ready to give those American swine something to do that that will keep them so busy they will not have time to ship troops and support to France." Jahnke suggested that Schwierz might have a place for him.

The Austrian physician now vacillated in the other direction, feigning interest to show his "true" patriotism. "I shall be most happy to accept anything that will give me an opportunity to do something for the Fatherland," Altendorf replied.

That evening they met for dinner at a restaurant and had a long conversation about the war and the United States. Once again Altendorf wavered. The meal ended with an agreement to meet the next morning when the doctor would provide his final decision about joining Schwierz's group.

Fate intervened and Altendorf awoke with typhoid fever, a vestige of his long journey from Mérida. An ambulance was called and he was taken to the Hospital General de México. Jahnke stopped by for a brief visit to say that he and Witzke were departing for Monterrey and Nuevo Laredo on an important mission. He was sorry that the doctor could not accompany them.

For the next three weeks while Altendorf convalesced at the hospital, Paglasch interceded tirelessly on his behalf. "He called on Ambassador von Eckhardt to announce that the doctor of whom Jahnke had spoken so highly was ill with typhoid fever . . . but he is such a valuable man that Jahnke left instructions that his bills should be paid out of German funds and that the doctor must have the best possible attention in order that he might realize that he had indeed fallen among friends. Von Eckhardt accordingly furnished the money for all expenses."

On visiting day, Paglasch paid Altendorf a call escorted by Major Ricardo Schwierz who brought flowers for the room and a bottle of port wine for the patient. After a friendly discussion, it was agreed that when Altendorf had sufficiently recovered he would join the staff of General Plutarco Elías Calles and serve as a doctor in Schwierz's regiment.

On September 13, 1917, Altendorf was discharged from the hospital, and Schwierz wired General Calles that he would soon arrive with a German doctor, Altendorf, who now held the rank of captain in the German army based on an arrangement with Minister von Eckhardt. Altendorf was assigned to work at the German-Mexican training camp at El Claro as an instructor. In the days that followed, Altendorf accompanied Schwierz on jaunts throughout Mexico City to purchase supplies for the proposed army of invasion, then they departed on a 950-mile journey by train and boat to Hermosillo, the capital of Sonora. When they appeared at Calles's headquarters, the governor was highly pleased with the newest member of his staff and granted Altendorf the rank of colonel in the Mexican army at a salary of $300 a month.

From October into November, Colonel Altendorf was stationed at the El Claro camp where he drilled recruits and acted as the medical officer for German members of the expansive colony. While ostensibly performing his duties, Altendorf worked behind the scenes generating phony evidence, and collecting real evidence, of corruption by Major Schwierz. When word of Schwierz's crooked dealings reached Calles, he angrily demoted the major to *"jefe de policía de la frontera,"* a commander of border police. ·

Weeks later, in a turbulent meeting at General Calles's office in Hermosillo, with both Schwierz and the governor present, Altendorf denounced the German agent as a corrupt thief, then leveled an infinitely more serious charge, accusing the major of being an American spy.

Schwierz gasped in astonishment.

"You are a traitor!" Altendorf screamed, jabbing his finger at the major for added effect. "This man, general, is an American spy. He has sold the secrets from your office, secrets from the office of the German ambassador [minister]. He has sold the German codes and the Mexican codes to an American agent named Page. If von Eckhardt knew what happened here he would have this man killed."

Schwierz sprang forward and swung a punch at Altendorf's face, which the doctor parried. In an instant, General Calles jumped to his feet, drew his revolver, and ordered the German officer to leave the room. Schwierz's days as a secret service agent in Mexico were at an end.

While he was scheming to discredit Major Schwierz as an American double agent, Altendorf had himself begun to pass information on German plans to U.S. Army military intelligence. In his travels around Mexico City with Schwierz, he had met a "Turk" named Joe Bru doing business with the Germans who he was certain was an American informant. ("A Turk who could speak perfect English was something of a novelty to me," Altendorf would recall.) Confronting Bru and pointing out the obvious flaws in his cover, the "trader" confessed to being a Romanian in American service and agreed to act as a go-between in delivering messages from Altendorf to American military intelligence in Nogales.

The first reports from the doctor landed on the desk of Byron Butcher, who was amazed at the insight they provided into the inner workings of the German secret service network in Mexico. He dispatched agents across the border to corroborate Altendorf's information and discovered that it was correct in all essential details.

Butcher sent a communiqué to Major Robert L. Barnes, department intelligence officer at Fort Sam Houston, requesting that Dr. Altendorf and Joe Bru be retained as paid intelligence operatives in Mexico.

Barnes contacted Major S. W. Anding, the intelligence officer in Nogales, and asked for his recommendations concerning hiring Altendorf and Bru on a full-time basis. Referring to Altendorf under the code name "A-1" and Bru as "B-2," Anding returned a positive endorsement:

This man [Altendorf, A-1] has been continuously investigated since his arrival in Sonora October 20th with R. W. Schwiertz. . . . To A-1 alone is due the credit that General Calles dropped Schwierz from his payroll. A-1 made a full report to Calles on the activities of Schwierz and demonstrated beyond question that the German agent was a rogue.

This office is convinced of his ability and reliability, considers him one of the most important finds, and predicts that he will prove an invaluable asset to the American government. He has already provided more information of real value than any other dozen informants. His information has been checked and rechecked and found to be correct.

Bru [B-2] is a "Rumanian Jew"; can pass for Austrian, German, Turk, or Italian; will secure his first [American nationalization] papers in three or four months.

A detailed statement of his antecedents have been secured from Bru [B-2] should the Department Intelligence Officer believe that his services in connection with those of Altendorf [A-1] should be secured temporarily or permanently.

Barnes sent an immediate response, directing Anding to hire Altendorf and Bru even before approval was received from Washington:

I forwarded a copy of your letter to the Chief, Military Intelligence Section, recommending that authority be given for the retention of the two informants recently employed by you. I deemed this course necessary for the reason that funds on hand at the present time are somewhat limited, but the information which your informants have been able to secure appears to me to be of such value that I am taking the liberty of authorizing you to continue them until you hear from me further.

On December 13, 1917, Altendorf was officially sworn in as an agent of the U.S. Army Military Intelligence Section by Byron Butcher at the U.S. consulate in Nogales. Butcher cautioned his new operative to be careful, that he would be held responsible for his conduct in the field. Altendorf told his new superior not to worry—nothing would ever be found on him if he should have the misfortune of being discovered, and he would commit suicide before ever being taken. Altendorf had procured a .32 revolver for that purpose, which he carried in a special holster under his left arm in addition to the .45 revolver that he carried in plain sight, as was the custom in Mexico.

The Austrian doctor was in an ideal position to keep American military intelligence informed about enemy operations in Mexico, and in the months to come Altendorf would supply a trove of valuable information.

After Jahnke placed him in charge of his estate on Calle Colonia, Altendorf copied the contents of secret correspondence and intelligence files, rifled through Jahnke's personal desk, and prepared reports on the German agents and couriers that came to visit the spymaster for transmission to Butcher. The secrets that Altendorf unearthed would result in a score of enemy plots and subterfuges being thwarted.

The German establishment in Mexico City was certain of Altendorf's loyalty. *They* had selected *him* as an agent, and at every turn in the recruitment process Altendorf had displayed a total lack of interest in becoming a spy. The doctor's spoken German was flawless—an instant sign of a faithful comrade. In contrast, Neunhoffer's German was tainted with an American accent, resulting in immediate distrust when he spoke. (When a true German agent of German-American ancestry named Fred Herrmann crossed into Mexico from the United States, he was unable to obtain any assistance from von Eckhardt due to his "bum German.") Although Neunhoffer claimed to have business interests in Tampico, he never seemed to work—or even leave his hotel—yet he was always flush with cash. In contrast, Altendorf worked as a doctor and appeared destitute, intentionally dressing in shabby clothes to gain sympathy. When von Eckhardt observed his poor attire, the minister instructed Jahnke to give Altendorf money to buy clothes. If the doctor was in the pay of a foreign power, they certainly weren't paying him much. Perhaps the most convincing sign of Altendorf's loyalty was that known American counterintelligence agents, Neunhoffer and Campbell, kept the doctor under surveillance, genuinely believing that he was a German operative.

Altendorf fooled almost everyone into believing that he was a dedicated German agent: Jahnke, von Eckhardt, Schwierz, Carranza, Calles, and a range of assorted subagents and middlemen. There was only one man who remained uncertain that he could be trusted.

Altendorf exited the American embassy after meeting with Campbell and disappeared into a throng of passing pedestrians. He was not being tailed and proceeded directly to Jahnke's house, arriving in good time for supper.

A dinner party had been organized for the agents leaving on the secret mission, with Jahnke, Goebel, Witzke, Kettenbach, and Altendorf in attendance. It was a boisterous affair, and as the evening wore on and the flow of schnapps increased, the conversation grew ever more spirited. Witzke had been notified that an award awaited him in Berlin, and he teased Jahnke that he had received no decorations. The spymaster responded with a smile and told the former naval cadet that he "admired him for what a plucky boy he was and for what he had done." Sensing an opportunity to draw out some useful information, Altendorf "baited the hook" with an outpouring of laudatory comments about the youthful saboteur.

Ordinarily tight lipped about secret operations, Witzke grew boastful in front of the festive gathering of comrades. "I have done wonderful things in San Francisco!" he proclaimed, telling of how a 250,000 pound (actually 127,660 pound) black powder magazine at Mare Island had been destroyed. He confided that he had once gotten a job at a huge lumber mill in Oregon producing spruce for American military aircraft and had "fixed the wood to burn down this big mill." He also took credit for ruining the boilers of an enormous cargo liner, the SS *Minnesota*, which put the ship out of commission for over a year. But his greatest accomplishment would always be the Jersey Terminal mission, where he and Jahnke "had caused the Black Tom explosion in New York harbor in July 1916, which caused a loss of many millions of dollars and several lives."

Witzke paused and grew reflective, then turned toward Altendorf and said, "I have laid many people in the cemetery. If you are not straightforward with me I will put you there."

Believing the comment to be the idle boast of a young man in his cups, Altendorf returned a good-natured smile. But he would soon learn that Witzke was dead serious.

5

"Get Down and Hang On!"

The house at Calle Colonia No. 4 came to life early on the morning of January 16, 1918, as preparations got underway for the departure of Witzke and Altendorf on their mission to the border. It would be an arduous trip. In the span of two weeks the agents would travel by rail from Mexico City to the port of Manzanillo on the Pacific coast, take a boat north to Mazatlán, and then travel up the western boundary of Mexico to Hermosillo before finally reaching Nogales, Sonora—a journey of 1,565 miles, the approximate distance from Boston to Miami. Along the way, Witzke was to perform courier duty, visiting German consulates to deliver confidential mail and convey verbal instructions from Jahnke and von Eckhardt to the consuls.

After an extempore breakfast, Jahnke called Witzke and Altendorf into his office. The spymaster went to the safe and withdrew a stack of currency from the cash reserve that he had received aboard the Spanish liner *Alfonso XIII* in Veracruz and counted out $1,000 in U.S. gold certificates and $500 in U.S. ten- and twenty-dollar bills. He handed the money to Witzke and then withdrew three hundred Mexican pesos which he gave to Altendorf. "If you need any more," he told the doctor, "you call on Witzke. He will give you money or whatever you want."

Jahnke put the currency that remained back in the safe and took out two slips of paper—coded documents that Altendorf had seen Kettenbach enciphering the day before, which Witzke would carry on the operation.

He slid the coded identification sheet across the desk to the young agent. Intended for presentation to German consuls along the route, it contained an introduction to Witzke, a description of the important mission, and an order to advance the agent up to one thousand pesos in Mexican gold upon demand. The second document was the cipher table that Witzke was to use in preparing the coded messages that he would send to Altendorf waiting on the Mexican side of the border in Hermosillo. The doctor would immediately transmit the coded reports to Jahnke in Mexico City. The spymaster emphasized that the documents must remain secure at all times.

Jahnke's demeanor was grave and he seemed almost depressed. "Pablo," he said quietly to the youth, "if anything happens in the United States and you are in danger of being caught, tear up these papers. Do not allow yourself to be arrested. Remember you are a sworn man [sworn-in German agent] and commit suicide first." Like Vice Admiral von Spee, his squadron commander in the Falklands battle who went down with his sinking cruiser rather than surrender, Witzke was expected to kill himself before being taken prisoner. Jahnke also directed Altendorf to commit suicide rather than be captured. "Jahnke, you have been more than a brother," the doctor said in reply. "I am going to show you what a man I am. You will never forget me." The three men shook hands, and then Witzke and Altendorf passed through the electrified fence that ringed Jahnke's estate and left to catch the 7 a.m. train.

Arriving at the station on time, they boarded their coach without incident and settled in for the first leg of the journey, a 168-mile ride to Iripuato. From a discreet vantage point, William Gleaves, the "third man" hired to act as a go-between in dealings with the IWW and black cavalry troops, watched them enter their car and boarded an adjoining coach.

The steam locomotive at the front of the train was a venerable wood burner, and it took most of the day rolling across a rugged, desolate landscape before their destination was reached. The agents were tense and guarded, each harboring his own private fears. Aside from the risks of the mission and the possibility of exposure and death in enemy territory, a trip by rail through revolutionary Mexico was itself a dangerous undertaking. Trains were attacked by bandits and revolutionaries on a daily basis and the passengers robbed or killed. The marauders would typically block the tracks and raise a rail, then open fire on the coaches from a concealed position alongside the road, or blow up the train with dynamite as it passed and then rummage through the wreckage for spoils. Passenger trains were often preceded by an armored train carrying federal troops, but this Sud Pacífico de Mexico train had no advance escort.

They reached Iripuato before dusk and disembarked; due to the danger of bandit attack, no trains traveled in Mexico at night. A car took Witzke and Altendorf into town, and they checked into the Hotel Reforma, sharing a room. Although Gleaves rode into town on the same car, Pablo Waberski from the Revolutionary Association did not display any recognition or acknowledge the black agent's presence.

In the morning, Witzke and the doctor rose early and after consuming a quick breakfast departed on the first train to Guadalajara. The 150-mile trip to the western metropolis was uneventful, and they pulled into the station in the late afternoon. As they exited the coach, Witzke noted Gleaves's presence on the platform but once again displayed no sign of recognition.

Altendorf and Witzke registered at the Hotel Cosmopolitan and after cleaning themselves up went out for dinner. The pressures of the operation were already beginning to tell on the former naval cadet. Crossing into the United States on a secret mission during wartime to meet contacts that he could not trust was bad enough, but within days Witzke would face the additional challenge of murdering an American intelligence agent in cold blood. The twenty-two-year old had taken a number of innocent lives, he knew, while carrying out sabotage in the United States—five at Black Tom, including the chief of the Lehigh Valley Railway Police and Arthur Tossen, the baby tossed from its crib by the blast, and another six at Mare Island, most from the MacKenzie family. But he hadn't *intended* to kill them, and after setting the explosives had been miles away when they died. It would be a different matter to look Byron Butcher in the eyes and shoot the unsuspecting intelligence man with a pistol, and escape without being caught.

The region around Guadalajara is famed for its tequila, and that night at dinner Witzke began sampling the local beverage—heavily. Observing his young companion's consumption rate gave Altendorf an idea. He confided to Witzke that he was unable to drink much himself, advising that he suffered from Bright's disease (a kidney ailment, today known as acute nephritis), but encouraged his fellow agent to drink at every opportunity.

"I have many lives on my conscience," the youth lamented, "and I have killed many people and will now kill more. I will receive my medal from the Kaiser for what I have done when I return to Germany and that will be my compensation."

Witzke proposed that they explore the city's night life and asked Altendorf if he was familiar with any brothels in the area. The doctor assured him that "he could find his way around Guadalajara blindfolded" and knew all the best resorts for engaging female company. Following a few discreet inquiries to the porter in Spanish, Altendorf suggested they make a night of it.

"You are right, doctor, perhaps I will never come back," Witzke replied.

A car was hired and the two traveling companions visited several of the local houses and became acquainted with the staff. As the evening progressed, Altendorf pushed more and more liquor on the intoxicated youth until he was nearly senseless. They went to a theater with two of the girls, and Witzke fell twice before they arrived at their box. When Witzke reached a state where he did not know if he was in a theater or a bar, Altendorf assisted his companion, stumbling and swaying, back to the bordello, undressed him, and put him to bed.

Altendorf stood for a while in the semidarkness watching the inebriated agent to ensure that he was truly unconscious and then set to work. Searching through Witzke's clothes he found an able seaman's card and lifeboat operation certificate, both in the name of Pablo Waberski, and the coded letter of introduction and cipher table that he had been given by Jahnke.

"I spent a large part of the night examining and copying the papers in his pockets," Altendorf later recalled, "and making up a report thereon for the intelligence department. That done, I watched over him until morning, not daring to sleep myself; for if any of those things had been missing he might have been tempted to carry out his threat to kill me."

When he finished with the documents, Altendorf returned them to Witzke's clothes exactly as they had been and left them there. Hours later, as the early morning sunlight filtered into the room, the youth groggily regained consciousness. Trying to think through a colossal hangover, Witzke suddenly rose with a start, aware that he had fallen asleep and left the secret papers unguarded. He quickly searched through the pockets of his clothes and was relieved to find that the documents were still in the same place he had put them.

"Doctor, has the door been closed here?" Witzke inquired. "I am carrying such valuable papers and have done such a foolish thing to get drunk."

Altendorf assured him the door had remained locked and no one had entered their room. Witzke thanked the doctor for taking such good care of him. "He said that wine and women were irresistible to him, that he had run great risks the night before, but that happily all was well."

They returned to the Cosmopolitan for breakfast, then Witzke announced that he was going to take a walk to the train station to find out when the next train for Colima would pass through. Altendorf watched the youth head off and after a brief interval shadowed him to the station, where he observed a black man that he had seen on the train from Mexico City follow Witzke into the depot. By this point, the number of chance encounters they'd had with the stranger made it apparent to Altendorf that he was the mysterious "third party" that Jahnke had said would accompany Witzke to the border. Advancing no further, the doctor hastily retraced his steps to the hotel.

Witzke returned to their room a short while later and informed Altendorf that there had been a gun battle between federal troops and bandits along the line, and as a result the train for the day had been canceled. He proposed they fill the time by visiting a local supplier working to obtain a motor that was urgently needed by the German government to power a new wireless station near Mexico City. The existing radio system at Chapultepec was able to receive messages from long distance but not transmit them. It was hoped that the new station would allow direct communication with Berlin.

When they called at the company, they were informed that all attempts to obtain the special engine had failed. Frustrated by the lack of progress, Witzke offered to pay twenty-five thousand pesos for delivery of the critical motor but was told that it was impossible; the only chance to obtain the unit was through the firm of Schumann & Shuckert in Buenos Aires. Witzke thanked them for the advice, saying that men had already been sent to Argentina with instructions to buy one, no matter the cost. Altendorf listened to the exchange in silence and made a mental note to include this interesting development in a report to Mr. Butcher.

After the fruitless meeting concluded, the agents retired to the German club and socialized with a pair of chemists employed at an ordnance factory in Guadalajara. Fifty rifles were being turned out each day at the plant with the aid of German technicians. One of the chemists mentioned that the factory lacked material that was needed from Spain for manufacturing gas masks, but were hoping to obtain a supply shortly. Witzke told them "they would [soon] need a lot of gas masks—and would want them quick."

The extended stopover in Guadalajara ended on January 19 with a one-hundred-mile train ride to Colima, where the agents remained overnight. The next morning they received news that another gun battle had occurred on the road between Colima and Manzanillo, and as a consequence no trains would be running that day. The delay posed a serious setback to their timetable since the biweekly boat from Manzanillo to Mazatlán departed on the 21st.

"I must leave . . . I've got to meet a man in Manzanillo," Witzke told the doctor anxiously. "You can speak Spanish, see if you can hire an engine to take us."

The agents hurried to the train station and, spotting an idle locomotive on a siding, hunted down the Mexican engineer and explained their predicament. The engine belonged to a German businessman from Guadalajara, and the driver proved sympathetic, offering to take them to Manzanillo in the locomotive at a charge of forty dollars per person.

"I don't mind the amount of money," Witzke said firmly. "I must arrive in Manzanillo before the consul's office closes."

The deal was finalized, and Witzke told the doctor that he needed to attend to some last-minute details before leaving Colima. He instructed Altendorf to offer the engine driver their three railway tickets to Manzanillo at no cost, for him to resell at a profit, if he would stop the engine on the other side of a bridge one half mile from the Colima station and wait for them there.

"I will do so," the engineer responded.

Witzke rushed to the hotel where Gleaves was staying and explained what had been arranged. The black agent was directed to pack his bags quickly; a taxi would arrive shortly to take him to the locomotive.

In a hired car, Witzke and Altendorf proceeded to the locomotive and tender, now waiting at the bridge. On their way to the rendezvous point, Altendorf saw the "third man" in a car ahead, racing fast to arrive at the locomotive before them. The agents boarded the engine, and the driver got underway.

The locomotive only traveled a short distance when the engineer brought it to a stop on the pretext of having to "oil around"—lubricate the rods and bearings, a common task in the day of steam engines. After a few moments walking about the machine, he reentered the cab and told Witzke, "There is a negro on the pilot ['cowcatcher' at the front of the locomotive] who refuses to pay his fare. He said his 'boss' was in the cab and would pay for him."

Livid that the identity of the "third party" had been revealed to Altendorf, Witzke shoved forty dollars at the engineer to cover Gleaves's share of the ride.

"Now, G-d damn you, you know who is with me," he said, glaring at the doctor.

"I know everything else," Altendorf replied nonchalantly. "I may as well know the 'third man.'"

When the locomotive reached a point ten miles from Colima, a fusillade of bullets struck the tender and ricocheted through the cab, signaling the start of a bandit attack. Witzke and Altendorf were sitting on the back of the tender with their legs dangling over the water tank when the shooting began. The engineer, a tough hombre, yelled out for them to "get down and hang on" to the opposite side of the tank from the rifle fire, then opened the throttle. With Gleaves hunched low on the exposed pilot at the front, and Witzke and Altendorf gripping the side of the water tank, the locomotive barreled down the track. Their luck held and no one was injured; the bandits had not expected a train to pass that day and neglected the usual precaution of removing a rail. In minutes they were out of danger and rolling down the line toward the coast.

They reached Manzanillo just before eleven on Sunday morning. Witzke told Gleaves to get a room at the Reforma Hotel and informed him that they would be staying at the Manzanillo Hotel. When Gleaves was out of sight, Witzke and Altendorf went to the hotel, deposited their bags, and hurried off for the German consulate.

The jovial consul, Adolfo Stoll, a former agent of the German Kosmos Steamship Line, was there to greet them.

"Is the doctor also in this case?" Stoll inquired, surprised that a physician was involved in the dangerous operation.

"Yes, he will help us at the border. I'm going across," Witzke responded. "He knows what's going to be done. He will be my secretary and stay in Hermosillo where he will make his headquarters."

For security reasons they gave their money and papers to Stoll for safekeeping while they were in the city.

"Here is my Russian passport," Witzke said, as he handed over the travel document.

Stoll flipped through the pages of the passport and glanced at the young agent in astonishment.

"By Jove, 'Waberski,'" he exclaimed, "we are a wonderful people! I have never heard of anything like that. To think that a [Russian] consul would dish out a Russian passport to a German subject—and to do a thing like that so secretly."

"The Minister is our friend," Witzke assured him with a straight face.

In reality the agent had stolen the papers of a sailor named Pablo Waberski who passed out after a drinking bout in a San Francisco bar. Witzke then used the documents to obtain an identification card from the Russian consul in Mexico City, which he took to the Russian embassy to obtain a genuine passport in the name of "Pablo Waberski." He later said of the episode, "Russia was giving signs even then of the breakup which came shortly afterward. Their officials at times were not so strict and the situation played into my hands."

Stoll locked the cash and documents in his safe and after spinning the tumbler informed Witzke that a letter had arrived for him. It was addressed to Pablo Waberski with the return address "José Iturbe, Box 306, Mexico City," one of Jahnke's aliases.

Witzke tore open the envelope and read the note:

Dear Friend Pablo,
I have noticed you left Mexico City with cold feet.
I was never accustomed to seeing you with cold feet.
How are the chickens on the road?
Are they young chickens or old chickens?
I hope when you get to Nogales your feet will be warm,
as I know you too well.
My best regards from yours,
Jahnke, Friend

Witzke frowned and read the letter with such concern that the consul asked, "What's wrong Witzke? Some bad news?"

"No, I just cannot understand this letter," the agent responded. Witzke held the note up to the light and examined it closely, looking for signs of secret ink. "Have you got some apple vinegar here?" he asked Stoll. The consul replied that he was sorry, but he didn't have any of the developing agent.

Altendorf and Witzke returned to the hotel, where the youth took out the letter once again. He gave it to Altendorf to read and then smiled.

"This letter is from Jahnke. I suppose when he gave me instructions in the office, about the work that I was going to do and the first time since I have been working with him that he asked me to carry a pistol, and if anything should happen to me I will have to commit suicide, that this made my feet cold. He ought to know me better after what I have done. My feet have never been cold." The agent quickly tore the letter into small pieces and threw the scraps away.

The next day Witzke departed for a private meeting with Stoll at the consulate, and Altendorf took the opportunity to go out in search of the "third party." He found the black agent in the city plaza and, on the pretext of booking their passage to Mazatlán on the steamer *Josefina*, was able to discover his name.

"I am Doctor Altendorf," he announced.

Gleaves hesitated before replying, "William Gleaves."

He had been directed "not to talk to any white man whatever; only to speak to negroes unless Witzke gave other instructions," and now he was violating orders.

"I see you carry a pistol," said Altendorf, gesturing toward the holstered revolver at Gleaves's waist.

"Yes, I am an official in the Mexican government," Gleaves responded, "and a lieutenant-colonel in the Carranza Army."

He told Altendorf that he was also headed north on the *Josefina* with his "boss," Pablo Waberski. At the ticket office the doctor purchased three tickets on the coastal steamer which was now scheduled to depart on January 22 instead of the 21st as originally planned.

Later that afternoon, when Witzke learned that Altendorf had spoken with Gleaves, he became furious and severely criticized the doctor for his carelessness.

"I told him that you were not of our party and going to some place in Colorado!" Witzke angrily exclaimed. "Now he knows that you're going to Sonora." Shaking his head in reproach, he continued: "Doctor, you are the only man who knows about this [operation]. You are a man who has to be very secret and be very careful with the negro in case he should be caught. He might give you away."

"Do you trust him?" asked Altendorf.

"I think I can," Witzke replied, eying the doctor. "But if he can't be trusted, then he's dead. I am going to use him in such a way that he will always be watched by our men. In case he would like to do something wrong he will find himself dead before he will do anything."

That afternoon Witzke and Altendorf went out to a bar for a drink. As they were passing the time in a game of dominoes, three naval officers from an American merchant ship entered the barroom and ordered a round of drinks. Seeing the agents' lively game, one of the men carried his glass over to where they were sitting and in a friendly way greeted Witzke in German.

"I do not understand what you're saying," the youth responded in English.

"I thought you were German," said the officer.

"No sir, I am a Russian and my friend is Swiss," Witzke replied. Then he introduced himself as Pablo Waberski and Altendorf as "Mr. Canet."

The American asked Witzke if he knew any girls in the area. Sensing an opportunity to obtain some secret information, Witzke said that he did and offered to take them to a local club called the Cinderella where they could meet women. The naval officers readily accepted, and with Witzke in the lead alongside the German-speaking officer and Altendorf in tow with the other two men, the group headed off for the club.

Altendorf watched Witzke step ahead of the group with his companion, certain that his intention was to collect intelligence from the unsuspecting American, and moved quickly to derail the plan. Speaking to the first engineer in a hushed tone, Altendorf warned him of the danger:

Listen, I will tell you something and you do what I am telling you. This man who is walking ahead with your friend is a German and I am sure that he will fool your friend to find something out. We will go to this place and have just one drink and you fellows ask for lemonade. Don't stay long in the place and then take your officer friend away from this man.

When they arrived at the Cinderella, Witzke insisted that his new acquaintances order beer rather than lemonade. The officer Altendorf had warned had a single bottle of beer and sipped it slowly, watching his friends down four bottles apiece. When two Mexican seamen from the gunboat *Guerrera* arrived and it appeared a serious bout of drinking would soon be underway, he advised his companions that it was time to get back to the ship. Witzke protested that they were leaving too soon, so the officer promised to return in the evening, as their freighter would be in port until the following day. Witzke and Altendorf walked the men to the pier.

After the Americans boarded their cargo ship, the two agents went to the German consulate where Witzke related the story of their encounter with the enemy officers to Stoll. The consul smiled and said to the youth, "What do you think about blowing up this little boat in the harbor? I can give you what you want [to destroy the ship] and I have my own gasoline boat."

"I can do it in five minutes," Witzke responded. "But my work which I am going to do now is more important, and you know as well as I that this would not be very wise to do because I could expose myself."

That ended any further discussion of the topic, and the American freighter sailed from Manzanillo without incident.

The next morning, Altendorf and Witzke boarded the steamship *Josefina* for the 440-mile voyage north to the port of Mazatlán. The vessel was owned by the German trading house Melchers Sucesores, which used the boat for hauling cargo between Mexican ports, but it also carried a small number of passengers as well. It would take three days for the oil-burning steamer to reach their destination. Continuing to maintain the fiction that they were not acquainted with the black agent, Gleaves boarded the ship separately. The only other passengers on the trip were two American traders that none of the men were familiar with.

Throughout the voyage, Altendorf displayed his customary relaxed, self-confident manner, but inside the doctor knew that he was playing a dangerous game. As he had told Neunhoffer in Mexico City: "A spy should be careful of what he says and when he says it." If Altendorf made the slightest error revealing that he was an American agent, he would be executed immediately, if not by Witzke, then certainly by his powerfully built henchman, Gleaves. A campaign of terror was about to be unleashed across the United States with plant bombings, an army mutiny, and violent uprisings, and he had yet to provide details to the Americans or even inform the U.S. authorities where Witzke and Gleaves would cross the frontier. Mr. Butcher was not even aware that he was the target of an assassination plot.

The coastal steamer proceeded slowly across the empty ocean toward their destination, the vast expanse an ironic backdrop for a double agent feeling "lost at sea." But Altendorf had no way of knowing the turn of events that awaited them on the road ahead, or that the situation was not what it appeared to be.

6

Placed Together, the Two Scraps of Paper Read: "NOVIA"

On January 24, 1918, the *Josefina* arrived at Mazatlán, the principal port of entry on the west coast of Mexico. The harbor was too shallow for ocean-going vessels to enter, so the small steamship anchored in the roadstead a mile offshore. There the *Josefina* was boarded by immigration officials who scrutinized the passengers' passports and interviewed the officers and crew before allowing them to land. Witzke, Gleaves, and Altendorf were taken ashore on lighters, gasoline-powered launches that brought them to the wharf. Their baggage was landed by lighters that followed.

Suggesting that they should not be seen together, but in reality wanting privacy to prepare a report for American military intelligence, Altendorf proposed that they stay at different hotels, and Witzke readily agreed. Once out of the doctor's hearing, Jahnke's lieutenant instructed a Mexican boatman to take Gleaves to a separate lodging. Witzke then departed for the Central Hotel, and Altendorf went to the Hotel Francia. The three agents welcomed the time apart, for unknown to the others, each had a secret appointment to keep in the city.

Mazatlán's favorable location on the northern Pacific coast of Mexico, together with the region's vast mineral and agricultural resources and the local demand for manufactured goods, had resulted in the port city dominating commercial trade in the area. Annual exports from Mazatlán exceeded $6 million and included gold and silver bullion, chickpeas, hides, and sugar, while imports primarily consisted of machinery for the mines and a variety of consumer goods. The largest firms controlling this trade were German owned, and an influx of German immigrants had left a strong Teutonic influence on the culture of Mazatlán. In 1900 a German brewery had been founded to produce a pilsner lager beer, and a German *biergarten* was built in which to drink it; Bavarian music transformed the sound of the local Banda music, and German-style architecture could be seen in buildings throughout the city, such as the ornate Gothic bandstand of the Plaza de la República in the central square.

Although Mazatlán had suffered heavily during the Mexican Revolution, by 1918 the days of hunger and privation were over, and the city was prospering once again. Yet beneath Mazatlán's peaceful and industrious exterior, a secret war was underway. The metropolis was a key junction linking the Mexican interior with the rail line that led to the U.S. border at Nogales, Arizona. German agents traveling to the United States or returning to Mexico City routinely passed through Mazatlán or were in temporary residence there. After America declared war against Germany, a Trading with the Enemy Act was passed by Congress that made it illegal for any person or entity in the United States to trade with a German-owned company. The government published a "blacklist" of known enemy companies and individuals with whom trade was forbidden that became known in Mexico as the "*Listas Negras.*" Violation of the act was punishable by a fine of $10,000 or ten years in jail or both. The German trading houses of Mazatlán sought ways to circumvent the American blacklist, not only for their financial survival, but to obtain material for German officials in Mexico to use in operations against the Allies.

The opposing "commanders" in this secret war were Friedrich Unger, the honorary German consul in Mazatlán, and William Chapman, the American consul and the U.S. State Department's senior official in the city.

Friedrich Heinrich "Fritz" Unger had arrived in Mazatlán in 1896 to take a position with Melchers Sucesores, the most powerful of the German trading houses. "Always immaculately attired in a fine suit with vest and gold watch chain, the 5-foot 10-inch Unger had short brown hair and a neatly trimmed moustache." He had risen rapidly at Casa Melchers (the House of Melchers) and in 1910 was elevated to managing partner. For decades Melchers thrived, dealing in a wide assortment of goods and commodities, from textiles to dynamite, plumbing supplies to fine wines; the trading house even imported Studebaker automobiles. Then the world war broke out in Europe. Britain's naval blockade instantly prevented the German-owned company from receiving any goods from Europe, and a second blow fell when America entered the war and both Melchers Sucesores and Friedrich Unger were placed on the U.S. blacklist. By 1918, Melchers' business had been reduced to 30 percent of its prewar volume.

Unger responded by engaging in a number of subterfuges to circumvent the *Listas Negras*, such as using intermediary Mexican companies to purchase goods in the United States for transshipment to Melchers' warehouse, and having business correspondence with U.S. firms addressed to staff with Mexican surnames. The consul also became an active participant in the clandestine war against the *norteamericanos*, employing the resources of Casa Melchers in support of a range of German intelligence operations. The trading house imported tons of lard for shipment to Mexico City where it was used in the manufacture of glycerin and converted into explosives. Supplies of dye woods for coloring army uniforms were bought by Melchers Sucesores to prevent their being acquired by the United States. Detailed economic and production maps showing important U.S. manufacturing centers were acquired by Unger and distributed to saboteurs leaving for America. Melchers Sucesores also acted as a conduit in channeling money to German agents engaged in clandestine operations. There were few activities that Fritz Unger would not undertake to oppose Melcher's archenemy, the United States.

The German consul's schemes were countered by the efforts of William Edgar Chapman, the U.S. consul in Mazatlán. Chapman was a dedicated State Department official whose rise in government service had come in the Horatio Alger tradition of hard work and fair play. Following service in the Philippines during the Spanish-American War, Chapman traveled to Washington, DC, and obtained a job as a clerk in the War Department. Burning with ambition, the former Arkansas farm boy received a bachelor's degree in law (LLB) from the Washington School of Law in 1914 and a master's (LLM) from the National University Law School in 1915. After passing the U.S. consular examination in 1916, Chapman was appointed a consul of class eight and posted as U.S. consul to Nogales and then Guaymas, before finally being assigned to Mazatlán in 1917.

Twenty years after serving in the Spanish-American War, Consul Chapman would again answer the call in defending the United States during the war with Germany. Chapman was a no-nonsense consular officer demanding strict adherence to U.S. laws and regulations—and reporting violations to the government for enforcement. After the war began, he organized a network of spies and confidential agents throughout Mazatlán to gather information on enemy activities, which he forwarded to his superiors at the State Department on a weekly basis:

As late as December 19, 1917, the firm of L. Dinkelspiel & Company of San Francisco, California, was taking orders from persons whom they knew were acting as covers for the enemies of the United States in violation of the Enemy Trading Act. It is suggested that the representatives of the Department of Justice at San Francisco be called . . . to investigate the matter set forth in the affidavit with the view of punishing any persons who may be found guilty of violating the Enemy Trading Act.

Large quantities of merchandise are going into San Blas from the United States and continually finding their way into the hands of Germans. As the large German firm of Deilius and Company own or control most of that section, some means should be adopted to offset this steady supply. . . .

M. Miranda, director general of Company Transportes Maritimos leaves for San Francisco on the steamer City of Para with letters of incorporation [for the firm]. Said company is trying to arrange business connections there. Capital is almost entirely that of Germans [in] Mazatlán under names of Mexicans connected with them. If United States objects . . . I have suggested secret service San Francisco to prevent them.

Chapman's greatest coup occurred when he obtained the first samples of German incendiary pencils ever seen by U.S. intelligence. This episode began when a Dutch seaman named Carl Jacobsen arrived at the consulate requesting approval to be "signed on" as a crewman aboard an American steamship leaving Mazatlán for the United States. The twenty-one-year-old Jacobsen resembled Lothar Witzke in appearance, with light hair and blue eyes, and also like Witzke, he carried a certificate attesting to his competence as an able seaman, in his case issued at Newport News, Virginia. The seaman's certificate and other papers that Jacobsen carried all appeared to be in order, as were his answers to Chapman's questions regarding his past service as a sailor. The consul was about to pass the youth for a shipboard assignment to the United States when a chance inquiry, "Why did you come to Mexico?" took Jacobsen by surprise and drew an improbable response. His suspicions instantly aroused and now uncertain of the young man's motives, Chapman refused to approve passage.

In the days that followed, Jacobsen returned to the consulate five times requesting approval for passage, growing increasingly more desperate with each rejection. In a final attempt to obtain a berth on an American ship, the anxious youth pleaded to sail on the SS *Fairhaven* (due to leave the next day), as he was now out of money. Once again, Chapman said no. Seeing no alternative, Jacobsen admitted to the consul that he *was* a German agent, revealing that there was a plot underway to burn U.S. shipyards, munitions plants, and supply ships using chemical bombs timed so that they would explode thirty-five minutes after being placed.

As Chapman related in a communiqué to the secretary of state:

> He admitted further that the German consul at Mazatlán [Friedrich Unger] had ordered him to go the United States on the *Fairhaven* in order that he might start the work of destruction in which he says a number of others are to be engaged.
>
> At this point he told me that he wanted to quit the Germans and looked to the Americans as his friends, [saying] that the Germans were not paying him well enough and that his life would be in danger if they should discover that he had betrayed them. He said that he wanted by all means to get to the United States, because now that he had told me what he was doing he could not continue with the Germans.
>
> I informed him that I would do nothing for him until he produced and delivered to me the materials which he had [received].

Jacobsen left the consulate and a short time later returned with a talcum powder can that contained six of the incendiary glass tubes. Chapman sent the sabotage devices and instructions on their use in a diplomatic pouch to the State Department. He gave Jacobsen twenty-four dollars to purchase a train ticket to Nogales, Arizona, and sent a coded telegram to the U.S. consul at Nogales with the saboteur's itinerary. On arrival in Nogales, Jacobsen was apprehended by U.S. Army military intelligence and escorted to the guardhouse.

But the Jacobsen episode was not the first time that Chapman worked with secret agents passing through Mazatlán for the border.

Altendorf rose early on the morning of January 25 and made his way down winding cobblestone streets to the American consulate on Olas Altas, a wide boulevard that fronted the ocean. He arrived unannounced at 4:30 a.m., but Chapman was only too pleased to receive his caller. They had met on a previous visit by Altendorf to the city, and Chapman was aware (and had confirmed) that the Austrian was an agent of U.S. military intelligence. The forty-two-year-old physician speaking English with a pronounced German accent and the forty-one-year-old Arkansas-born bureaucrat who responded in a southern drawl made an incongruous pair, but they got along well. Altendorf quickly briefed Chapman on Witzke's mission and delivered a written report that he had prepared the night before for dispatch to Nogales in the diplomatic pouch. To ensure that the information arrived in time, the pair composed a coded message for Chapman to wire to the American consul in Nogales "that he [Altendorf] was en route with two German spies who would appear at the [Nogales] consulate to arrange their papers for entering the United States." Altendorf told Chapman that it would be too dangerous for him to return during daylight hours with so many enemy operatives about; if he obtained any additional information, he would come back at the same time the following morning. The coded draft complete, Altendorf left the U.S. consulate and headed for Unger's office at Melchers Sucesores on Calle Arsenal, which served as the German consulate.

The doctor entered the fortresslike headquarters of the German trading company and came upon Unger, Witzke, and an agent named Boeder engaged in light conversation following a meeting that had just concluded. Unger and Witzke were close comrades from previous stopovers the youth had made to the city, and a minor quarrel from a previous visit had apparently just been settled.

"Well, we are good friends now," said Witzke, shaking hands with the consul.

"Yes," Unger responded with a smile, "but have you forgotten about this?" He gestured toward Witzke's coded letter of introduction.

It was standard procedure for German agents to present their credentials upon arrival at a post. The agent sat down, and after several attempts to decode the difficult identification card cipher, managed to complete the task. (Cryptography historian David Kahn would later note: "The Waberski cipher proved to be an immensely complicated system; one wonders how the German officials worked it.") He presented a translated copy to Unger and asked the consul to provide Boeder with $100 in cash on the authority outlined in his credentials. Boeder was shortly to leave for Mexico City with a message from Witzke for hand delivery to Jahnke, and the $100 would cover expenses. Unger handed the cash to Boeder, and Witzke gave him an additional $100 from his own funds. Then he collected the worksheet used to decode the message, along with the translated copy, and tossed both into the fire. "I must not lose this," he announced firmly.

Witzke asked Unger about "some items that would be sent to him when he got on the border." The businessman led the group through the administrative offices of Melchers Sucesores into a warehouse at the side of the building where seven hundred rifles imported by the trading house for the impending German-Mexican invasion of the United States were being stored. Altendorf was amazed by the size of the arsenal—more rifles than he had ever seen in one place before. During the discussion that followed, he learned that an agent named Reinmann was to deliver the weapons to Witzke after the sabotage campaign had been launched.

They returned to the administration building, and Witzke deposited his papers with Unger for safekeeping, then went off to a public bath. Altendorf and Boeder retired to the city plaza where they joined Gaedke and Reinmann for a beer. While they were talking, Gleaves walked past and saluted.

"That is Waberski's man, I know him," said Boeder, nodding toward Gleaves.

Altendorf gave the "third man" a casual glance as he departed down the walkway, not revealing his concern about Witzke's powerful attendant who always seemed to be hovering in the background. Since their arrival, Gleaves had called on Jahnke's lieutenant unfailingly each morning at 7 a.m. for instructions.

Witzke reappeared and ordered a beer, then entered into a conversation with Reinmann about the stockpile of rifles at Melchers' warehouse. It would require significant effort to move such a large quantity of weapons to the border in secrecy, and Reinmann was anxious for the operation to get underway.

"You must have patience and wait," Witzke cautioned the agent. "I will let you know immediately upon arriving at the border [when it will be safe to deliver them]." Suddenly aware of the tremendous opportunity this chance gathering of enemy operatives presented, Altendorf had an inspiration:

> Before leaving Mazatlán I contrived to buy three rolls of photographic film of a size to fit Waberski's camera. Then I found an opportunity to borrow his camera to photograph him with Max Boeder and a group of the boys. Some trivial pretext enabled me to step out of sight long enough to substitute one of my rolls of film for the roll of six negatives.

The doctor-spy returned to his hotel and found a note from Chapman waiting for him. The consul had an urgent matter to discuss and requested that Altendorf meet him at the American consulate the next morning at 4:45 a.m.

An hour before sunrise, Altendorf once again followed the cobblestone streets to the consulate. Chapman indeed had important news to report. He had been informed by his counterpart at the British consulate, Vice Consul Theodore E. S. Watson, that the German operative Gleaves had called and claimed to be an agent in the employ of the British legation in Mexico City. Altendorf was stunned. Jahnke's "third party," the pistol-carrying strongman, a double agent?

Chapman advised that "Gleaves had informed the Vice-Consul that Waberski and party were on the way to the United States to do something terrible and kill many people." The operative wanted a means of identifying himself to the American authorities when he reached Nogales to report the plot and proposed a simple identification method. Chapman showed Altendorf the torn half of a sheet of paper that read "VIA," advising that "the negro had the other half reading 'NO,' which he was to present to the U.S. authorities in Nogales to identify himself as a British agent." Placed together, the two scraps of paper read "NOVIA," the Spanish word for "girl-friend," which would be the countersign to prove that he was a British spy. As of yet, Watson had been unable to verify Gleaves's claim.

Altendorf's survival as a double agent depended on his keen ability to judge people and situations. He had served with the British cavalry during the Boer War and was highly skeptical that the black laborer was an opera-tive of the elite British secret service. Just as Jahnke had visited the U.S. Justice Department before the Mare Island explosion to report a German agent seeking information about the shipyard, Gleaves's visit to the British consulate could be part of the German border plot. The "NOVIA" torn pa-per identification might be the method used by Gleaves (or Witzke) to gain access to U.S. military intelligence headquarters in Nogales to assassinate Butcher or another American agent. If that were the case, the intelligence officer displaying the "VIA" slip at the other end of the line would be hold-ing his own death warrant. Until events proved otherwise, Altendorf would note Gleaves's claim but not act upon it, and Chapman did not forward the "VIA" paper slip to Nogales.

Altendorf asked the consul if he had received a response to the telegram sent the previous day. There had been no reply. Concerned that the warn-ing message might have been delayed or lost in transit and that Butcher now had no knowledge of the assassin en route to take his life, a second coded message was composed for Chapman to wire to military intelligence:

JANUARY 26—
TO BUTCHER FROM A1—
I ARRIVED FROM MEXICO CITY LAST THURSDAY LEAVING FOR HERMOSILLO ON SATURDAY TWENTY SIX WITH TWO GERMAN SPIES ONE A. NUDING.[*] BOTH ARE PLOTTING ASSASSINATION SOME OFFICIALS IN NOGALES WHERE THEY ARE TO ARRIVE NEXT MONDAY STOP CATCH NUDING IF POSSIBLE USE CARE AS HE IS DANGEROUS I WILL BE IN HERMOSILLO ONE DAY WOULD YOU NOT HAVE JOE BRU MEET ME AT COHEN HOTEL THERE AT ONCE GOT NEWS FOR YOU.
I HAVE CORROBORATIVE EVIDENCE AS TO DANGER OF NUDING.
CHAPMAN

[*The name "Nuding" was garbled in transmission. Altendorf almost certainly meant "Witzke."]

Outside the sky had begun to lighten; it was time for Altendorf to leave. Chapman escorted the agent to the door and wished him safe passage to the border. Altendorf retraced his steps to the Francia and reached the hotel unobserved as dawn broke over the city.

Hours later, Witzke, Gleaves, and Altendorf boarded a train for the next leg of the journey, a 475-mile ride up the west coast of Mexico to Guaymas. They reached the port city near midnight, an unusual arrival time given the level of bandit activity, and called on Vice Consul Otto Rademacher.

Like Friedrich Unger in Mazatlán, Rademacher was the principal of a trading house, Rademacher, Mueller & Company, similarly struggling to evade the American blacklist and remain in business. Also like Unger, the vice consul was an ardent supporter of German clandestine operations. Rademacher & Company bought merchandise in the United States through a "cloak" intermediary, W. Loaisa & Company, a Mexican export-import firm with offices in San Francisco and Guaymas that shipped the goods to "La Constancia," the cover name for Rademacher's trading house. The black-market purchases provided the funds to finance German espionage. Rademacher directed some of the covert activities himself; at various times German agents such as Ricardo Schwierz and Adam Siegel had reported to Rademacher, and a German secret service agent named Weebe was on his company payroll.

The visit to Guaymas was a brief stopover for Witzke to deliver instructions and a quantity of official correspondence to Rademacher. The vice consul was in high spirits; a celebration of the kaiser's birthday had been underway all afternoon, and he proudly displayed a register book with the names of local dignitaries who had called to drink to the kaiser's health. Rademacher pointed out the name of a Frenchman who had come to drink a toast and said he would send it to the emperor "to show him even the French sympathized with them." (Presumably the Frenchman had not visited France recently.) The two agents raised a stein to the kaiser, Witzke somewhat dejectedly, unhappy that he had missed the afternoon celebration.

After a few hours of sleep, the agents caught the morning express train to Hermosillo, the capital of Sonora. Before boarding, Witzke instructed Gleaves to sit in an obscure location on the train and maintain a low profile. When he entered and saw that the black agent, in violation of security, had taken a seat in the same car in which he and Altendorf would be riding, he heatedly ordered him to move to another coach.

When the train got underway, Altendorf watched Witzke rise from his seat and disappear into an adjoining car. Unknown to the doctor, four other German agents had been accompanying them undercover since their departure from Mexico City, at times traveling on a different train or boat—Dietz, Schmidt, and two operatives who will forever remain nameless. Dietz was the most dangerous of the group; Gleaves considered him to be a far more dangerous agent than Witzke. Working with Schmidt, Dietz had set incendiary fires in the Tampico oil fields in October 1917. His present assignment was to cross into the New Mexico coal country and organize IWW sabotage activity in the mines; the other agents had been given similar tasks to carry out in support of the campaign of destruction. Witzke passed through the coaches meeting with the members of his team and discreetly slipped a payment to each of the agents.

He returned thirty minutes later and took a seat next to Altendorf. "I have gotten rid of over one hundred dollars," he said, smiling triumphantly. "I have six men going north with me [including Gleaves and Altendorf]. The work is moving splendidly."

The train pulled into the Hermosillo station in the late afternoon where, despite Witzke's growing optimism about the mission, they arrived on a sour note. Gleaves had a fondness for tequila, and wanting to ensure a ready supply of the potent liquor, he carried a quart barrel in his luggage. It was illegal at the time for an individual to possess a quart of tequila in Mexico, and when they reached their destination, Gleaves was promptly arrested. Witzke was forced to pay a fifty-dollar fine to obtain Gleaves's release from custody, but not before giving the agent a "thorough dressing down." Witzke and Altendorf then exited the train, while Gleaves and the other agents continued on to Nogales, Sonora.

Since he was traveling under the persona "Pablo Waberski," a Russian-American sailor returning to the United States, Witzke insisted on staying at an American hotel and registered at the Arcadia. He displayed his Russian-issued passport at the front desk and told the staff that he had lived in the United States for seventeen years. Witzke spoke of American military camps and installations with such authority that his remarks drew an amazed comment from the proprietor.

The Mexican official they had come to meet would have an important role to play in the secret operation. Plutarco Elías Calles was one of the most powerful political figures in the country. He had been a supporter of Venustiano Carranza during the revolution and had risen swiftly through the Constitutionalist ranks to become a general. Calles was an able strategist and commander in the early years of the conflict and had inflicted a devastating defeat on the army of Pancho Villa at the battle of Agua Prieta. In 1915, General Calles became governor of Sonora, where he gained a reputation as an iron-willed, often ruthless strongman.

Altendorf checked into the Cohen Hotel and telephoned Calles, his superior in the Mexican army, informing him that he had arrived in Hermosillo with a German agent named Waberski that he wanted him to meet. The general instructed Colonel Altendorf to report to the Palacio de Gobierno that afternoon—without fail, at three o'clock—his response making it clear that he had already been informed about Witzke's trip to Sonora.

The two agents arrived at the government "palace," a two-story barnlike building of sand-colored brick, at the appointed hour. After being "passed" by the sentries guarding the entrance, they ascended a flight of wooden stairs to an anteroom where the governor's staff of some twenty men were engaged in clerical work. An aide opened the door to Calles's inner office, and Altendorf and Witzke were announced; two or three minutes later they were told to enter.

Calles was a big man standing well over six feet tall, heavily built, with slate-gray hair and mustache. He rose from his rolltop desk and received them cordially. Calling into the anteroom that no one was to be admitted to the room, the general closed the door and the three men settled down to business. Since Witzke did not speak Spanish, Altendorf served as interpreter.

"This gentleman is Lothar Witzke," said Altendorf. "He is a German but goes on a Russian passport as 'Pablo Waberski,' and will operate on the border against the United States."

"Yes, you know that I am pro-German," Calles responded. "I am for Germany and I shall do everything possible to help him."

The governor was briefed regarding the campaign of destruction that Witzke would lead in the United States in preparation for the larger military operation that was to follow.

"We have got every man we can," Witzke told the general, "but if we should want some more men from you [would that be possible]?"

"I will do everything to help you," Calles repeated, "but be very careful so that you do not get exposed."

"I have done some wonderful [sabotage] work before," Witzke said proudly. "Everything is safe. I will just send the doctor some letters and messages, and he will send them to Mexico City."

"That will be all right," Calles responded.

"Witzke, with Altendorf acting as interpreter, informed Calles that he should not be fearful of sending coded telegrams to Mexico City 'as everything had been arranged.' . . . Calles would receive instructions from Mexico City . . . to send his coded telegrams [provided by Altendorf] from Calles' private telegraph office in the palace in order to avoid the American censorship." The governor would receive further direction on the particulars of all this from Carranza.

Recently a German agent had been found dead in a hotel room on the Mexican side of the line at Laredo, his death being blamed on the Americans. Concerned that there might be an attempt on his life while he was in Nogales, Witzke asked the governor if he could provide security for the operation. Calles responded that he would provide protection for Witzke while he was in Mexico, but he could not be responsible for his safety on the American side.

"I also have an order for you to issue him a pistol," Altendorf said respectfully.

Calles touched a button to summon his chief of staff, Colonel Garcia. When Garcia appeared, the general said, "I want, immediately, a good pistol for this man."

The colonel returned with a Smith & Wesson .38 Military & Police revolver in a brown leather holster. The handgun was over a decade old but in excellent working condition, with a bright blue finish. Garcia handed the pistol to Witzke, who was also given a permit from the municipal president of Hermosillo allowing him to legally carry the weapon in Sonora, which read:

Republica Mexicana. Ayuntamiento de Hermosillo.
Estado de Sonora.
Num. 254
Esta Presidencia de mi cargo, en acuerdode hoy, ha
tenido a bien conceder permiso al senor Pablo Waberski,
para que porte una pistola marca "Smith Wesson"
numero 65184, para su defensa personal.

Mexican Republic. Hermosillo City Council.
Sonora State.
Number 254
The President of this office has today kindly granted Mr. Pablo Waberski
permission to bear one pistol marked "Smith Wesson"
number 65184 for his personal defense.

Witzke turned to Altendorf. "Tell him I don't want it for a present, but will pay for it." Altendorf translated the message into Spanish for Calles, and Witzke was accordingly charged 150 pesos ($60) for the revolver. The meeting drew to a close, and after a few casual parting comments the two agents went to their hotels.

The following day Witzke returned to the Palacio for a private conversation with the governor. The second meeting went equally well, and when Witzke reappeared he was carrying a picture of General Calles. The agent who once threatened Altendorf with the warning, "I have laid many people in the cemetery; if you are not straightforward with me I will put you there," was now full of praise for the doctor's close relationship with the governor.

"I can say now, doctor, that I can see your influence with General Calles," he said approvingly.

Witzke assured Altendorf that he would send a letter to Jahnke letting him know what a fine man he was. The doctor smiled and humbly responded that he was only too happy to assist and would take care of anything Witzke needed to have done while he was on station in Hermosillo.

Altendorf borrowed the youth's camera, and they toured the city taking snapshots. One of the photographs captured by Altendorf shows Witzke standing like a western gunfighter on an empty Hermosillo street, the .38 revolver in a holster at his waist near a row of gleaming bullets. The German agent's face holds no emotion; his eyes stare out blankly beneath a tilted fedora, as if he was about to draw the pistol on an unsuspecting Byron Butcher and blast him into eternity.

"The ambassador and Jahnke think very highly of me for my work and I am very proud to have done it," Witzke had said to the doctor. "I am a man they know they can depend on."

Shortly before one o'clock on the afternoon of January 30, 1918, Witzke purchased a one-way fare and boarded the afternoon train to Nogales.

In the stillness of his hotel room, Dr. Altendorf began to shave off his mustache.

7

Crossing the Line

There are two towns named Nogales at the U.S.-Mexico border, Nogales, Senora, and Nogales, Arizona. The communities of Ambos Nogales (Spanish for "Both Nogales") had been founded in the early 1880s and were divided by an international boundary that ran along a wide road called International Street, patrolled by U.S. Army troops and Mexican border guards. Crossing between the two Nogaleses was only permitted at the customs stations and a few designated border posts. When the world war began, the U.S. government introduced a higher level of security by requiring that foreign visitors entering the country possess a visa issued by a U.S. consulate. But even with the new visa requirement, Ambos Nogales remained a popular base for German agents to operate from.

Gleaves arrived in Nogales, Sonora, late on the night of January 28 and checked into a hotel. Before Witzke disembarked at Hermosillo, he had given Gleaves a sealed envelope and instructed him to walk up and down the sidewalk in front of the Central Hotel in Nogales the following day at noon, saying that someone would appear and ask for the message. On January 29, Gleaves went to the hotel at the appointed time and began pacing the sidewalk. After two hours of roaming, a short, chunky American approached him—"kind of sporty looking," in a dark gray checked suit and a derby hat—and asked for the note. Gleaves handed it to him and the man disappeared, never to be seen again.

Witzke also directed Gleaves to circulate around the plaza until he arrived, where he was to "look for committeemen" (IWW members) who would probably be there to meet him. Accordingly, Gleaves remained in the plaza after the American left, and a few hours later two other men approached—Germans—who inquired if he had arrived on the Southern Pacific train. Gleaves said that he had.

"Where is the man who was with you?" one of the men asked.

"Who was that?" Gleaves responded.

"The man who was sent out of Mexico City with you."

"He stopped off in Hermosillo," said Gleaves.

"Well, go stay in your room and be comfortable," the other German told him. "We'll take care of you here."

"All right," Gleaves said and returned to his room as instructed.

On the third day after arriving in Nogales, Gleaves spotted Witzke walking across the street from his hotel. He greeted his superior and told him where he was staying. Witzke eyed the entrance of the hotel apprehensively and said that he couldn't go inside; Gleaves would need to move to a different hotel, which he subsequently did. Witzke provided Gleaves with his room number at the Central Hotel.

"Get some good colored men," Witzke said to Gleaves. "Pick out men you think are all right, and get those colored committeemen that were down at Mexico City." (Apparently a reference to black IWW members Gleaves had introduced to Witzke in Mexico City.)

They parted company, and a short while later Gleaves met Witzke in his room accompanied by an army deserter who, he informed the agent, would assist in creating a mutiny among the "negro" troops of the U.S. 10th Cavalry at Fort Huachuca. The defector was going to cross the border that night to foment disobedience among the American troops on patrol.

"There is no river there, and he can talk to them," Gleaves advised.

Witzke eyed the deserter with suspicion, a black man dressed in "some kind of uniform over which he wore a United States military overcoat." Gleaves had formerly introduced Witzke to another black man in Guaymas, also a U.S. Army deserter, of whom he had been equally wary. After interviewing the renegade, he drew Gleaves aside and said, "I don't know about him—whether I can trust him or not; leave him out a few minutes and you and I can talk it over."

Gleaves asked the ex-soldier to wait in the hallway. When the man was out of earshot, Witzke reiterated that he wasn't sure he could use the deserter, and told his subordinate to "get the other men" and bring them in for a conference. He also instructed Gleaves to secure a horse or automobile within the next few days to reconnoiter the road between Nogales and Naco, Arizona; agents involved in the operation were planning to pass that way shortly. Then he gave Gleaves fifty dollars to cover expenses.

In the afternoon, Witzke presided over a gathering of local men being considered for sabotage work in the United States. The meeting was held at the Root Beer Garden on Calle Arizpe, a local watering hole and rendezvous for foreigners run by a German émigré named Oskar Sholars, located near the international line. Behind the one-story bar was a garden where patrons could socialize in private. Witzke arrived with a group of four or five prospective saboteurs, bought them a round of drinks, and then retired to the garden where a lengthy meeting was held. Gleaves soon arrived with a man named Carter who had come from Naco at the agent's request. Witzke told the gathering that although he had come to the border to assess the chances for creating a revolt among the American troops stationed there, the chief object of his visit was to continue the work of blowing up munitions plants and military installations in the United States.

In the discussion that followed, Witzke tried to gauge each man's potential for sabotage. "Are you afraid to take chances?" he asked William Colton, an expatriate Alabamian called "Big Hat" because of the large hats he wore.

Colton responded, "I'm not afraid to die"—a reply that seemed to satisfy the agent.

Witzke then circulated among the others and had a long conversation with Gleaves's man Carter, in whom he appeared to place great confidence. When the gathering dispersed, the men agreed to meet again at a later date.

That evening Gleaves reported to Witzke in his hotel room and saw that the agent was now carrying a large quantity of U.S. currency. Witzke withdrew his .38 Smith & Wesson revolver and tossed it onto the bed, then raised his breeches and removed two handkerchiefs stuffed with banknotes that had been bound to his calves.

"I have a considerable amount of money, but I can't give you right now what is necessary," he told Gleaves. "I have to go back to Hermosillo to get what is needed. This money I have is in gold certificates and you can't use it."

In two days (on February 2) Witzke would be leaving for Hermosillo to receive $5,000 for making payoffs and other ancillaries in support of the operation. Part of the funds were earmarked for the propaganda materials that Gleaves would distribute "to the colored soldiers and colored population" to cause mutiny and insurrection. The two made plans to meet again upon his return from Hermosillo.

Witzke informed Gleaves that on Friday morning he was going to cross the border into the United States to take care of some business for the Revolutionary Association.

A look of surprise crossed Gleaves's face. "Aren't you scared to cross the American border?"

"No, I have been prepared with papers in the City of Mexico," Witzke replied confidently. "I have everything ready."

He didn't mention that he had crossed the border twice that day already without encountering any problems. There seemed to be no cause for concern, yet beneath his outward bravado, Witzke had a deep sense of foreboding that danger loomed across the line.

After Altendorf finished shaving off his mustache, he changed his clothes and donned a chauffeur's uniform. Then he applied iodine to his hands and face to acquire a Mexican complexion. He was playing for high stakes now—his very life—and couldn't take any chances. If the warning messages had not been received by the Americans, the potential for death and destruction posed by Witzke was too great for him to remain in Hermosillo. He would travel to Nogales and warn them in person. But if Dr. Altendorf, the German agent on General Calles's staff, was recognized at the train station by Mexican officers or German agents, the consequences would be severe.

Altendorf rushed to the station and caught a freight train to Nogales that left half an hour after the train on which Witzke traveled. His disguise proved successful, and he wasn't spotted at the depot. It would take almost two days for the slow-moving freight to reach the border. There would be little chance for sleep in the rumbling boxcar as he watched Mexican towns roll by, while anxiously wondering whether he would arrive in time to warn Mr. Butcher about the plot on his life—or arrive for Mr. Butcher's funeral.

At that moment Special Agent Byron Butcher was in the military intelligence office at Nogales making plans for Witzke's reception in the United States. Days before, Butcher had received the urgent telegram from Agent A-1, "that he was on his way to the line with two German spies in tow," transmitted by Chapman in Mazatlán. He contacted Ezra Lawton, the American consul at Nogales, Sonora, and made arrangements to ensure that when the German agents appeared at the consulate to obtain their visas for entry into the United States, there would be a problem with their papers, and an "immigration official"—Butcher—would be called to render assistance.

Based on past surveillance of German spies operating in Nogales, Butcher believed the Central Hotel was the most likely place the agents would stay. He assigned a German-speaking informant given the code name "M-2" to maintain watch at the hotel for the arrival of the enemy operatives. (Based on informant M-2's uncanny ability to report Witzke's intentions, it seems likely that M-2 either planted a Dictaphone recorder or wired a microphone in the youth's hotel room.)

With his plans in place, Butcher waited for news that the German agents had arrived.

The leading newspaper in Nogales, Arizona, was the *Border Vidette*, an eight-page weekly that provided news of interest to Santa Cruz County. The January 26 edition of the *Vidette*, on newsstands the week that Witzke planned to visit Nogales, featured a number of stories that highlighted the town's patriotic support of the war. Printed on page 1 was a list of the young men from the county who had been "called to the colors"—registered for the draft and been found fit to serve in the army. Prominent at the top of the list were John R. McIntyre and Lon Pyett, now "entrained" for training camps. On the opposite side of the front page under the title "Not Slackers Yet" was a list of shame—the names of young men from the county who had not returned their "questionnaires."

Under the draft registration regulations of June 5, 1917, all men aged twenty-one to thirty-one were required to register for the draft at their local draft board. Each registrant was then given a questionnaire with a set of questions to be answered that enabled the board to classify the individual as eligible or ineligible for military service. Any man who failed to return the questionnaire within seven days of registration was automatically classified as Class I, "fit to serve," and his name was sent to the local police with a request that he be delivered to the draft board for processing into military service.

Apart from the risk of being identified as a "slacker" (draft dodger) by their draft board and publicly humiliated for not returning their questionnaire, young men of draft age walking the streets of America in 1918 also faced the possibility of being stopped by the police to learn whether they had registered for the draft and completed their questionnaire.

On page 2 of that week's *Border Vidette*, surrounded by a variety of other advertisements, was a mail-in membership coupon for a local vigilance association, the "100% American Club":

TO WIN THIS WAR GERMAN SPIES MUST BE JAILED
WILL YOU HELP?

If you cannot go to the trenches you should join this club. If you have a friend or relative fighting for his country you should join. Crops, munition and manufacturing plants, grain elevators and buildings are being destroyed by German agents. You can do your part in stopping this by joining. STOP GERMAN ACTIVITIES.

The coupon urged prospective members residing in Nogales to send their name and address to the "Secretary of the 100 Per Cent American Club" for immediate enrollment. "The reports of all members concerning suspected spies and German agents will be strictly confidential and thoroughly investigated." It was a remarkable coincidence that the notice should appear while one of the most deadly German saboteurs in the hemisphere was on his way to the small border town.

On the night of January 30, informant M-2 located Witzke at the Central Hotel in Nogales, Sonora, and booked into an adjoining room. Butcher's informant would maintain continuous surveillance of the enemy agent for the next twenty-four hours without being detected.

The next morning Consul Ezra Lawton was at work in his office when a man in his early twenties with "the appearance of a well-educated, debonair and prosperous foreigner" entered the consulate and requested a visa to cross into the United States. Lawton asked for his passport, noticing that the young man carried a holstered revolver. The passport was the Russian type—always regarded by consular officials with suspicion, issued in Mexico City to "Pablo Waberski," twenty-two-year-old Russian mechanic and automobile engineer. The passport had been "seen" (reviewed) by the U.S. vice consul in Mexico City, Harold A. Paschal. Witzke also gave Lawton his "Declaration of an Alien about to Enter the United States" form, a necessary companion to the passport for entering the United States, and a draft registration card in the name of Pablo Waberski.

Lawton asked Pablo what his intentions were in coming to the United States. The youth responded that he had registered for the draft in San Francisco but had not completed his questionnaire. Since he didn't want to be considered a slacker, he was going to the city hall in Nogales, Arizona, to fill out the classification document.

Lawton frowned and pointed out that when the passport had been endorsed by Paschal in Mexico City, the vice consul had added the notation: "Bearer is to depart for the United States of America between Dec. 25, 1917 and Dec. 31, 1918."

"This passport is overdue by three weeks," the consul said.

"Mr. Lawton, you know how it is," Witzke replied. "The trains are late and getting held up in Mexico, and [now] I am pretty near three weeks late."

"I can't fix it up for you until you see a man from the other side, a man from the Immigration Service."

The consul also advised Witzke that he would need to remove his pistol before crossing the U.S.-Mexican border; he would be in trouble otherwise.

Witzke unbuckled his gun belt and passed the holstered Smith & Wesson revolver to Lawton for safekeeping until he returned from city hall.

Lawton went to the telephone and called Butcher, informing him that "Pablo Waberski" had arrived at the consulate. The intelligence officer arrived a short time later and was introduced to Witzke as an official from the Immigration Service who could help him gain entry into the United States. The saboteur-assassin was unaware that he was now facing the man that he had received orders to kill. Observing that Witzke had no baggage or packages—and therefore likely no evidence of being a spy—Butcher made a snap decision to allow Witzke to "walk." He would bide his time, waiting for the right moment to capture the enemy agent and his luggage together.

Butcher nodded understandingly as he listened to the youth's story about wanting to return to the United States to complete his questionnaire, and offered to escort him across the border to the customs office where his visa could be amended for entry.

At the nearby customs station, Butcher presented Waberski to Mr. Milliken, the inspector in charge, and then departed, assuming that after his paperwork was sorted out the German would return to Mexico, collect his baggage, and return.

But Witzke had other ideas.

Milliken passed the young traveler to immigrant inspector Charles L. Beatty for processing. Beatty asked Waberski why he wanted to enter the United States and was told:

> His business in Mexico was to look up a location for a garage, and that he had seen a great many places in Mexico, but the one that suited him best was Mazatlán, and that he was going to consult with a friend in San Francisco, and that it was possible he would return and open up a garage, and that it was also possible that he would enlist in the army if accepted, and that he was undecided about the matter.

Beatty scanned Witzke's passport and alien entry declaration, then filled out an Immigration Service manifest to allow Waberski to cross the border into the United States. The German agent signed the document which noted his reason for arrival as "Going to join friend—name and address; James Karale, San Francisco, California," and then solemnly swore an oath to its truthfulness. Beatty stamped the passport and approved the visitor for entry into the United States.

Witzke made two trips over the border that day. On his first crossing he went to the Nogales city hall and completed a draft questionnaire. Now if stopped by the authorities he could provide proof of his reason for return-ing to the United States and not be detained for draft evasion.

With each crossing, Butcher observed that Witzke remained empty-handed, his luggage still at the hotel in Sonora, safely out of reach on the Mexican side of the line. That evening the situation took a turn for the better when Butcher was contacted by informant M-2 at the Central Ho-tel, who advised that Waberski would be crossing over again the following morning at 10 a.m. He was going to visit the First National Bank on Morley Avenue in Nogales to transact some business. Butcher instructed M-2 to abandon his post at the hotel as soon as the enemy agent departed for the border, and to immediately cross the line and give him the news in person. Luggage or no luggage, the special agent was determined to apprehend Witzke before he had a chance to act.

Butcher knew that he would need assistance in capturing the athletic youth who, given the penalty for espionage in wartime, would probably not be taken without a fight. A few days before, he had enlisted the help of Harry Smart, a U.S. customs inspector with a reputation for dependability, and a man who could readily handle Witzke if a struggle should ensue. He telephoned Smart and told him that the German spy would be crossing the border in the morning, and advised him where to report with *his* revolver the following day.

After Witzke was taken into custody, they would need someone with an automobile to drive them to a military camp where the enemy agent could be placed in confinement. Butcher contacted a friend, Wirt Bowman, the prosperous owner of the Bowman Mercantile Company, who eagerly vol-unteered for the task.

W. G. "Wirt" Bowman was the proverbial "local boy makes good"—in Bowman's case, *very* good. He had come to Nogales from Guaymas twenty years before as a station agent and telegrapher for the Southern Pacific Rail-road, earning seventy-five dollars a month. Struggling to support a growing family, Bowman became a commission agent on the side, selling agricultural products and forage to the Mexican government on a percentage basis. He extended generous credit terms to the Carranza regime at a time when few others would, and grateful for his assistance, the Carrancistas made Bowman their purchasing agent, allowing him to charge the market price on day of delivery. As commodity prices continued to rise during the world war, Bow-man had made a fortune on the inflated margin and commission he earned.

Now a pillar of the community, Wirt Bowman became active in local politics and founded the 100% American Club to rally Nogales citizens in defense of the home front. (According to the *Santa Cruz Patagonian*, the

100% American Club "stands for the extermination of German spies. The secretary of the club reports that applications are pouring in.") He also devoted time and money to assisting law enforcement efforts. When federal agents needed to search the houses of suspected Mexican revolutionists in a distant part of the state for arms and ammunition, Bowman volunteered to drive them over twenty-five miles of rough mountain roads to reach the desolate location. Upon learning of the episode, the sheriff of Santa Cruz County commented, "That's what Wirt Bowman likes. Just let him get on the trail of anybody the government is after and he's as happy as a little boy with a new red wagon."

Bowman assured Butcher that he would be waiting in the morning with a powerful automobile to help capture the German spy.

At nine o'clock that night, the freight train on which Altendorf was traveling rolled into the station at Nogales, Sonora. Unshaven and exhausted after two days on the slow-moving freight, the doctor went directly to the home of consul Ezra Lawton.

"Consul, everything is OK with Waberski?" he anxiously inquired, uncertain whether his messages had been received.

"Yes, everything is arranged according to your instructions by wire," Lawton assured him. "He is coming across at ten o'clock [tomorrow morning] to put some money in the bank."

The consul guided Altendorf across the border to the American Club in Nogales where Butcher was staying. Greatly relieved at discovering his superior alive and well, Agent A-1 detailed the journey from Mexico City to Hermosillo, filling in any missing gaps about the enemy operation. When asked about Witzke's documentation, Altendorf said "the German always carried his papers on his person." Butcher put the weary agent up for the night in his quarters to ensure that A-1 remained out of sight.

On the morning of February 1, Lothar Witzke rose early and prepared for his next trip across the border. Opening an account at an American savings bank was an important task; it would provide ready access to a safe source of currency to pay off the committeemen for organizing strike activity and to enlist saboteurs. The agent was now carrying almost $1,000 in U.S. gold certificates and Mexican gold, and the following day he would receive $5,000 more in Hermosillo. It was too much money to keep on his person or to take across the border when needed, with only a .38 revolver for protection.

Witzke checked the gold coins in his money belt and once again wrapped the gold certificates in handkerchiefs which he strapped to his calves. With a sense of foreboding, he decided to take an extra precaution:

I had a very real premonition of danger. I removed the cipher message I was [now] carrying in my necktie and hid it in the lining of my suitcase, which I left in the hotel, planning to have the message retrieved as soon as I was safely across the border.

Then Jahnke's lieutenant left his hotel and headed for the international line.

Morley Avenue was one of the busiest streets in Nogales. Although modern automobiles were parked in front of the businesses lining the broad avenue and telephone poles ran throughout the district, the street had otherwise changed little since the days of the Old West. Antiquated store awnings shielded the wooden walkways from the sun, and desert winds blew dust across the unpaved roadway.

Shortly before nine o'clock, Bowman pulled his car into a parking space near the First National Bank building. Butcher and Smart exited the vehicle and proceeded to the U.S. customs station on International Street, where they took up a discreet vantage point not far from the crossing station.

For nearly an hour they stood watching the border post as the minutes ticked slowly by, until just before ten when M-2 appeared and informed Butcher that the enemy spy was on his way over.

The intelligence officer directed Smart to "go on duty" at the customs station and ensure that Witzke had no difficulty crossing with his Russian passport. The German agent soon arrived and presented his passport to Smart, who displayed only cursory interest and passed him through. Witzke then left the station and started walking down Morley Avenue, unaware that he was now being shadowed by two determined men.

From the window of Butcher's quarters at the American Club, Altendorf had a clear view of the national bank and watched the drama unfolding before him with spellbound fascination.

As Witzke neared the bank, his pursuers quickened their pace until they were directly behind him; then Butcher and Smart whipped out their revolvers and shoved them hard into the German agent's back.

"Halt! Hands up!" Butcher ordered.

Witzke froze and slowly raised his hands. Glancing over his shoulder, the youth was stunned to see the "customs official" who had assisted him the day before and the inspector who had just cleared him across the border, now holding revolvers pressed against his ribs. Their cold, hard-eyed stares left no doubt that any attempt to resist would be ill advised.

Witzke drew a quick breath and forced a half smile. "I suppose you think you have caught a German spy," he said.

"We know what we've caught," Butcher responded evenly.

The enemy agent was spun around, and then Butcher, the man Witzke had come to Nogales to kill, snapped handcuffs on his wrists. The arrest occurred so quickly that no one on Morley Avenue knew what had happened, and much too fast for the youth to follow Jahnke's directive to commit suicide before being captured. The prisoner was shoved into the backseat of Bowman's waiting automobile, with Bucher and Smart piling in alongside. Bowman fired up the engine, and then the eager volunteer raced off to Camp Stephen D. Little, the home of the U.S. Army's 35th Infantry Regiment, located a mile from where Witzke was captured.

At the base intelligence office, Butcher searched the German agent while Smart and Captain Joel A. Lipscomb, assistant intelligence officer, looked on. They found Witzke's Russian passport and entry manifest; a Mexican passport issued to Pablo Waberski at the Mexican consulate in Laredo dated November 15, 1917; the able seaman and lifeboat operator certificates; a notebook listing various payments in pesos, such as "hotel Guadalajara 23" and "ticket Mazatlán 40"; the U.S. draft registration card; a driver's license issued in San Francisco; and an amorous letter addressed to Miss Sarah Gillespie of Berkeley, California. They also discovered the gold coins in Witzke's money belt, the handkerchiefs containing U.S. gold certificates bound around the calves of his legs, two opals, and a wristwatch. The codes that Altendorf reported finding in Witzke's clothes while he was unconscious in Guadalajara were missing, as was the revolver provided by General Calles. None of the items identified "Pablo Waberski" as an enemy spy or provided any information about his mission.

Witzke refused to answer any questions, and no attempt was made to interrogate him on his first day in captivity. He was turned over to the officer of the day, who led the dazed prisoner to the guardhouse in handcuffs. Four soldiers detailed to guard the enemy agent were instructed: "If he makes a wrong move shoot him."

Butcher knew they would now have to move fast. The secret codes, plans, maps, and whatever else Witzke was using to coordinate the operation were still on the other side of the line in Sonora, either in his luggage or hidden in his hotel room. Once the Germans discovered he was missing, there would be a no-holds-barred scramble to recover the vital documents, which would be lost forever if enemy operatives reached the hotel first.

Within hours Butcher and Lipscomb crossed the border in plain clothes and headed for the Central Hotel. They were in luck. At the hotel no opposition was encountered, and "by a little bluffing and greasing of hands" they succeeded in obtaining Witzke's suitcase. Returning to Camp Little with their prize, the intelligence officers searched the bag and found the .38

Smith & Wesson revolver, gun belt, and holster and the permit to carry the pistol that the agent had received in Hermosillo, together with the youth's clothing, personal effects, and shaving kit. Searching the lining of the bag they located the cipher table of German and Spanish words with code numbers, and the coded identification sheet.

Escorted from his cell to view the items, the prisoner was asked if they were his, specifically the cipher and code key. The sight of the code materials left Witzke stunned:

> The Americans were successful in obtaining a sheet of paper containing the cipher message, in a series of 10-letter groups, from the suitcase in the hotel. When I was suddenly confronted with it I admitted its ownership, but I was positive also that the contents could not be deciphered. It was a German transposition cipher with the address, signature, and the message itself first written in German and then the letters mixed up.

Beyond admitting that the seized items were his, Witzke refused to provide any further explanation and was returned to the guardhouse.

Butcher's satisfaction at obtaining a German code key, along with a message in cipher, proved to be short-lived. To his disappointment, a comparison of the message and the code key showed that there was no connection between the two.

Over the next two days, Captain Lipscomb made "true copies" of each of the recovered documents and forwarded the originals to Major Barnes, intelligence officer at Fort Sam Houston in Texas. Barnes made additional copies, which he sent to the military intelligence coding section in Washington known as MI-8, requesting that an effort be made to decipher the message. Then he locked the original documents in his office safe.

In Sonora, Pablo's sudden disappearance left Gleaves in a quandary. He now had no means of communicating with the members of the Revolutionary Association in Mexico City, or any source of funds. Gleaves wandered about Nogales for several days, uncertain how to proceed. He was soon spotted by U.S. military intelligence operatives who briefly shadowed "Witzke's accomplice" before inviting the wayward agent to the American consulate for an interview. Butcher held two meetings with Gleaves at the consulate on February 2 and 3, during which Gleaves asserted that he was a secret service agent in the employ of a "Mr. Place" at the British embassy in Mexico. Unaware of Dr. Altendorf's true identity as an agent of U.S. military intelligence, Gleaves's account of the journey from Mexico City to Sonora matched almost every detail of the report provided by "Agent A-1." A telegram was sent to Major Campbell at the American embassy in Mexico City asking that he check on Gleaves's claims with the British embassy.

The response confirmed Gleaves's story: "Mr. Place" was the cover name of Major Alfred Mason, and Gleaves was, in fact, a British intelligence agent.

William H. Gleaves had been born on May 1, 1870, in Montreal, Canada. Although his boyhood was spent working as a laborer in Pennsylvania and he lived in Mexico for almost thirty years, as a Canadian citizen Gleaves remained a subject of Great Britain. Since 1914, Gleaves had been employed by the British embassy in Mexico City, first by William Cummings, the chargé d'affaires at the legation, and then by famed novelist and former member of Parliament, now major, Alfred Edward Woodley Mason, the naval attaché. Mason was in charge of British naval intelligence in Mexico and reported to Admiral Sir Reginald Hall, chief of naval intelligence, tasked with "surveillance of movements of oil, submarines, and generally of German plots and endeavors in that part of the world." Gleaves's assignment was to infiltrate the German espionage establishment and obtain information about clandestine activities in Mexico. Like Altendorf, the black agent had taken considerable risks in carrying out his work. After successfully penetrating the enemy camp, Gleaves had been instrumental in identifying methods of wireless communication being used by the Germans and obtaining information on other activities, such as plans to sabotage the Tampico oil fields. Mason attested that Gleaves was an intelligent, reliable, and trustworthy operative whose information could be relied upon.

Jahnke had dispatched his faithful lieutenant to the border in the company of not one, but *two* Allied double agents. Witzke's mission of sabotage, insurrection, and murder had been doomed from the start.

After being debriefed by Butcher, the British agent agreed to place himself under the direction of American intelligence. Gleaves was asked to continue to circulate throughout Nogales, Sonora, pending new developments and to keep watch for German activity.

On the night of February 1, Gleaves was contacted by Dietz, who had returned to Nogales in an automobile with Schmidt and another man Gleaves had never met. The three enemy agents remained in the border town overnight and left early the next morning without learning that Witzke had been arrested. When Dietz inquired about Waberski's present whereabouts, Gleaves told him that "he thought Waberski had gone up to the mines in Arizona."

Captain Lipscomb advanced the British operative fifty dollars and re-quested that he travel to San Antonio for a conference with Major Barnes. At the meeting, Gleaves informed Barnes that Dietz was expected to arrive in Eagle Pass, Texas, sometime around February 15 to rendezvous with members of the IWW, and a plan was hatched to keep tabs on the danger-ous enemy agent. Barnes instructed Gleaves to cross into Mexico at Eagle Pass and locate Dietz, pretending to have had some difficulty escaping from the United States, and intimate that the American authorities had probably captured Witzke. It was believed that news of Witzke's arrest would leak out in time anyway, and this would help to keep Gleaves in good stead with the Germans. He was then to remain in Piedras Negras for several days and report on any action taken by Dietz in connection with the IWW.

Gleaves headed off for Nogales, and Barnes reported to his superiors in Washington, "It was impressed upon him that the important thing to do was keep well under cover. This he promised to do. He appears rather bright and if he is able to do this will doubtless develop additional information."

In the weeks that followed his capture, Witzke was repeatedly ques-tioned at Camp Little, but to his interrogators' frustration, the prisoner continued to maintain that he was just a Russian-American sailor who had returned to the United States to complete his questionnaire. The youth claimed that his original intention had been to travel to San Francisco to fill out the draft document because that was where he registered, in accor-dance with the law.

Although the prisoner initially refused to make any comment about the cipher message and code key that had been seized in Mexico, a few days after his arrest Witzke informed his guards that he wanted to discuss the coded items. Lipscomb had Witzke brought to the intelligence office, where the youth explained that he was having second thoughts about the documents. "He was afraid that his possession of the papers and his refusal to explain them might get him into trouble—more serious trouble than he was in, and that he desired to explain them."

Witzke told Lipscomb that he had entered into an employment agree-ment with Mexican newspapers to provide them with stories about the progress of the Mexican army campaign against the Yaqui Indians that was underway in the state of Sonora. The words in the code key had been agreed upon with representatives of the newspapers, the meaning of the phrases allowing him to inform them about the state of the campaign. The cipher message was merely a "memorandum of identification" that would be used to "identify him as being in good faith with the agents of these newspapers and their influences . . . which he was to serve by furnishing news to them. He stated that if it bore any other significance he did not know of it, but that the way he knew it [the card] was simply a card of understanding."

After enlightening Lipscomb on the reason he was carrying coded documents at the time of his arrest, the "newsman" was returned to his cell.

On February 14, Witzke was transferred from Camp Steven D. Little to Fort Sam Houston in San Antonio, Texas, under the escort of Byron Butcher and Special Agent Van Curtis of the Justice Department. While Butcher stood waiting with the prisoner on the open platform at Calabasas Station near Nogales, the two bantered about "spy work," and Witzke lowered his guard. While not admitting to being a German agent or revealing any secret information, he acknowledged that he had "done his duty," for which he would now likely pay with his life.

"Well, I am in a pretty hard position. What do you think they will do with me?"

"Pablo, I tried to tell you the other day that the best thing for you would be to tell the whole thing," Butcher replied. "If you keep on the way you are now and do not tell the truth and all you know, you have no chance at all. As you have already guessed we know nearly all about you. We are in a war now and also as you know spies are hung. Americans are sometimes strange in their actions and I will tell you again the only possible chance you have is after a week or ten days in San Antonio, and after you have thought it over, tell them all you know."

"No, I can't do that. I am very young to die, 22 years. But I have done my duty. If I told, I would be a traitor and that I will never be."

"Pablo, that is the chance we all take who do this work," said Butcher. "It is legitimate as long as you do not get caught, but when caught, you have to pay the penalty."

"Yes, I know it. I will probably be the first man to die in the United States for my country, won't I?" Witzke asked.

"Yes, probably the first, though I hear that one or two more have been caught since you were. You think it over, for the way I see it, your only way now is to tell all."

"No, I think I will go through with it. I had planned to live in Mexico after the war, but now I can never do that."

"Is there any word or message I can give to Lupe, if she should come to the border?" Butcher inquired. (Possibly to gain sympathy, Witzke had claimed that a woman named Lupe Garcia of Mazatlán was his fiancée.)

"No, she won't come to the border."

"Then, anything if I go to Mazatlán?" Butcher asked.

"You can tell her that I will never come back."

"It is great work, Pablo, and I have treated you as I would expect you to treat me under the same circumstances," said Butcher.

"If you are ever my prisoner, I will also take good care of you. No, to tell would make me a traitor, I can't do it."

"I hope to get the rest of your party in the next few days, including Schwierz," Butcher said confidently.

"Where is that Major?" Witzke inquired facetiously.

"He was over around Mulegé, Lower California, a few days ago waiting for money to get out."

"He's a no-good crook. I hope you get him," Witzke responded in disgust.

"I may have Schwierz, Dietz, the Doctor, Schmidt, and the negro along with you in a short time, and also Siegel.'

"I hope you do get that Major. Of course, I don't know much about him, but from what I have heard he is no good. The most I can say is that I wish you luck. You are doing your work and I have been doing mine. What kind of a trial will I get?"

"I do not know as yet how they will try you," said Butcher.

"Will it be published in the papers?"

"I don't know, probably not."

"You know all the details all right, and I think it was that Dr. Altendorf who told you, as I told him a lot of things in conversation," Witzke replied with venom.

"I think the Doctor and Siegel will talk when I get them and tell all they know."

"How much did you pay the Doctor to do this on me?" asked Witzke.

"If we get him he will probably get the same pay as you."

These would be the last words spoken between Witzke and Butcher. On his arrival at the Fort Sam Houston prison, the captured saboteur-assassin was placed in a steel cage and kept under close guard. After considerable debate between the army and the Department of Justice, it was decided that the prisoner would stand trial for espionage before a U.S. Army general court-martial.

Although his captors were certain that Witzke was a German agent, establishing that fact in court was going to be a difficult proposition based on the evidence at hand. Two Allied informants had made separate, unsubstantiated claims that Witzke was an enemy operative sent on a mission of destruction, but at the time of his capture, the young man in civilian clothes was carrying only identification papers and money, no weapons or explosives. He had been arrested in downtown Nogales a mile from the nearest U.S. military installation, and nothing was found on his person to suggest that he was any guiltier of being an enemy spy than any other person walking along Morley Avenue that day. In a covert operation of questionable legality, army intelligence officers had crossed into Mexico and retrieved a handgun—with a license for its legal possession—and a few documents that appeared to be in code, but the code had not been broken.

The fate of one of Germany's most dangerous secret agents would now rest in the hands of two middle-aged English professors from the University of Chicago—a man and a woman who had spent most of their lives studying the works of William Shakespeare and Geoffrey Chaucer.

The only German warship to survive the battle of the Falkland Islands in 1914, the SMS *Dresden* played cat and mouse with British cruisers for months in the fjords and channels of Chile. Naval Cadet Lothar Witzke was a member of the *Dresden*'s crew. (Courtesy of the author)

The *Dresden* was cornered by British cruisers at the Chilean island of Más a Tierra and scuttled after a brief engagement. Pictured, a grave marker for the eight German sailors killed. Interned with a serious leg wound, Witzke escaped aboard a steamship bound for San Francisco. (Courtesy of the author)

Seal trapper Albert Pagels became a volunteer agent for the German consul in Punta Arenas, helping to keep the *Dresden* well supplied and safely hidden. Photo taken in 1939. (Courtesy of the author)

The only known photograph of master saboteur and spymaster Kurt Jahnke, taken surreptitiously by U.S. Army military intelligence. In 1918, German naval intelligence appointed Jahnke sole confidential agent in Mexico—*Bevollmächtigter Geheimagent*, head of the espionage system for the American continent. (NARA, RG111, Records of the Office of the Chief Signal Officer 1860–1985, German Propaganda in Mexico, National Archives Identifier 86711636)

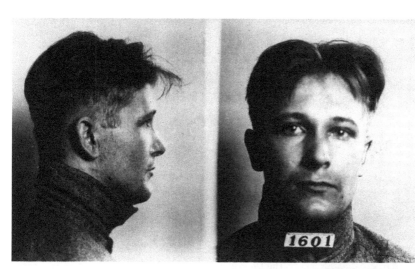

Above, police photograph of Lothar Witzke, aka Pablo Waberski, taken in February 1918. (NARA, RG165, Records of the War Department and Special Staffs, Military Intelligence Division, File 51-45)

At right, the police Bertillon card for Lothar Witzke. (NARA, RG165, Records of the War Department and Special Staffs, Military Intelligence Division, File 51-45)

The SS *Minnesota* was the largest ocean liner ever built in the United States when launched in 1903. The steamship could carry 28,000 tons of cargo, equal to 100 trains with 25 freight cars each. In 1915 the *Minnesota* departed for the Atlantic to carry vital commodities to England. (Courtesy of the author)

In November 1915 the *Minnesota*'s boilers failed at sea and the crippled ship was towed to San Francisco. Witzke claimed credit for wrecking the steamship's machinery. For over a year, the largest cargo carrier in the world remained under repair, unable to transport war supplies to Britain. (Courtesy of the author)

At a Jersey City pier in 1916, crates of explosives and ammunition are transferred from rail cars to a barge similar to the *Johnson 17* barge sabotaged by Jahnke and Witzke at Black Tom Island. The *Johnson 17* carried 100,000 pounds of TNT and 417 cases of artillery fuzes when it detonated, setting off a chain of explosions across the munitions depot. (Courtesy of the author)

The morning after Black Tom was destroyed, a burned-out freight car stands at a shattered pier landing. In the distance, one of the storage warehouses flattened by the blast can be seen. (Courtesy of the author)

Firefighters from the Jersey City Fire Department battle the flames on Black Tom. (NARA, RG165, Records of the War Department and Special Staffs, 1860–1952, Enemy Activities, Black Tom explosion, burning barges being cut loose from the docks at Black Tom, New Jersey, National Archives Identifier 31478108)

The explosion of 2 million pounds of munitions devastated the warehouses, piers, and rail terminal on Black Tom. Total damages were estimated at $20 million. (NARA, RG165, Records of the War Department and Special Staffs, 1860–1952, Enemy Activities, scene after explosion at Black Tom, New Jersey, National Archives Identifier 31478104)

The ammunition magazine at Mare Island Naval Shipyard in 1917. When U.S. warships visited the station for service or overhaul, artillery shells filled with explosives from the magazine were loaded aboard ship. (Courtesy of the author)

Wrecked buildings litter the landscape after a storehouse at the magazine containing 127,660 pounds of black powder exploded. Witzke would later boast that he was the saboteur who triggered the blast. (NARA, RG165, Records of the War Department and Special Staffs, 1860–1952, Navy Yards—Scene of the Mare Island Navy Yard Explosion, National Archives Identifier 45511828)

Dr. Scheele's incendiary "cigars" provided German saboteurs with a deadly tool for attacking munitions supply ships. Items seized from the machine shop of the interned German liner *Kaiser Friedrich der Grosse* by New York City police: several incendiary "cigars," chemicals, and a small press for inserting copper disk dividers. (Courtesy of the author)

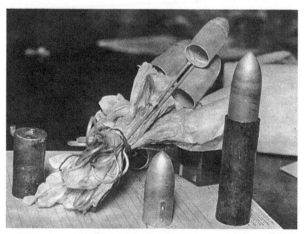

Early-model incendiary "cigars" consisted of a simple lead tube plugged at either end. A later version equipped with a hollow aluminum nose cone gave the appearance of an artillery shell, making the devices less conspicuous when discovered in the hold of a munitions ship. (Courtesy of the author)

Inspector Thomas J. Tunney of the New York City Police Department's bomb squad. (Courtesy of the author)

At the top of the page is shown a bomb in the form of a glass tube, which is used by German agents to set fire to property.

The upper chamber as designed to be filled with sulphuric acid is that nearest the sharp point. This chamber is filled first, and the sharp tubular point sealed by melting the glass and closing the opening. The lower chamber is then filled with a mixture of two-thirds potassium chloride and one third finest powdered sugar. The bottom also is then closed in any convenient way. The tiny passage between the two chambers is so small that after the sealing of the top of the tube by the melting process, the sulphuric acid will not pass through it to the contents of the lower chamber so long as it remains in this state.

When thus prepared the tube is usually wrapped in cloth or paper and carried in the upper left coat, blouse, or shirt pocket until there is an opportunity to place it in position to do the damage desired. When a place is selected for its work, the culprit breaks off the sealed upper end, unstops the bottom, sets it top upwards and leaves it for the action of the air and gravity to carry the contents of the upper chamber into the lower, when, as explosion takes place and fire is set to whatever inflammable material may be adjacent to the tube. The explosion usually takes place thirty-five minutes after the two ends are opened, thus giving the person placing the tube plenty of time to get away from the danger and to avoid being detected.

The English authorities have found many of these tubes sealed in lead pencils, fountain pens and similar objects in searching suspects. Great vigilance should be exercised to see if he has any such tool in his baggage or on his person.

M. Churchill,
Lt. Colonel, General Staff,
Chief, Military Intelligence Branch,
Executive Division.

Developed by Abteilung III B, German army intelligence, the glass pencil incendiary made Dr. Scheele's lead pipe "cigars" seem primitive in comparison. Sometimes called "tubes" or "glasses" by German saboteurs, pencil incendiaries were a concealable, highly effective means of sabotage. Above, a warning notice issued to U.S. military intelligence officers concerning the deadly devices. Below, a glass pencil incendiary concealed within a wooden pencil. (NARA, M1085, Investigating Case Files of the Bureau of Investigation 1908–1922, Pencil in glass tube used by enemy aliens to destroy works of Entente Allies, Roll boi_german_257-850_0121, Case No. 8000-196474). (Søhr, Johan. *Spioner og bomber. Fra opdagelsespolitiets arbeide under verdenskrigen.* Oslo: Johan Grundt Tanum)

The Washington Post.

MOB SHOOTS AND BURNS NEGROES BY SCORES IN EAST ST. LOUIS RIOTS

Victims Fired On as They Flee From Blazing Houses Throughout City.

Several Lynchings Also Mark Outbreak—Torch Is Applied in Four Sections of City as Rioters Gather Around Burning Areas—Two White Men Lose Lives in Rioting Earlier in Day, Hundred Injured Taken to Hospital—Guardsmen Practically Powerless at First to Quell Trouble—Women and Girls of Both Races Participate—Property Loss $3,000,000.

TUNG AGAIN EMPEROR

Occupies the Palace at Peking Surrounded by Military Chiefs.

FATE OF PRESIDENT UNKNOWN

Li Declared He Couldn't Resign in Favor of Young Ruler.

Czar's Old Blacklist Bars Bernstein Till Lansing Acts

Quickly Admitted to Russia on Washington's Request. State Department Makes Record by Prompt Dealing With Situation.

By HERMAN BERNSTEIN

200-MILE DRIVE IS ON

Kerensky Leads Russian Army to Attack in Person.

GALICIAN LINE BATHED IN FIRE

Ten Thousand Teuton Prisoners Taken on First Day.

CLOTURE

Chamberlain Day; Expec

FIRST USE

Debate to Be Pending

Kerensky Calls on All Russian Armies to Strike; Warns of Delay

HITS AT DEFENSE BOARD

Senator Reed Assails Method of Awarding Contracts.

ARTHUR V. DAVIS HIS TARGET

Some of the worst incidents of racial violence ever to occur in American history took place in 1917. German intelligence hoped to take advantage of the racial unrest to raise a black insurrection that would disrupt the U.S. war effort. (Courtesy of the author)

Dr. Paul Bernardo Altendorf. (NARA, RG165, Records of the War Department and Special Staffs, Military Intelligence Division, File 51-45)

Special Agent Byron S. Butcher, U.S. Army Military Intelligence. (Courtesy of the Library of Congress)

On January 16, 1918, Witzke, Altendorf, and Gleaves departed Mexico City by train bound for Sonora. In Colima, Witzke hired a locomotive and tender to transport the agents to Manzanillo. (Courtesy of the author)

The German trading house Melchers Sucesores was also the headquarters of the German consul in Mazatlán. Within the one-story warehouse in the foreground, seven hundred rifles imported for a German-Mexican invasion of the United States were stored. (Courtesy of the author)

William Edgar Chapman, U.S. consul in Mazatlán. (Courtesy of the Library of Congress)

Nogales,
Sonora

Nogales,
Arizona

The Nogales border crossing on International Street. (Courtesy of the author)

General Plutarco Elías Calles, governor of Sonora. (Courtesy of the Library of Congress)

A photo of Witzke taken by Dr. Altendorf the day before he left for the border. The German agent wears the Smith & Wesson .38 revolver provided by General Calles. (NARA, RG76, Mixed Claims Commission United States and Germany 1922–1939, Printed United States Exhibits, Exhibit 103, "Photographs of Lothar Witzke."

Morley Avenue in Nogales, Arizona, circa 1918. (Courtesy of the author)

Byron Butcher passport photo, 1918. (NARA, U.S. Passport Applications 1795–1925, Roll 547, Certificates 25000–25299, 8 July 1918–8 July 1919)

"He had the appearance of a well-educated, debonair, and prosperous foreigner." Lothar Witzke shortly after his capture; the look of a man facing the gallows. (NARA, RG111, Records of the Office of the Chief Signal Officer 1860–1985, German Propaganda in Mexico, National Archives Identifier 86711632)

Captain John Matthews Manly, the brilliant MI-8 cryptanalyst who broke the "Waberski cipher." (Courtesy of the Hanna Holborn Gray Special Collections Research Center, University of Chicago Library)

Edith Rickert, also an expert cryptanalyst, assisted Manly in solving the immensely complex cipher. (Courtesy of the Hanna Holborn Gray Special Collections Research Center, University of Chicago Library)

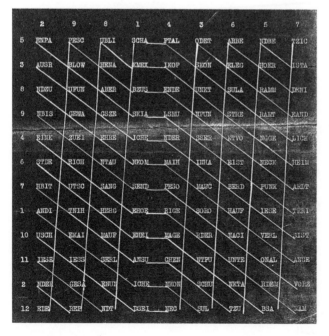

A diagram prepared by Manly shows how the deciphered four-letter code groups of the Waberski cipher were reassembled to form the plaintext message. (Courtesy of the George C. Marshall Foundation, Lexington, Virginia)

The military prison at Fort Sam Houston. On the night of August 1, 1919, Witzke and two confederates escaped from the prison building at left, traversed the roof of the two-story barracks in the foreground, and disappeared into the darkness. (Courtesy of the author)

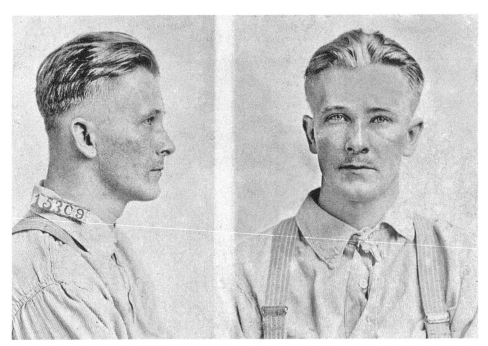

Lothar Witzke, Inmate No. 15309 at Leavenworth Penitentiary. (NARA, Inmate File of Lothar Witzke (aka Luther Witzke, aka Lather Witcke), RG129, Records of the Bureau of Prisons, 1870–2009, Series Inmate Case Files, 7/31/1895–11/5/1957)

8

Breaking the Code

Shortly after midnight on August 5, 1914, only a few hours after England declared war on Germany, a tired forty-three-year-old paddle-wheel steamer named the HMTS *Alert* departed Dover on a secret mission that would change the course of history. Under cover of darkness, the *Alert* steamed across the North Sea to a position chosen years before off the coast of Emden, Germany. There was a flurry of activity on her deck as lines with heavy iron grappling hooks were lowered into the black water, and then the *Alert* surged forward, dragging them on the ocean floor until they finally snagged the "catch" they were after. The hooks were reeled to the surface, and five rubbery communications cables dripping mud and seaweed were pulled from the sea and lowered onto the ship's deck, where they were hacked to pieces and the ends dropped back into the water. By the time the first rays of sunshine broke over the horizon, the *Alert* was already steaming back to port, having severed Germany's transatlantic cables, her only secure means of telegraphic communication with Europe and the United States.

The secret cable-cutting operation had been planned by the British "Committee of Imperial Defense" in 1912 as a means of disrupting Germany's foreign communications. Now instead of sending messages securely over the private cables that they controlled, the German government was forced to communicate using the powerful radio transmitter at Nauen, Grossfunkstelle Nauen, located a few miles from Berlin, or over the cables of friendly neutral countries like Sweden. Although their messages would be transmitted in code, they were no longer private; German communiqués could now be intercepted by her enemies on a continuous basis, and in volume. This in turn would lead to a new era in cryptanalysis. The Allied nations formed cryptanalytic bureaus to crack the German intercepts, with code breakers working in teams to solve the encrypted messages by applying mathematical techniques and a knowledge of the idiosyncrasies of the German language, as well as local or geopolitical factors related to individual intercepts.

The French War Ministry created the "Bureau du Chiffre" to attack German naval codes, diplomatic systems, and the strategic cryptograms of the kaiser's army. Throughout the course of the war, the French code-breaking bureau "intercepted more than 100,000,000 words, or enough to make a library of a thousand average-sized novels." The Bureau du Chiffre were the pioneers of radio traffic analysis, and its cryptanalysts became expert at deciphering enemy battlefield communications. One of its code breakers, Lieutenant Georges Painvin, decrypted the highly complicated German ADFGVX system—so named because only those letters appeared in the coded messages—which helped prevent a French defeat in 1918. Painvin would be recognized as the greatest cryptanalyst of the war.

Besieged by a flood of coded German wireless intercepts after hostilities began, the British Admiralty's director of naval intelligence established a cryptanalytic section that would be forever known by its location at the Admiralty building, "Room 40." By the end of 1914, the cryptanalysts of Room 40 were receiving over two hundred German intercepts a day, and its staff increased correspondingly, with "university dons, barristers, linguists, [and] accountants with a flair for mathematical pattern" joining the unit, all with the unique mind-set needed for unraveling cryptographic puzzles. The decoding capabilities of Room 40 were enhanced by a library of captured enemy codebooks that came into its possession, which included the codebook of the German light cruiser SMS *Magdeburg* that grounded on an island in the Gulf of Finland—taken from the arms of a dead German signalman by the Russians and sent to Britain; the codebook from a sunken German destroyer found in the net of an English fishing trawler; the diplomatic codebook abandoned by German agent Wilhelm Wassmuss while escaping from Persia in 1915; a badly burned but still legible codebook taken from the downed Zeppelin L-32; and numerous codebooks removed from sunken U-boats by Royal Navy divers. It has been estimated that between October 1914 and February 1919, Room 40 decoded fifteen thousand secret German communications. The staff of the code-breaking section had grown to eight hundred wireless operators intercepting coded messages at stations throughout Britain, and seventy to eighty cryptographers and clerks to decrypt them, when the most famous coded message of the war arrived at Room 40: the "Zimmerman Telegram."

On a routine morning in January 1917, two Room 40 cryptanalysts, William Montgomery and Nigel de Grey, were given a very long message comprising one thousand numerical code groups for decoding. The cable was encrypted in a new diplomatic code known as 0075, which the pair had been working to break for six months, and had been sent by German foreign minister Arthur Zimmerman to Ambassador von Bernstorff in Washington, DC, "to be handed to the Imperial Minister in Mexico [von Eckhardt]." As they worked to unravel the secret message, Montgomery and de Grey soon realized that they were onto something important.

By this point in the war, Germany had lost over one million men killed and an even greater number wounded, and her annual military spending had risen to an astronomic twenty-eight billion marks. The British naval blockade was causing widespread starvation, and during the summer of 1916 food riots broke out across Germany. The conflict was in its third year, with no end in sight. Germany's leaders came to the conclusion that their only hope for victory was to launch a new campaign of unrestricted submarine warfare, which they believed would strangle Britain and France into submission within six months. Although unleashing the U-boat fleet might result in the United States entering the war on the side of the Allies, it seemed a risk worth taking, since hostilities were expected to be over before an American army could reach Europe. Still, it would help to ensure a German victory if a means were found to focus American attention elsewhere.

Zimmerman's telegram notified von Eckhardt that unrestricted submarine warfare would begin on February 1 and instructed him to advise President Carranza that if war should break out with the United States, Germany proposed a military alliance that would enable Mexico to reconquer its lost territory in Texas, New Mexico, and Arizona. Zimmerman also suggested that Carranza should, on his own initiative, invite Japan into the coalition. The coded message was sent to von Bernstorff (for relay to von Eckhardt) via two routes: with the consent of Sweden as a Swedish diplomatic cable, and reencrypted within the American diplomatic code as an official American cable. To encourage the exchange of peace initiatives, the U.S. government had decided to allow messages between Germany and the United States to be sent under American diplomatic auspices. But unknown to Germany, the Swedish and American diplomatic cables passed through England, where the communications were intercepted and forwarded to Room 40.

When Captain William Reginald "Blinker" Hall, Britain's director of naval intelligence, was given a partially decoded copy of the telegram from Montgomery and de Grey, it left him in a quandary. The message from Zimmerman was political dynamite. The revelation that Germany was secretly working to incite Mexico to attack the United States to regain her lost territories, and was trying to involve Japan in the scheme by means of a dispatch sent over the United States' own diplomatic cable, was certain to bring America into the war. But how could the contents of the telegram be made public without revealing that Britain was intercepting the diplomatic communications of neutral countries or alerting the Germans that their codes were being broken by British cryptanalysts?

Captain Hall devised a brilliant subterfuge that solved both problems. An English agent known only as "T" was instructed to obtain a copy of the coded telegram sent by von Bernstorff to von Eckhardt from the telegraph office in Mexico City. This follow-on message to the original wire was forwarded by von Bernstorff to Mexico encrypted in an earlier diplomatic code that Room 40 could fully decipher. With the approval of the British foreign office, Hall provided a decoded copy of the telegram with the same preamble and serial number as when received in Mexico to Edward Bell, a secretary of the American embassy. When the message was made public and caused the expected uproar in the United States, the Germans concluded that a plaintext copy of the telegram had fallen into their enemies' hands through the carelessness of their diplomatic staff in Washington or by theft in Mexico City. Little did Hall realize that his successful ruse would lead the Germans in Mexico City to believe that Butcher's men were behind the theft of the vital cable and mark the intelligence officer for assassination by Witzke. As the admiral anticipated, the Zimmerman Telegram would prove to be a significant factor in America's declaration of war against Germany.

Three months after the United States entered the conflict, Major Ralph Van Deman, the head of the newly formed Military Intelligence Section of the U.S. Army War College, received an unexpected visitor. The young man did not make a strong first impression, standing just five feet five inches tall, 125 pounds in weight, and, at twenty-seven years of age, prematurely balding. But what Herbert O. Yardley lacked in physical stature he more than made up for in enthusiasm, and the proposal that he came to deliver was of great interest to Van Deman—the need for an American cryptanalytic bureau. Yardley was a telegrapher with the U.S. State Department and an expert amateur cryptographer. He had amazed his superiors by producing a one-hundred-page monograph that outlined the methods by which a foreign power could break U.S. diplomatic codes, appropriately titled "Solution of American Diplomatic Codes." Armed with letters of recommendation from his boss and several military officers that confirmed his code-breaking prowess, Yardley called on the military intelligence director and persuasively expounded on the reasons why the United States should form a bureau of cryptanalysts to break the codes of foreign governments. When he completed his discourse, Yardley offered to establish a code-breaking department within military intelligence. Van Deman was impressed. "This is a pretty big job you've picked out for yourself," the major concluded. "You talk as if you think you can do it."

The military intelligence director scribbled a note for Yardley to deliver to a staff member, arranging for him to be commissioned a first lieutenant in the U.S. Army Signal Corps. The former code clerk was then tasked with creating MI-8, Military Intelligence Section 8, "Code and Ciphers." MI-8 would become the U.S. government's chief cryptanalytic service during the First World War and achieve a notable string of successes. Yardley began his mission by assembling a cadre of men and women with the rare gift of "cipher brains" who would form the core of his code-breaking team.

The first person that Yardley hired would be counted among the very best. John Matthews Manly was the fifty-two-year-old head of the English Department at the University of Chicago. Manly had received a master's degree in mathematics at the age of eighteen from Furman University and a doctorate from Harvard University in philology, the study of the structure, development, and relationship of languages. Because Harvard did not offer a curriculum in philology at the time, Manly collected professors from different fields and created a curriculum for his own field of study. After receiving his pioneering degree in 1890, he taught at Brown University for eight years before being lured away by the president of the University of Chicago to chair its English Department. Manly had been reading German since the late 1880s, and in 1909 the university sent him as an exchange professor for five months to the University of Göttingen where he expanded his knowledge of the German language.

As a teenager Manly was fascinated by codes and ciphers, and cryptography became a lifelong interest. He gathered a collection of French texts on the subject (then the most authoritative available) and worked briefly for George Fabyan, an eccentric multimillionaire who formed a cryptanalytic research laboratory at his estate outside Chicago that assisted government decryption efforts. In March 1917, Manly traveled to Washington and offered his services to Major Van Deman, "if they could be of any value to him during the war." Van Deman directed the college professor to see Lieutenant Yardley at the Cipher Bureau.

David Stevens, a PhD code breaker who worked alongside Manly at MI-8, would note: "One trait of his [Manly's] that is known to us all was an intense directness to an idea. Trivial or obtuse, any question had his complete attention immediately. He then applied all his knowledge to its solution. . . . His knowledge of language and his understanding of [mathematical] probabilities supported a developed power of deduction." Herbert Yardley said of Manly: "He was destined to develop into the most skillful and brilliant of all our cryptographers. It is to Captain Manly that I owe a great deal of the success I achieved as head of the War Department Cipher Bureau."

Once established in his new position, Manly brought a colleague from the University of Chicago to work at MI-8, Edith Rickert, an assistant professor in the English Department. Rickert completed her undergraduate studies at Vassar in 1891 and received a doctorate from the University of Chicago in 1899. Aware of Rickert's knowledge of language, particularly her ability in German, Manly arranged for her to join the staff of code breakers. Like Manly, Rickert would become a brilliant and expert cryptanalyst. On an academic level, the two were intellectual soul mates with a shared interest in the writings of Shakespeare and Chaucer and would collaborate on two major studies of Chaucer's work, the *Chaucer Life-Records* and the eight-volume *Text of the Canterbury Tales*. Recent evidence suggests that they were more than academic colleagues with a passion for medieval literature, but lovers as well. Rickert closed one letter written to Manly on September 6, 1919, with the remark: "With no more love than usual, but something of a wish that I had you here this minute." Their secret relationship—neither was married—likely enhanced the quality of their collaborative writing and the results they would achieve as a code-breaking team at MI-8.

The dispatch from Major Barnes containing copies of Witzke's code key and cipher message was delivered to military intelligence headquarters in late January 1918, within days of the agent's arrest. The army officer who received the documents was so impressed by their importance that in the interest of secrecy he forwarded them to (now) Captain Yardley for decipherment without providing any indication of their source or significance. Since the items were not marked for priority attention and the staff at MI-8 was preoccupied with other coded intercepts, the Waberski documents, nameless and undescribed, languished in a pile of undeciphered material for months. When a senior official finally sent an inquiry to MI-8 asking whether the Waberski letter had been deciphered, "no one remembered anything about the message, as it had attracted no special attention."

For the first time, the code breakers learned the crucial significance of the captured sheets, and deciphering Witzke's message became a top priority. In the weeks that followed, a succession of MI-8 cryptanalysts, including Yardley, attempted to break the message without achieving any success. By the end of April, the pressure to solve the cryptogram grew intense. Apart from its importance to the government's case against Witzke, the U.S. Army's chief of staff and members of a congressional committee were scheduled to make an inspection tour of military intelligence headquarters on a coming Sunday, and decryption of the Waberski document would be sure to impress them. Van Deman directed Yardley to concentrate all of the code-breaking group's energies to solving the cipher before the important delegation arrived. With only three days left until the deadline, Yardley assigned the Waberski message to Manly.

The encrypted identification sheet that Jahnke had given Witzke in Mexico City was a tremendously complicated cipher that contained no signature or identifying words to guide the cryptanalyst, only a plaintext numeric date. Figure 1 shows the document as received by Manly.

The first step in deciphering the document would be for the code breakers to determine whether it was a substitution cipher or a transposition cipher. In a substitution cipher, the letters of the original message are replaced by other letters of the alphabet, or by numeric figures or symbols. For example, an *a* might be replaced by an *s*, or by the number 8, or a triangle. In a transposition cipher, the letters of the original message remain unchanged but are moved from their normal positions in the words of the

		15-1-18
seofnatupk	asiheihbbn	uersdausnn
lrseggiesn	nkleznsimn	ehneshmppb
asueasriht	hteurmvnsm	eaincouasi
insnrnvegd	esnbtnnrcn	dtdrzbemuk
kolselzdnn	auebfkbpsa	tasecisdgt
ihuknaeie	tiebaeuera	thnoieaeen
hsdaeaiakn	ethnnneecd	ckdkonesdu
eszadehpea	bbilsesooe	etnouzkdml
neuiiurmrn	zwhneegver	eodhicsiac
niusnrdnso	drgsurriec	egrcsuassp
eatgrsheho	etruseelca	umtpaatlee
cicxrnprga	awsutemair	nasnutedea
errreoheim	eahktmuhdt	cokdtgceio
eefighihre	litfiueunl	eelserunma
znai		

Figure I. Waberski cipher message
Courtesy of the George C. Marshall Foundation, Lexington, Virginia.

message to other positions according to an encoding system. A defined system must be used in disarranging the transposed letters to ensure that they can be returned to their normal positions forming the words of the original message when deciphered.

To determine whether the Waberski message was a substitution or transposition cipher, Manly and Rickert created a "frequency table" showing how many times each letter appeared in the document and then compared it with a table displaying how frequently letters appear in normal use. If the frequency is similar, the cipher is a transposition; if not, it's a substitution. Experience had shown that although intercepted cipher messages were usually around one hundred to five hundred letters long, and a "normal use" frequency table was based on an examination of around ten thousand letters, any statistical comparison would still be reliable, but not absolute. MI-8 had created different "normal use" frequency tables for foreign languages based on deviations in the way characters were used in those languages. Because the Waberski note had been found in the hands of an alleged German agent who had been operating in the United States but had arrived from a Spanish-speaking country, the frequency of the characters in the Waberski message were compared with "normal use" frequency tables for English, German, and Spanish.

The frequency table comparison revealed that without a doubt the message was a transposition cipher, and the original text had probably been composed in the German language. The two professors concluded that it had been written in German based on their knowledge of languages. Since the message had no q's, they ruled out Spanish because the word *que* is very common in Spanish. Since the cipher document contained only two w's, it had probably not been written in English; if it were, in a message of this size there should have been approximately six w's based on normal English frequency. Finally, the very high frequency of e's and n's that appeared suggested strongly that the original message had been written in German.

After establishing that the cipher was likely a German transposition, the next step in its solution was for the professors to uncover the system by which the letters had been disarranged. In the German language there are certain letters that almost always appear before certain other letters. The task would now be to identify the numeric distance or "interval" between these typically combined letters in the message, which might help reveal the process by which the letter pairs had been separated. To accomplish this, they numbered all the letters of the cipher message in sequence from beginning to end (see figure 2).

Manly knew that in German there are two pairs of letters that always form an "inseparable group"—the letter *c* never occurs except when placed

s-1	e-44	u-87	n-130	n-173	e-216	c-259	a-302	t-345	e-388
e-2	v-45	a-88	a-131	o-174	h-217	r-260	t-303	e-346	i-389
o-3	n-46	s-89	u-132	i-175	p-218	e-261	g-304	m-347	o-390
f-4	s-47	i-90	e-133	e-176	e-219	o-262	r-305	a-348	e-391
n-5	i-48	i-91	b-134	a-177	a-220	d-263	s-306	i-349	e-392
a-6	m-49	n-92	f-135	e-178	b-221	h-264	h-307	r-350	f-393
t-7	n-50	s-93	k-136	e-179	b-222	i-265	e-308	n-351	i-394
u-8	e-51	n-94	b-137	n-180	i-223	c-266	h-309	a-352	g-395
p-9	h-52	r-95	p-138	h-181	l-224	s-267	o-310	s-353	h-396
k-10	n-53	n-96	s-139	s-182	s-225	i-268	e-311	n-354	i-397
a-11	e-54	v-97	a-140	e-226	a-269	t-312	u-355	h-398
s-12	s-55	e-98	t-141	a-184	s-227	c-270	r-313	t-356	r-399
i-13	h-56	g-99	a-142	e-185	o-228	n-271	u-314	e-357	e-400
h-14	m-57	d-100	s-143	a-186	o-229	i-272	s-315	d-358	l-401
e-15	p-58	e-101	e-144	i-187	e-230	u-273	e-316	e-359	i-402
i-16	p-59	s-102	c-145	a-188	e-231	s-274	e-317	a-360	t-403
h-17	b-60	n-103	i-146	k-189	t-232	n-275	l-318	e-361	f-404
b-18	a-61	b-104	s-147	n-190	n-233	r-276	c-319	r-362	i-405
b-19	s-62	t-105	d-148	e-191	o-234	d-277	a-320	r-363	u-406
n-20	u-63	n-106	g-149	t-192	u-235	n-278	u-321	r-364	e-407
u-21	e-64	n-107	t-150	h-193	z-236	s-279	m-322	e-365	u-408
e-22	a-65	r-108	i-151	n-194	k-237	o-280	t-323	o-366	n-409
r-23	s-66	c-109	h-152	n-195	d-238	d-281	p-324	h-367	l-410
s-24	r-67	n-110	u-153	n-196	m-239	r-282	a-325	e-368	e-411
d-25	i-68	d-111	k-154	e-197	l-240	g-283	a-326	i-369	e-412
a-26	h-69	t-112	t-155	e-198	n-241	s-284	t-327	m-370	l-413
u-27	t-70	d-113	n-156	c-199	e-242	u-285	l-328	e-371	s-414
s-28	h-71	r-114	a-157	d-200	u-243	r-286	e-329	a-372	e-415
n-29	t-72	z-115	e-158	c-201	i-244	r-287	e-330	h-373	f-416
n-30	e-73	b-116	i-159	k-202	i-245	i-288	c-331	k-374	u-417
l-31	u-74	e-117	e-160	d-203	u-246	e-289	i-332	t-375	n-418
r-32	r-75	m-118	t-161	k-204	r-247	c-290	c-333	m-376	m-419
s-33	m-76	u-119	i-162	o-205	m-248	e-290	x-334	u-377	a-420
e-34	v-77	k-120	e-163	n-206	r-249	g-292	r-335	h-378	z-421
g-35	n-78	k-121	b-164	e-207	n-250	r-293	n-336	d-379	n-422
g-36	s-79	o-122	a-165	s-208	z-251	c-294	p-337	t-380	a-423
i-37	m-80	l-123	e-166	d-209	w-252	s-295	r-338	c-381	i-424
e-38	e-81	s-124	u-167	u-210	h-253	u-296	g-339	o-382	
s-39	a-82	e-125	e-168	e-211	n-254	a-297	a-340	k-383	
n-40	i-83	l-126	r-169	s-212	e-255	s-298	a-341	d-384	
n-41	n-84	z-127	a-170	z-213	e-256	s-299	w-342	t-385	
k-42	c-85	d-128	t-171	a-214	g-257	p-300	s-343	g-386	
l-43	o-86	n-129	h-172	d-215	v-258	e-301	u-344	c-387	

Figure 2. Waberski cipher letters are numbered (in order) to measure C–H–K intervals.

Courtesy of the George C. Marshall Foundation, Lexington, Virginia.

before an *h* or a *k*. So they next prepared a list of all the *c*'s in the document with their location number showing where they were positioned in the message, and similar lists for the *h*'s and *k*'s with their location numbers.

As Manly later noted, this revealed an important discovery:

[It was found] that the interval between certain occurrences of the letter "c" matched exactly with the occurrences of the letter "h." Thus for "c's" the interval between c-109 and c-145 is 24, and the interval between c-145 and c-199 is 36. In the lists of "h's" these same intervals appear between the numbers h-193, h-217, and h-253. It would seem probable, then, that these three "c's" were originally joined with these three "h's," and this was confirmed by the fact that fifty-four letters further on in each case appeared another pair of equal intervals; that is, in the "c's" between c-199, c-201, and c- 259, and in the "h's" between h-307, h-309, and h-367, the pair of intervals being 2 and 58. . . .

It was quite clear that six "c's" had been correctly matched with six "h's," and subtracting the [assigned] number of each "c" from that of the corresponding "h" it was found that there was an interval between them of 108. Thus h-217 minus c-109 equals 108, h-253 minus c-145 equals 108, h-309 minus c-201 equals 108, h-367 minus c-259 equals 108. It was safe to conclude that the first step in the transposition of the original message had resulted in moving each letter 108 spaces from the letter preceding it.

After achieving this breakthrough, the professors decided to write the letters of the message sequentially in vertical columns of 108 letters, beginning with the first letter of the message and then starting a new column when the 109th letter was reached, and so on. This resulted in four columns with 108 letters per column, except for the last column. Because there were 424 letters in the message, the final column did not reach 108 letters in length and was therefore short by eight letters (see figure 3).

It was immediately apparent to Manly and Rickert that the four-letter groups created by this operation might well be segments of German words. Their task would now be to match the groups together and determine the rest of the system on which the disarrangement (encryption) was based.

Scanning through the letter groups for a group that could definitely be matched with another, their attention focused on group 10, *kmex*, in which the last three letters suggested the beginning of the word *Mexico*. Since the bearer of the document had just come from Mexico, this seemed a likely word to appear in the message. The rest of the word could be spelled *ico*, or more probably *iko* since based on the letter groups the message was clearly in German. Their search for a group beginning with *ico* or *iko* directed their attention to group 13, where it was noted that *ikop* could be a continuation of group 10, *kmex*. Examination of the message showed that this was the only group of the 108 groups that began with these letters, and it was therefore almost a certainty that group 13 should be joined with group 10.

Based on this apparently positive outcome, the professors examined the subsequent letter groups to see whether other groups could be joined to make German words, or parts of them. It seemed obvious to them that the *sul* in group 24, *sula*, would make a good continuation of *kon* in group 12, *skon*, forming the Teutonic word *konsul*. Similarly, the *zus* in group 19, *kzus*, could be combined with the *ende* of group 22 to form the word *zusende*, German for "send."

	Column 1	Column 2	Column 3	Column 4			Column 1	Column 2	Column 3	Column 4			Column 1	Column 2	Column 3	Column 4
1	s	c	h	a		37	i	c	h	e		73	e	h	e	i
2	e	n	p	a		38	e	i	n	r		74	u	s	c	h
3	o	d	e	t		39	s	s	e	r		75	r	d	e	r
4	f	t	a	l		40	n	d	e	r		76	m	a	g	e
5	n	d	b	e		41	n	g	g	e		77	v	e	r	l
6	a	r	b	e		42	k	t	v	o		78	n	a	c	i
7	t	z	i	c		43	l	i	c	h		79	s	i	c	t
8	u	b	l	i		44	e	h	r	e		80	m	a	u	f
9	p	e	s	c		45	z	u	e	i		81	e	k	a	i
10	k	m	e	x		46	n	k	o	m		82	a	n	s	u
11	a	u	s	r		47	s	t	d	e		83	i	e	s	e
12	s	k	o	n		48	i	n	h	a		84	n	t	p	u
13	i	k	o	p		49	m	a	i	h		85	c	h	e	n
14	h	o	e	r		50	n	e	c	k		86	o	n	a	l
15	e	l	e	g		51	e	i	s	t		87	u	n	t	e
16	i	s	t	a		52	h	e	i	m		88	a	n	g	e
17	h	e	n	a		53	n	t	a	u		89	s	e	r	l
18	b	l	o	w		54	e	i	c	h		90	i	e	s	s
19	b	z	u	s		55	s	e	n	d		91	i	c	h	e
20	n	d	z	a		56	h	b	i	t		92	n	d	e	r
21	u	n	k	t		57	m	a	u	c		93	s	c	h	u
22	e	n	d	e		58	p	e	s	o		94	n	k	o	n
23	r	a	m	m		59	p	u	n	k		95	r	d	e	m
24	s	u	l	a		60	b	e	r	d		96	n	k	t	a
25	d	e	n	i		61	a	r	d	t		97	v	o	r	z
26	a	b	e	r		62	s	a	n	g		98	e	n	u	n
27	u	f	u	n		63	u	t	s	c		99	g	e	s	a
28	s	k	i	a		64	e	h	o	e		100	d	s	e	i
29	n	b	i	s		65	a	n	d	i		101	e	d	e	
30	n	p	u	n		66	s	o	r	o		102	s	u	l	
31	l	s	r	u		67	r	i	g	e		103	n	e	c	
32	r	a	m	t		68	i	e	s	e		104	b	s	a	
33	s	t	r	e		69	h	a	u	f		105	t	z	u	
34	e	a	n	d		70	t	e	r	i		106	n	a	m	
35	g	s	z	e		71	h	e	r	g		107	n	d	t	
36	g	e	w	a		72	t	e	i	h		108	r	e	p	

Figure 3. Waberski cipher written sequentially in 108-letter columns.
Courtesy of the George C. Marshall Foundation, Lexington, Virginia.

Manly concluded:

After a good many groups had been matched in this way it became clear that the system [by which the message had been encrypted] was very complicated indeed, and the best way to discover it was to bring to light as many uniformities as possible in the intervals between the groups. The process was long and

difficult. It was easy to bring together groups which would make interchange-
able German words and parts of sentences, but it was necessary to bring them
together in accordance with some system or we could not be sure that the
result was the original arrangement.

We experimented with arranging the groups into columns, because a
transposition by columns is a very common form of [creating a] cipher. As
there were 108 groups in the message, this would give either three columns
of thirty-six groups each, or six columns of eighteen groups each, or nine columns of twelve groups each, or twelve columns of ten groups each. We tried
the arrangement of twelve blocks or columns of nine groups each as being
the most probable arrangement, and this proved to be correct [see figure 4].

The outcome of long hours spent in analytical thinking and computa-
tion, the success achieved in forming the four-letter groups convinced the
two professors that they were on the right track. They found the hunt for a
solution to the German spy's cipher exhilarating. It was noon on Saturday
before they reached the point at which they were able to search in earnest
for the system underlying the arrangement of the groups, but by now they
were certain that the solution of the message was just a matter of careful
scientific investigation.

They discovered that the group *kmex* with which they had started put-
ting together possible words stood in the first line of the second column,
and group *ikop*, which they decided must follow it, was in the fourth line

	Col 1	Col 2	Col 3	Col 4	Col 5	Col 6	Col 7	Col 8	Col 9	Col 10	Col 11	Col 12
	1	10	19	28	37	46	55	64	73	82	91	100
Line 1	scha	kmex	bzus	skia	iche	nkom	send	ehoe	ehei	ansu	iche	dsei
	2	11	20	29	38	47	56	65	74	83	92	101
Line 2	enpa	ausr	ndza	nbis	einr	stde	hbit	andi	usch	iese	nder	ede
	3	12	21	30	39	48	57	66	75	84	93	102
Line 3	odet	skon	unkt	npun	sser	inha	mauc	soro	rder	ntpu	schu	sul
	4	13	22	31	40	49	58	67	76	85	94	103
Line 4	ftal	ikop	ende	lsru	nder	maih	peso	rige	mage	chen	nkon	nec
	5	14	23	32	41	50	59	68	77	86	95	104
Line 5	ndbe	hoer	ramm	ramt	ngge	neck	punk	iese	verl	onal	rdem	bsa
	6	15	24	33	42	51	60	69	78	87	96	105
Line 6	arbe	eleg	sula	stre	ktvo	eist	berd	hauf	naci	unte	nkta	tzu
	7	16	25	34	43	52	61	70	79	88	97	106
Line 7	tzic	ista	deni	eand	lich	heim	ardt	teri	sist	ange	vorz	nam
	8	17	26	35	44	53	62	71	80	89	98	107
Line 8	ubli	hena	aber	gsze	ehre	ntau	sang	herg	mauf	serl	enun	ndt
	9	18	27	36	45	54	63	72	81	90	99	108
Line 9	pesc	blow	ufun	gewa	zuei	eich	utsc	teih	ekai	iess	gesa	rep

**Figure 4. Waberski cipher arranged in twelve columns of nine groups per
column.**
Courtesy of the George C. Marshall Foundation, Lexington, Virginia.

of the same column. Combining the first and fourth lines of each column produced the following pairings: (1) *schaft/al*, (2) *k/mexico/p*, (3) *b/zusende*, (4) *ski/als/ru*, (5) *ichen/der*, (6) *n/komma/ih*, (7) *send/peso*, (8) *ehoerige*, (9) *eheim/age*, (10) *ansuchen*, (11) *ichen/kon*, and (12) *d/seine/c*. It was clear that all of these combinations formed parts of a German sentence. The professors next started looking for the group that followed each of these pairings to continue the process of uncovering the system "rules."

In the combination that formed *konsul*, the *sul* in the third line of column 12 had been matched with the *nkon* in the fourth line of column 11. Manly and Rickert wondered what would happen if the third line of each column were combined with the fourth line of the preceding column. Experimentation proved that it resulted in additional correct word fragment pairings. (The continuation of column 12 was naturally found in column 1.)

Following the same rules, when they combined (100) *dsei* with (103) *nec* to (3) *odet*, the extended pairing became *d/seine/code/t*, resulting in the German words meaning "his code" and the beginning of a word which might be "telegram." Searching column 2 for the rest of the word "telegram," they found it in line 6 of column 2, *eleg*, and then discovered the continuation in line 5 of column 3, *ramm*. This generated yet other rules to apply throughout the columns of the message.

Analysis would show that in every case, the sequence of lines established created an intelligent and correct sequence of letters and words. Excitedly, the professors realized they had uncovered the beginning of the German's encryption system—applying the same process would reveal the entire system!

Manly and Rickert continued working on the Waberski decipherment for the remainder of Saturday afternoon but were not finished at six o'clock, the usual close of a working day at MI-8. With success so close at hand, they decided to take a break and stepped out to a local restaurant for dinner before returning to work late into the evening.

By examining the groups and the rules that they had established to decipher individual segments of sentences, they came to the realization that it would be necessary to reorient the horizontal lines (of figure 4) into vertical columns and then reorder the new columns into the sequence 2-9-8-1-4-3-6-5-7 to replicate the system (see figure 5). This produced twelve exactly similar series moving diagonally one space to the right and down, except between the fourth and fifth columns (new columns 1 and 4) where the movement was horizontal. By starting at the eighth row down on the left in figure 5 (labeled 1) and following the directional arrows across to the end of the sequence, then resuming at the beginning of sequence 2 at the left and

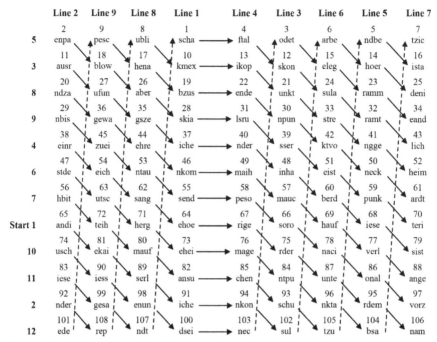

Figure 5. Waberski cipher lines reoriented as columns in revised order
Courtesy of the George C. Marshall Foundation, Lexington, Virginia.

following the directional arrows to the end of this sequence, and resuming with succeeding sequences labeled at the left 3, 4, 5, and so on, the full text of the original document could now be written in order. Discovery of the system that the Germans had used to create the cipher left no doubt that the only correct meaning of the message had at last been found.

As the plaintext letters were transcribed from the matrix, the words of Witzke's coded identification card leapt off the page:

> An die Kaiserlichen Konsular-Behoerden in der Republik Mexiko Punkt.
> Srenggeheim Ausrufungszeichen!

> Der Inhaber dieses ist ein Reichsangehoeriger der unter dem namen Pablo Waberski als Russe reist punkt Er ist deutscher geheim-agent punkt Absatz ich bittn ihm auf ansuchen schutz und Beistand zu gewaehren komma ihm auch auf, Verlangen bis zu ein tausend pesos oro nacional vorzuschiessen und seine Code-telegramme an diese Gesandtschaft als konsularamtliche Depeschen abzusenden punkt

> Von Eck[h]ardt

Translated into English the message read:

> To the Imperial Consular Authorities in the Republic of Mexico
> Strictly Secret!
>
> The bearer of this is a subject of the Empire who travels as a Russian under the name of Pablo Waberski. He is a German secret agent. Please furnish him on request protection and assistance, also advance him on demand up to one thousand pesos of Mexican gold and send his code telegrams to this embassy as official consular dispatches.
>
> Von Eckhardt

Long before the invention of electronic computers, using only their intellects, paper, and pencils, Manly and Rickert had deciphered the immensely complex double-key transposition cipher of the German secret service in just three days. The message had been enciphered in a 12-step process "with its multiple horizontal shiftings of three- and four-letter plaintext groups ripped apart by a final vertical transcription." It was a code-breaking tour de force.

The triumphant professors prepared several typewritten copies of the coded message as it had originally been received, a brief overview describing how the decipherment was obtained, and the final translation. They left the documents on Yardley's desk before departing wearily for their homes in the early morning darkness.

When Major Van Deman arrived at the office at ten o'clock that Sunday morning to prepare for the inspection, the intelligence director was surprised to find Yardley waiting for him. Yardley handed him a copy of the translated identification card message, and Van Deman read it over and over in silent amazement.

"Please offer my sincere congratulations to the personnel of MI-8," he said to Yardley. "If for no other reason, the decipherment of this document justifies your bureau."

The inspection tour of military intelligence headquarters by the chief of staff and members of the congressional committee was a success. Van Deman could not only "point to a well-organized, smoothly working division, but he could cite a fresh achievement of the Code and Cipher Section" as proof of its capabilities.

In August, Captain Manly and Miss Rickert departed Washington for Fort Sam Houston in Texas to testify at the Witzke trial and explain the method by which the decipherment had been accomplished. Their journey by train from the nation's capital to the southwest was not only long, but very hot. The country was suffering from one of the worst heat waves experienced in recent years, and they passed through towns wracked by clouds of dust and scorching heat before arriving in San Antonio, where the expert witnesses were guided to their temporary residence.

Not far from their quarters, on the second floor of a hastily constructed building at the army post, a large meeting room sat empty, awaiting the court-martial that was to determine whether a captured German agent would live or die.

9

The Court-Martial of Lothar Witzke

The temperature had risen to ninety-nine degrees Fahrenheit on the afternoon of August 16 when Lothar Witzke entered the courtroom. Under military guard, he was escorted to a chair at the center of the room facing an assembled committee of U.S. Army officers.

The court-martial of the alleged spy would be unlike a typical court proceeding, with its judge and jury, witness stand, and public audience. While courts-martial in the United States were almost invariably open to the public during trial, due to the sensitive nature of the Witzke espionage trial at which active-duty intelligence agents would give testimony, it was carried out as a secret tribunal without public notice or spectators. Seated behind a long table piled with evidence, military records, and law books were the members of the military commission appointed to hear the case: the presiding officer, Brigadier General James A. Ryan, National Army, at the center, and on his right and left according to rank, Brigadier General James J. Hornbrook, National Army; Colonel Augustus C. Macomb, 14th Cavalry; and Colonel Erwin L. Phillips, 307th Cavalry. The judge advocate, or prosecutor, was Major A. J. Burgwin, who would be assisted by Captain T. H. Brown, assistant judge advocate. Witzke was represented by Colonel W. J. Glasgow, 14th Cavalry. Apart from the commission, the accused, his counsel, and a single witness chair, the courtroom was empty.

The mandatory punishment if convicted of spying in wartime was death. As stated in *A Manual for Courts-Martial* released by the U.S. Army judge advocate general in 1917, "death by hanging is considered more ignominious than death by shooting and is the usual method of execution being designated in the case of spies."

Duty bound to judge a case in which a man's life hung in the balance, the commission members were humorless, almost grim, while after six months of solitary confinement Witzke was "pale and nervous, but quiet as a stone."

The army order designating the commission was read to the accused, and he was asked if he objected to being tried by any of the members named. Witzke replied that he had no objections to any of the members of the commission.

The prisoner was told to stand and was arraigned on the charge and specification:

Violation of the 82nd Article of War

In that Lothar Witzke, alias Pablo Waberski, did, at or near Nogales, Arizona, United States of America, on or about the 31st day of January, 1918, act as a spy in and about an encampment there situated, of the Army of the United States, and did, then and there attempt to collect material information in regard to the numbers, resources and operations of the military forces of the United States, with intent to communicate the same to the enemy.

The commission asked for Witzke's response, and the accused pled not guilty to the charge and specification. Major Burgwin rose and called the first witness for the prosecution, Dr. Paul Bernardo Altendorf.

As the only person to testify with firsthand knowledge of the enemy plan and the actions of the defendant in carrying it out, Altendorf would be a key witness for the prosecution. He began by describing his past history and recruitment by the German espionage establishment. Then the doctor detailed the journey from Mexico City to Hermosillo, explaining what had occurred at each stage of the operation.

"What was Waberski to do on the other side of the border?" Burgwin inquired.

"He was to go to the other side of the border to mutiny the negroes there, at Huachuka, and get his German agents together," Altendorf replied. "Also, the IWW people, he was to get them out, and burn and kill everybody they could halt—to go against the United States in the war; that he had these men from South America, and from everywhere, to go against the United States."

"Was there any conversation with reference to any certain one?"

"Yes, sir, the principal thing was to get Mr. Butcher, who was against us, and he [Jahnke] said he was going to play hell with him, and he swung around and said, 'You have to kill him first, he is one of the intelligence officers.'"

"Did Waberski at any time tell you how he expected to cross the border at Nogales?" asked Burgwin.

"Yes, sir, through his Russian passport; that he could work very freely in the United States then, and meet his people and his agents, and arrange everything."

"I do not understand where those men were all to come from," Colonel Glasgow interjected.

"They were coming from South America, and everywhere," Altendorf responded. "Everything was ready there."

"Did he tell you why they wanted to create disorder and raids along the American border?" Burgwin continued.

"Yes, sir, so that they would not lose the war in Europe, because America would then have to stop shipping men across to Europe on account of the trouble in her own country. He told me that I should be very, very, secretly. He says, 'Doctor, you are the only man who knows this, and you are a man who has got to be very secretly, and be very careful.'"

When the prosecutor announced that he had no further questions, Glasgow addressed the committee, requesting that cross-examination of Altendorf be delayed until the following morning so that he could review the transcript of the doctor's long and complex testimony. The commission granted his request, and the trial was adjourned for the day.

At eight o'clock the next morning, Altendorf returned to the witness stand. Attempting to cast doubt on the doctor's story, Glasgow focused his attention on the testimony in which Altendorf had described being recruited by the German secret service.

"You said yesterday that in August 1917, you went to the Juarez Hotel in Mexico City?" Glasgow stated.

"Yes, sir," Altendorf responded.

"You also said that the next day Mr. Paglasch found your name and told you that he had 'two gentlemen here' he would like to introduce you to?"

"Yes, sir."

"Do you say that Paglasch said they would be interested in meeting you, both of them, as they were both working in the German secret service?" Glasgow inquired.

"Yes, sir."

"Do you mean to say, that you came to the Juarez Hotel and registered, and that the very next day the owner of that hotel told you that he was going to introduce you to two German secret service men?" Glasgow asked skeptically.

"Yes, sir, the very same word," said Altendorf.

"Has this any bearing on the case?" the president of the commission questioned.

"I am trying, gentlemen, to attack—at least slightly—the credibility of the witness," the defense counsel replied. "He has treated us, yesterday, to a very interesting little bit of fiction. It seems most remarkable to me that the accredited German agents in Mexico City would so open their hearts within twenty-four hours to a perfect stranger, no matter whom he claimed to be, to tell him their most intimate secrets."

The cavalry officer had in fact identified the Achilles' heel of Jahnke's espionage organization—the spymaster's failure to probe into the background of prospective agents like Altendorf and Gleaves. But despite Glasgow's incredulity, the casual approach to recruiting new agents described by the witness had actually occurred in Mexico City, and he was unable to cast doubt on Altendorf's testimony.

Further cross-examination proved ineffectual, and Altendorf was excused.

The next witness to be called was William Gleaves. Under questioning from Burgwin, Gleaves told the court that he was a Canadian citizen employed by the British government. He described how he had infiltrated German intelligence and revealed details of the Witzke mission unknown to Altendorf, including the late-night meeting with the Revolutionary Association in Mexico City, before providing his own account of the journey to Nogales, Senora.

"What was to be done when you got up to the border?" Burgwin inquired.

"I were there to obey all orders of Mr. Pablo Waberski, and the men in charge, and were not to have anything to say to them, unless by authority from him."

"You were then, to be under the express instructions of Waberski?" Burgwin asked.

"Yes, sir."

"What were you to do?"

"I were to go see the colored soldiers and the colored population," said Gleaves, "and explain to them some literature which I were to receive at Nogales, and explain what we were going to carry out, and that we were going to carry out a revolution."

"Do you remember any particular mine or fort you were to go to?"

"I were to go up to the line by horseback to Fort Huachuca and see those delegates."

"What were you to do among the delegates?" Burgwin asked.

"I were to arrange to bring the delegates to see him, and he would arrange to do whatever he was supposed to do, and furnish them whatever amount of money he seen fit to, and go ahead with whatever instructions he got from Mexico City."

"What was the expressed object in visiting these negro soldiers?"

"There was supposed to be a strike through the mining district about Globe [Arizona], and men were coming out on strike, and I were to see the negroes, all the negro soldiers, and see that they did not come in against those strikers, and place enough money in the hands of the negro soldiers to bribe them to turn [sides] over to us, and Waberski was to furnish enough money for me to give to them, and to bring down the delegates, and when they got there he was to turn over enough money to them to place them in this revolutionary movement."

When the prosecution finished questioning the British operative, Glasgow began his cross-examination, asking a few irrelevant questions about a $300 payment that Gleaves had made for an automobile.

In frustration, Witzke addressed the witness himself.

"How did you know these gentlemen you met in Mexico City were Germans?" the agent demanded.

"Why, I had been knowing some of them, several of them that were delegates, because I had been with them and working for them since September 1917," said Gleaves.

"How did you know I was a German?"

"They told me that they had a man coming from the States whom they wanted to send me with, and I waited from December until January," Gleaves replied.

"Then somebody told you Pablo was not a Russian but a German?" asked Glasgow, taking over the questioning.

"They did not tell me whether he was a German or not. They said that one of the men they had under their employment would be there, and for me to wait, and that as soon as he got there, they would notify me."

When this line of questioning reached a dead end, Glasgow asked the witness about a range of other topics, from the name of the German consul in Mexico City to the composition of the Revolutionary Association, which did little to diminish Gleaves's testimony.

"There seems to be nothing further," the commission president said at length. "The witness will be excused."

Major R. M. Campbell, the U.S. military attaché in Mexico City, took the stand next and gave the court an overview of his counterintelligence duties in the Mexican capital. Under questioning from Burgwin, he described his meeting with Altendorf at the embassy and told the commission that the doctor had said he would be leaving for the border the following day with a German agent named Pablo Waberski. Doctor Altendorf was called into the courtroom, and Campbell identified him as the man he had met.

The next witness called by the prosecution was Charles L. Beatty, immigrant inspector at the U.S. customs station at Nogales. Beatty detailed Witzke's arrival at the border station on the morning of January 31 and the manner in which he had been admitted into the United States. The inspector identified Witzke's Russian passport and draft registration card as documents that had been presented for identification, as well as the manifest he had prepared that day.

After Beatty was excused, Byron S. Butcher was called to testify, and under questioning from Burgwin he outlined his history as a special agent for the military intelligence office in Nogales, Arizona, and the events that occurred before, during, and after the capture of Witzke. Butcher told the commission that he had personally discovered the government's exhibits on the German agent or in his suitcase.

"Do you know a man by the name of Dr. Altendorf?" the prosecutor asked.

"I do."

"How long have you known him?" Burgwin inquired.

"I have known the doctor indirectly since last October."

"When did you first know him directly?"

"Last December," Butcher replied.

"What was the occasion of your meeting him?"

"I employed him as an agent of the American government at that time."

"For the secret service?" the prosecutor inquired.

"Yes, sir, for the American secret service and to operate in Mexico."

"Was he sworn in by you?"

"He was."

"Did he either after or before he was sworn in make reports to you?" Burgwin inquired.

"He had been reporting to me, I believe, some two months before I employed him."

"Did you have any conversation with Pablo Waberski at any time after you searched him at the intelligence office in Nogales?"

"I had several conversations with him."

"Did he ever at any time after or before his apprehension make any statement to you as to what his real name was?" Burgwin inquired.

"He told me that he used the name 'Lothar Witzke.'"

"He did not say then what his real name and what his false name was?"

"No."

"Did Pablo Waberski at any time make any statement as to the cipher message?" Burgwin inquired, gesturing toward Witzke's identification card.

"He identified that as being his property."

"Did the accused admit to you that he was a spy?"

"Indirectly, but not directly," Butcher responded.

"When he said that he had been doing his duty to his country, to what country did he refer?"

"I took it as a matter of fact that he referred to Germany, but Germany was not mentioned in the conversation, at all, at the time."

"Then you got the impression that he went into Mexico to become a spy and work against the United States as such?" the prosecutor asked.

"Yes, sir, that Mexico was his base to work in the United States."

"Did he bring the suitcase containing some of these exhibits, himself, into this country?" Burgwin inquired.

"No, sir."

Burgwin paused, the response having taken him by surprise. "How was it brought over?"

"I brought it over."

"Into the United States?" the prosecutor inquired.

"Yes, sir."

"He did not bring it himself?"

"No, sir, he did not."

With no further questions from the prosecutor, Butcher was excused.

U.S. consul Ezra Lawton was the next witness called to testify for the prosecution. Lawton described Witzke's visit to the American consulate and identified several of the government exhibits, including the Russian passport, draft registration card, and alien entry form, as having been presented to him by Witzke at the consulate.

Captain Joel Lipscomb was called to the stand and questioned about the composition of the military units in the area around Nogales, Arizona. The intelligence officer confirmed that the 10th Cavalry at Fort Huachuca was composed of "Negro" troops. Lipscomb also testified that all of the exhibits entered as evidence, including the identification sheet cipher, were found among Witzke's effects when the agent and his suitcase were searched at Camp Little. Lipscomb told the commission that Witzke had told him that the identification card cipher and code sheet were credentials that identified him as a reporter for use in communicating with Mexico City newspapers.

Major Robert L. Barnes, intelligence officer at Fort Sam Houston, advised the court that he received the documents taken from Witzke by registered mail. He arranged for copies to be made, which were sent to military intelligence headquarters in Washington, and had locked the originals (now government exhibits) in his office safe. They had remained securely in his possession until transferred to the judge advocate for the trial.

Special Agent William Neunhoffer testified that while engaged in undercover work in Mexico City he had seen Witzke in the company of Dr. Altendorf at the Cosmos Hotel. He had not learned Witzke's name or that he was a German agent.

The final witness to be called by the prosecution was Captain John Matthews Manly. When questioned by Burgwin, Manly responded in a clear, scholarly tone that made a strong impression on the bench. He informed the court that he was the chairman of the English Department at the University of Chicago and had developed a lifelong interest in cryptography. He had been commissioned in 1917 and joined the Code and Cipher Section of MI-8. In the spring of 1918, after several individuals had attempted to decipher the Witzke message without success, the intercept was assigned to him.

"Did you finally solve it?" Burgwin asked.

"I did," Manly replied.

"If you will state the result of the decipherment," the prosecutor requested.

Manly raised a copy of the deciphered identification card and calmly read the message, first in German and then in English:

> To the Imperial Consular Authorities in the Republic of Mexico. Strictly Secret! The bearer of this is a subject of the Empire who travels as a Russian under the name of Pablo Waberski. He is a German secret agent.

The impact on the court was explosive. Up to that moment, the question of Witzke's guilt or innocence had been based entirely on the testimony of individual witnesses who *claimed* he was a German agent; the deciphered identification card provided irrefutable proof that he *was* a German operative—and Witzke had publicly admitted the document was his property.

As if delivering a college lecture, Manly calmly recited the sequence of steps that he and Rickert had performed to decipher the message. He then explained the system that a German agent would have used to encipher it.

"Is there any other special method by which this cipher could be deciphered?" Burgwin asked.

"I could not say, but there is no possibility of its being deciphered to show anything else. There might be a conceivable variation in which the particular form for these same results could be secured; just as if you were going from one place to another, you can go north and then go west, or you can go west and then go north, and still arrive at the same point."

Captain Manly was excused from the witness stand. Burgwin turned to the commission and announced, "The prosecution rests."

The judge advocate had proven beyond any reasonable doubt that Lothar Witzke, aka "Pablo Waberski," was a German agent. Captured on American soil during wartime while preparing to attack the United States, Witzke's fate seemed sealed. In contrast, the opposing counsel had been unable to summon any witnesses from Mexico to appear at the secret tribunal, virtually eliminating the possibility of mounting a proper defense.

No one recognized that the odds now favored a death sentence more than the defendant himself. In desperation, Witzke took the stand and was sworn in as a witness on his own behalf. He then launched into a long and rambling tale that was so fantastic, so beyond the realm of possibility, that it could only have been told by a man with no alternatives left.

I was born in Winski, Dziatozin, Russia. My father and mother were both Russians, but my mother came from the German Provinces, German-talking provinces in Russia, and I learned to talk German; but I still talk Polish. My father talked Polish and I talk Polish, too. So far as I know, we emigrated from Russia about seventeen years ago, as well as I remember, and came to New York. My father died a short time after that, and a friend of my father took me on board a steamer as kitchen helper. I was only about eight or ten years old at the time, and since then I was traveling mostly on steamers as a sailor; and about two or three years ago I landed with a steamer in Peru, and took up mining, and kept mining and worked as a miner there for the last time, and I did not go as a sailor any more either.

About a year and a half ago I landed in Mexico, in a southern state of Mexico, and worked my way up to Mexico City, and I went up to a mine near Guadalajara in a big mining district to go to work there, and I went up there and met a man by the name of Ramirez, and this man Ramirez went with me to Mexico City, and we started a business there. We did not start a business, but went more out to get gold bullion; that means he was acquainted with some Mexican bandits about thirty miles outside Mexico City in the mountains, some disbanded soldiers that were robbing mines, in that business, and intended to send the gold and silver bullion to Ramirez, and Ramirez needed a man as a go-between, and he sent me out with a machine about thirty miles out of Mexico City, and I would bring one or two, or even five or six, bullions mostly consisting of silver, sometimes gold, into Mexico City at night.

I lived in the Hotel Juarez, Calle Cuba 81, which is owned by Otto Paglasch, and Paglasch told me to take work in the hotel, as I did not have anything to do in the daytime, and he told me to help him, registering the people who arrived at the hotel, and I did so. I got pretty good acquainted with him, and I trusted him, and there are no banks in Mexico, and I had to give my money to him to keep for me because he had a safe. Then I had about one thousand dollars in money on me, and something went wrong with this man Ramirez, and I intended to beat it to the United States, and so I went to the United States about the middle of July last year, and went to San Francisco because I was registered there, and I got acquainted with the wrong bunch of people, and they cheated me, and one day last summer when I was drunk, I had an automobile and a lot of money, and in a short time I got broke and only had about a hundred and fifty dollars left, and a second-hand Ford automobile.

I then decided to go back to Mexico City, and I took the same railroad down, the Southern Pacific, to Nuevo Laredo, and went to Mexico City, and went back to the Hotel Juarez again, and I asked the proprietor where this man Ramirez was, and he said Ramirez was working at a mine at Guadalajara and he gave me his address and I went off and got in connection with him again, and we started in the same business again. That was in November of last year, 1917. When I went up to the United States the first time, Otto Paglasch, the hotel man, offered me to do some work for the German government. He did not say it exactly, but talked around this way, and I knew where he was at, and I would not talk to him at all about it, only in English. I wanted to have a place where I could go if anything happened in Mexico, because I wanted to be prepared, and I refused to do any of that work which he wanted me to. And when I came back to Mexico City again he offered me again something like that, and I said, "No, I will not have anything to do with that." Then I kept on at this business, this bullion business, and one night when I went out to get this five or six bullions they told me, the man who brought them to me, said that Ramirez got shot, and I went back to Mexico City and went to the hotel, and I thought the best thing for me to do was to beat it back to the United States again, and I went to the American Consul and asked him if I could cross to the United States, and he said, "You have to get a passport, and it will take at least fourteen days to get it" and I put in an application to get it, and when he told me it would take fourteen days to get it I was quite disappointed, and I went and told my friend Ramirez that I would have to wait fourteen days, and that I could do something in the meantime, and he said, "How would it do to switch everything over to the west coast, there is a big mining state over there, the State of Sinaloa, and if the mining is not good over there, why, there are plenty of bandits over there, and you and I have got enough money, we can start a mining business ourselves."

So I left on the 20th of December 1917 for Mazatlán to see if I could get anything from the miners in Mazatlán, and I got acquainted with a girl, and her father had two mines, one was a very good mine, and he took me and showed me his mines, and I got better acquainted with the girl, and we were engaged to each other, and a short time later I went back to Mexico City and told Ramirez everything about it, and he said it was a good proposition and that we had better start all over again. When I came back to Mexico City on the 11th of January 1918, I went up the next day to the American Consulate and asked for my passport and he said, "You were supposed to leave about fourteen days ago already; you can't leave on this passport at all. You will have to stay here on this and fill out a new application." I said, "my only intention to go to the United States was to get my military questionnaire and to know definitely whether I would have to go back to the United States at all, and whether I would be kept for the draft, as I don't want to be held for a draft deserter"; and he said, "You will have to wait fourteen days, because we can't help you now."

Now I was quite well acquainted with this man Paglasch at the hotel, and he talked with other people; and I talked German, but he did not know that, and one day I was talking in German with another fellow and he said, "Well, you talk German all the time?" He said, "Why did you not tell me you talked German?" I said, "Well, I am going to the United States and I don't want to get in bad"; and he said, "You can talk German?" I said, "Yes"; he said, "Did you ever hear me once talking German about some people?" I said, "No, I never heard it." He said, "What do you intend to do next?" I said, "I think I will go back to Mazatlán and stay there." He said, "Don't you think you'd better go to the United States and do some work for our people?" I said, "No, I haven't got anything to do with that." He said, "When do you intend to leave?" I said probably on the 16th, day after tomorrow." So the next day he met me, it was on the 15th of January, and he said, "Well, there is a man here that I met yesterday, and he wanted to talk to you, and he said he had a proposition for work on the west coast of Mexico." I said, "Is he a German?" He said, "No he is not a German, he is a Mexican; you go down to the saloon there and ask for a man named Ramon Alderate, this man he will have some work for you"; and I went down and met this man, and he said, "Have you any military knowledge?" I said, "No I never was a soldier in my life." He said, "Anyway, you can report to me about military matters." I said, "I could do it, probably, if I could get in communication with military people." He said, "There is a big Yaqui campaign on in the State of Sonora, and there are three armies fighting against the Indians and we would like to have information about them, would you like to furnish it?" I said, "If there is nothing wrong with it I should like to." He said, "You will have to keep the matter a little quiet, it is anti-government work, and in order to make it safe for you there I would like to give you a code, you could send a code message before you could send a letter and the Mexican government will not allow you to send real words, you have to fix a code up so that you can write words so that it looks like any ordinary telegram," and that afternoon he gave me this code. And he also told me exactly how to work this code—it was on both sides, in Spanish, and he said, "If you talk another language you had better translate one side into German, or whatever other language you talk; and if it gets into the hands of the Mexican authorities they will want to find out what it is right away." And I promised to do that, and did right away, and then he gave me another code, a small code, and told me that was an identification card, and for me to present this identification card to people in Mazatlán, a big merchandise house, the name of it was La Voista de Puebla, or something like that, and he told me to tell them I am from Ramon Alderate, and that they would then help me out with whatever I needed, and I promised to do that. I asked him if there was any meaning to this letter code, and he said, "No, you will see that all this man will do, he takes it and takes another piece of paper exactly like it and puts it up against it and reads the letters over on one side to the other, and if he says 'all right' it will be all right for you to get out." I asked him for an introduction letter, but he did not give me no list of names whatever.

The next day I left Mexico City for Mazatlán, and on the first day out we went through Irapuato and there at Irapuato I had to stay overnight, because the trains only run in daytime in Mexico. I met a man there in Irapuato by the name of Altendorf, and the next morning we traveled together and he told me that he was from Hermosillo and lived a high life while in Hermosillo, and was acquainted with lots of people, and I said, "Are you acquainted with the military people there?" He said, "Yes, for pretty near two months I was a doctor to General Calles, and I know all the German people, and everybody of military influence." I said, "You might be useful to me, to make me acquainted with those people," and he said that he was in a very poor fix and did not have much money because he had got broke by a Mexican major, and I had pity with him and paid sometimes his hotel bill and I took him out and spent time and money for drinks with him.

We went out together to Colima, and at Colima we could not get a train, there was no train running between there and Manzanillo, and I heard that the steamer would leave that same afternoon, and I went to the station office and asked the agent about what was the chance to go down to Manzanillo, and he said there was an engine leaving, and "if you will pay that engine driver something maybe he will take you along." I went and talked to the engine driver and he said he would take me, and the doctor came, and said "How much did you pay him?" I said, "So and so," and he said "Maybe that will do for two of us." The engine driver would not agree to that and made us pay him something to take him, and while hanging around there waiting for that engine all at once there was a negro came up; he walked right up and said, "Did you hire this engine here?" I said, "No, but I paid the amount of money so the man would take me to Manzanillo." He said, "I am in a hurry to get down to Manzanillo myself." I said, "I am in a hurry to get down there too," and I said, "Maybe you can fix it with the engine driver," and he did so and went on the same train, and the doctor and I traveled together to Manzanillo, and I saw this negro on the steamer and he seemed to be quite well acquainted with the doctor, and also tried to talk with me, but I did not talk to him. At Mazatlán I took the doctor over and made him acquainted with my fiancée. I met her father, Mr. Garcia, and he asked me if I was going to the United States, and I told him "no," and I told him I could not go. He said, "Are you an American citizen?" and I said "no," and I said, "if I don't have a passport they won't let me go," and he said, "if we could go and see if these two mines were any good. I have got friend in San Francisco, some mining friends, and they might be mining here, and if you can marry my daughter you can get in business yourself." I said, "Probably I can fix it up and go to the United States, and have something to do and as Hermosillo is only three hours away from Nogales, and I can go right away to see the German Consul in Mazatlan, I went and looked him up, and the next day I left for Hermosillo, and then I got off the train there with Altendorf, and I said, "I am acquainted with this hotel," and I wanted him to stick together with me, and he went to the Cohen Hotel and I stayed at the Hotel Alcalde. Then on the same day I told him to keep in mind his promise to make me acquainted with those people, but he backed out and said he could not do it, and I said, "What's the matter, I thought you knew them?" He said that some of them were not there, and that the Governor was in Nogales, and he had an excuse for pretty near everything, and I got quite mad with him and told him I had spent a lot of money and time on him. And while I was in the hotel there they told me a lot of things about him, that he was a big crook and had a bad reputation, and I think the newspapers in Hermosillo would be quite interested in this story, "if you don't keep your promise to me" is what I told him, "I intend to make it known," and he was kind of scared and he told me to go to Nogales first and see about my business and that when I came back to Hermosillo he would see what he could do there. I asked him to get me a pistol, and he went out and got it, and said he got it from some major or colonel there and he went to the Presidente of the Municipality and got me a permit also, and the next day I met a fellow at the hotel and he told me that the doctor was a supposed German spy and that I had better keep away from him because the owner of the hotel was an American, and that the doctor had a bad reputation, and that he was always in the crowd around with Governor Calles and other Mexican generals and colonels and majors and that he was no good to the man who wanted to keep in good standing with the United States. I paid no attention to it, but in the afternoon I went to the doctor and told him that and he denied it. We went out to the jewelers and I had thirteen pearls examined, and they said they were worth about three hundred dollars—I paid twenty-five or thirty dollars for them, and the next day I left my hotel and went to his hotel and took my suitcase along, and I said, "Here are the thirteen pearls, take them and sell them," he had a man who would buy them, he said. And I said, "Here is my suitcase, you keep it and I will be back on the next train," and he said that would be all right. I told him there was some shirts there—he was quite poor—and if he needed one he could take one of them, and he opened the suitcase to get the shirt and he saw these two codes laying in there, and he handed them to me and said, "There are your two codes"—he knew about them—and I said, "I don't need them." He also said, "You'd better take your suitcase along, you can't tell when the Yaquis will hold the train up, and you will need your clothes," and after a while he begged me so hard, I took it, and when I got in Nogales, Sonora, and left it there.

I got there the 30th of January, and the next morning about 10 o'clock I went to the American Consul, Mr. Lawton, and showed him my passport and asked him if I could go across on it, and he said, "This passport is overdue three weeks," and I said, "Mr. Lawton, you know how it is, the trains are late and are getting held up in Mexico, and I am pretty near three weeks late"; and he said, "I can't fix it up for you until I see a man from the other side, a man from the Immigration Service," and then he phoned over and got Mr. Butcher from the other side, and introduced me to him, and said "This is Mr. Butcher, he will help you get across," and Mr. Butcher took me right across to the customs office, and he asked me what intention I had in coming to the United States, and I said the only purpose I had was to get my questionnaire fixed up so that I would not be considered as a deserter or slacker, and they sent me right from the customs office there to the city hall, and at the city hall a man gave me a questionnaire, and told me to take it and fill it out and answer, and asked me if I had answered one, and I told him no, and he told me I ought to have filled it out at least two months ago, and I told him I had been in Mexico, and he was satisfied with that. He sent me to a lawyer and he filled it out quite complete and I went back to city hall, and he told me I should go back to the Immigration Office and send it away, it had to go to San Francisco. I went there and they told me to bring it back to the city hall, that it was their business, and I got back there and it was nearly 12 o'clock and the city hall was closed, and I went over on the Mexican side, I had my baggage over there, and I intended to go back over at 3 o'clock in the afternoon, and at half past three I went to the American Consul and got my pistol back—I had given it in his care, and I went over to the United States, to the city hall and left my questionnaire. They asked me a couple of questions and looked at it, and it was all right, and I then went down the street to get some cigarettes and then went right back across to Mexico and stayed there. The next morning there was a man asked me to get him some paste, said he could not get it in Mexico there, because they didn't make it over there, and I went over to the United States side and walked about half a block and got arrested. That is about all I have got to say.

After Witzke concluded his statement, the courtroom fell silent.

Burgwin rose and began his cross-examination. The prosecutor focused on the statements that Witzke had made that were clearly disproven by the government's evidence, such as receiving the identification cipher from a newspaperman and not having been acquainted with William Gleaves. In each instance the defendant clung to his story, further weakening his case. When asked if he knew the content of the cipher message, whether he had been a cadet in the German navy, what U.S. Army camps were located near Nogales, and even the name of the inspector who had filled out his entry manifest, Witzke denied having any knowledge. His ill-considered testimony now fully discredited, the sole witness for the defense was excused.

The closing arguments of the court-martial were less an orderly summation by a prosecutor and defense counsel than an open debate. Glasgow called the commission's attention to the difficulty he had encountered in defending the accused when "we cannot get any witnesses from Mexico" and attacked the credibility of the government's witnesses: "Now you take Dr. Altendorf and take Gleaves; they are confessed men who have sold to both sides, and I really don't know now which side paid them the most, I assume we did."

The defense counsel also expressed doubt that twenty-four hours after meeting Altendorf the German secret service "immediately began disclosing all their secrets [to him], what they had done and had proposed to do, and began trusting him like a brother."

Assistant Judge Advocate Brown countered that Altendorf had joined the German espionage ring on the express instructions of Mr. Butcher and that nothing could explain away the cipher identification card that Witzke admitted belonged to him. "What did the possession of that cipher code upon the accused mean?" Brown asked. "It meant only this—taken in connection of the testimony of Mr. Gleaves, Dr. Altendorf, and Mr. Neunhoffer who saw that man in Mexico City with Dr. Altendorf . . . corroborated by the testimony of Mr. Butcher, that this man is a spy and an employee of the Imperial German Government."

Glasgow called the commission's attention to the charge and specification that required a violator to "act as a spy in and about an encampment . . . and there attempt to collect material information."

"The man himself says that he went up to the city hall and back," said the defense counsel, "but the encampment is a mile away—there is testimony to that effect, you are all probably familiar with that anyway—he never went anywhere near it. Well, of course, there is [also] no evidence, whatever, to show that he attempted to collect any material information."

To which Major Burgwin responded: "In the Manual for Courts-Martial, on page 236, it says 'Being a Spy—The principal characteristic of this offense is a clandestine dissimilation of the true object sought, which object is an endeavor to obtain information with the intention of communicating it to the hostile party.' The proof is that the accused was found at a certain place within our lines, acting clandestinely, or under false pretenses. It is the contention of the Government in this case that this accused was within the American lines for a certain purpose; that his object among others . . . was for the purpose of obtaining valuable information on the American side with reference to American encampments, American soldiers, and American miners, and by the arrangements which he had perfected transmit that information back to the enemy in Mexico City."

Burgwin and Glasgow continued to spar into the afternoon, introducing argument and counterargument, until at last the prosecutor ended the debate by responding: "We have no desire to reply to the counsel's last remarks."

After seven hours and twenty minutes of testimony, the proceedings were closed. In accordance with the regulations for courts-martial, the commission took a vote on the guilt or innocence of the accused to the charge and specification. The first vote was taken from the most junior member of the commission in rank, Colonel Macomb, and continued to the highest rank. Each member wrote their decision on a slip of paper which was handed to the presiding officer, Brigadier General Ryan. Since spying in wartime was a capital offense, it would be necessary for two-thirds of the commission members to concur for a conviction.

When the votes were tallied, the commission found Witzke guilty as charged.

Brigadier General Ryan addressed the court: "The commission sentence the accused, Lothar Witzke, alias Pablo Waberski, to be hanged by the neck until dead, two-thirds of the members concurring therein."

10

The Jailbreak of Lothar Witzke

The trial concluded, Witzke returned to his cell a condemned man. There would be no execution at daybreak. He learned that his case was to be reviewed by a U.S. Army judicial review board. But their ruling seemed a foregone conclusion, the delay a temporary stay of execution. There now appeared to be only one course open to avoid the hangman's noose—a breakout.

This seemed a likely possibility to his captors as well. The officer in charge of the custody squad at Fort Sam Houston, Lieutenant Charles F. Miller, was instructed to take special precautions to prevent Witzke's escape and ensure that the inmate did not commit suicide. Only the most reliable men were selected to guard the prisoner, and every twenty-four hours a guard entered Witzke's cell to examine his clothing, bedding, and toiletries for weapons, saws, or other contraband.

Late one night, Corporal Roy Stephens, a sentry posted at the door to Witzke's cell in the darkened prison block, notified Lieutenant Miller that he had heard unusual activity and suspected the enemy agent was up to something. Near midnight the prisoner was removed from his cell, stripped to his underwear, and a thorough search was made of his clothes and the lockup area. Nothing was found, but as a precaution it was decided to keep Witzke in his underwear for the remainder of the night.

The prisoner was escorted back to his cell, and when he entered, they saw him immediately glance upward at a remote corner of the barred room.

Stephens grabbed a chair to stand on, then probed around the steel sheeting and molding in the area. Lodged between a metal sheet and the wall he found a safety razor blade and a folded wad of brown paper. Unraveling the crumpled paper, the soldiers saw that it was brown cigarette paper on which a message in German had been penciled. Translated, the note read:

> My name is Lothar Witzke. Born in Posen and for that reason I only understand Polish and not Russian. I was lieutenant on cruiser *Dresden* that was sunk near Valparaiso, Chile. I lay two months in the hospital, which is the reason I escaped internment. The rest of the crew is interned.

It appeared to his jailers that Witzke hoped to smuggle the note to someone on the outside, possibly to other agents sent to find out what had become of him. When asked why he had written the message, Witzke just shrugged his shoulders and laughed. Now on their guard, the security detail for the special prisoner was doubled in size, and the German operative was permanently confined with his top clothes removed.

The days slowly passed, and Witzke's incarceration turned from weeks into months. An armistice was signed ending hostilities on November 11, 1918, but Witzke still remained a prisoner. On May 20, 1919, his court-martial record was examined by the military review board, which decided that the evidence proved the agent's guilt beyond a reasonable doubt. However, the board also recommended that his sentence be commuted to confinement at hard labor, and this was sent to the president for a decision.

In 1917, Woodrow Wilson had asked for a declaration of war against Germany, outraged over her "criminal intrigues." The following year he signed the Espionage Act, introducing stiff penalties for espionage activity, and the severe Alien and Sedition Acts to suppress public expression or actions in opposition to the war, legitimate or otherwise. It seemed highly unlikely that Wilson would stay the German agent's execution by hanging.

Languishing in his prison cell while awaiting the final verdict, Witzke tried to entice his captors into helping him escape. He told one of the officers on the custody squad, Lieutenant George Haslam, that "every American has his price," advising that he had between $7,000 and $8,000 hidden in Mexico which he wanted to retrieve; Haslam could obtain a share of the money if he helped him break jail. The lieutenant immediately reported the conversation to his superior. On another occasion, a corporal of the guard with whom Witzke was friendly was sitting on a cot in his cell when the prisoner offhandedly remarked that he would pay the corporal $5,000 for helping to turn him loose. That conversation was also reported.

Guarding the enemy agent had descended into a monotonous routine, when on the night of August 1, 1919, a curious sequence of events began to unfold on the second floor of the prison.

The military prison at Fort Sam Houston was a three-story brick building flanked on either side by a long two-story wing used as a barracks. The first floor of the structure housed offices for the custody guard officer, a guardroom, kitchen, dining room, and a sally port (controlled entrance to the prison). At the bottom of a stairway leading from the first floor of the prison to the cells on the second and third floors was a wicket, or steel door, that provided the only entry to the upper stories. The wicket was always locked and required a pass key for access that was only carried by the corporal of the guard, the sergeant of the guard, and the prison officer. At the top of the stairway was an anteroom containing six cells, and on either side of the anteroom was a large room containing a steel cage. There were no other enclosed compartments on the second floor of the prison except a bathroom and a toilet room. The steel cage to the left of the anteroom was divided by a steel partition; on one side of the partition, a large common cell held several prisoners, while the other side was subdivided into several small individual cells. Confined in one of these smaller cells at the northeast corner was Lothar Witzke.

The ceiling at the top of each cage was a steel latticework. It was possible for a prisoner in one of the individual cells to stand on their cot and communicate over the partition with a prisoner in the large common cell. A passageway ran around the common cage to allow the guard on duty to patrol around its perimeter, but guards were ordered not to pass down the side of the cage containing the small cells. The reason for this rule was that with postwar demobilizations, few prison guards were available. Untrained Mexican immigrants were often enlisted as guards, and it was thought unwise for them to speak with the prisoners in the small cells, and definitely not to converse with Witzke who was recognized to be a dangerous individual. No prisoner was ever assigned to a cell next to Witzke.

At midnight on that particular August night, a prisoner in the cage to the right of the anteroom told the guard that he needed to use the toilet. The procedure in such a circumstance was for the guard to walk to the head of the stairs and call down to the corporal of the guard, who would unlock the steel wicket, ascend the stairs, unlock the cage containing the prisoner, and accompany both the guard and the prisoner to the toilet. On this night, however, the corporal beckoned the guard to the foot of the stairs and handed him the keys to the cage through the doorway. The guard then unlocked the cage holding the prisoner, took him to the toilet, and left him there. At that moment, another prisoner said that he also needed to use the toilet, and the guard took him there, leaving both prisoners in the toilet at the same time. Suddenly Witzke, from his cell on the left of the anteroom, called out that he too wanted to use the toilet. The guard, a recent arrival from Mexico with limited knowledge of military procedures, unlocked Witzke's cell and walked him to the toilet also. As soon as the German agent reached the latrine, all three prisoners jumped out and attacked the guard, wrestling his rifle away from him. The unfortunate victim was bound and gagged with towels, and then the three escapees raced up the stairs to the third story, where parole prisoners were held.

In an anteroom on the third story of the prison, the bars in one of the windows had been sawn through, an action that had taken place surreptitiously since their last inspection an hour before. The escapees ran to this window, which looked out onto the roof of the barracks, and wrenched away the sawn bars, then leapt through the opening onto the roof of the barracks and ran to the far end.

The moon was a thin crescent in the sky as they peered over the edge of the roof. In the dim moonlight, the grass-covered ground could be seen two stories below. It was a drop that no sane person would attempt, but the three men were desperate, none more so than Witzke, who with a death sentence hanging over his head had little to lose. One after another they dropped from the roof of the barracks and slammed onto the lawn beneath them. Miraculously, none of the escaping prisoners was killed or injured, and each man rose and ran off into the darkness.

Meanwhile, inside the prison, the guard who had been bound managed to wriggle free of the towels that restrained him and alerted the corporal of the guard about the escape. A sergeant who had been asleep on the second floor of the adjoining barracks, roused by the sound of the escapees running across the roof above him, also raised an alarm.

The telephone soon began to ring in the prison office, and Lieutenant Haslam was awakened. Upon learning of the escape, he contacted Colonel Gray, the commander of the post, requesting permission to call out a company of soldiers to search for the missing prisoners. This was approved, and Haslam issued an order for the two hundred men of Company G, 3rd Infantry, to mount a search for the escapees. The soldiers were divided into individual patrols of three to four men each and sent off in all directions to search the camp and surrounding districts.

Stumbling through the dark night in bare feet while dressed only in his underclothes, and still 150 miles from the Mexican border, Witzke was in a tough situation. Capture meant being returned to an almost certain death, and it was fortunate that the desperate fugitive did not run into any passersby in the early morning hours. On the outskirts of the post, he came to a small shantytown. Entering an unlit shack, Witzke began a frantic search for clothes, but the shelter was nearly empty, with few spare garments. He hurriedly grabbed a man's Mexican breeches, a woman's coat, and a pair of ill-fitting shoes and rushed outside.

The directive that Witzke remain confined in his underwear proved to be his undoing. As he exited the shack clad in the odd attire he had managed to scavenge, the agent ran straight into one of the armed 3rd Infantry patrols searching for him and was taken into custody. The other two escapees disappeared into the night and were never recaptured.

Witzke was returned to the lockup with a guard posted outside his cell to monitor his activities day and night. His only chance of escape thwarted, it now appeared that nothing would delay his appointment with the hangman.

The following month Witzke was interrogated by U.S. Army military intelligence. The examination was conducted by Special Investigator Thomas J. Tunney, the tough former New York City police detective whose bomb squad had solved the case of ships being sabotaged with Dr. Scheele's incendiary "cigars." Tunney had joined the Military Intelligence Section shortly after the United States entered the war.

Tunney's interrogation of the German agent took place over a four-day period from September 16 to 19, 1919, and was carried out in the presence of Major R. B. Woodruff, Captain F. P. Stretton, and Corporal Henry A. O'Brien. Addressing the prisoner in a calm, almost soothing tone, Tunney asked Witzke questions from a prepared list of interrogatories on a wide range of topics, from his personal history to the secret operations of the German espionage establishment.

"Paul," Tunney began, "I want you to tell me in detail and as accurately and truthfully as you can, what you accomplished as a sworn agent of the German government in the United States, and what the other secret German agents accomplished in the United States, commencing from your first arrival into this country." (Note: "Paul" is the English equivalent of "Pablo.")

Witzke's answers to Tunney's questions varied from truthful responses to total fabrications. If he thought the information being requested was already known to his captors, his replies were factual; if he thought it was unknown, he responded with disinformation. The agent admitted that his name was Lothar Witzke, that he was a former German naval cadet who had been promoted to lieutenant while in Mexico, and that he had come to the United States from Valparaiso, Chile. He denied having any knowledge of the Black Tom or Mare Island explosions and attempted to discredit the abilities of Dr. Altendorf and William Gleaves as intelligence operatives.

Witzke told Tunney that he had not met any agents employed by Jahnke, only messengers. He even claimed to having been sent on a mission to the east coast of Mexico to discover whether American and British agents were conspiring to blow up the Mexican oil fields in Tampico in order to implicate Germany, suggesting that the British secret service would destroy one of the Royal Navy's principal sources of fuel.

By the second day of the interrogation, Tunney had become aware that Witzke was leading him astray. The agent initially claimed to have met Jahnke "around September 1916," but trapped in a lie, he later corrected his statement to "about June or July 1916."

"Have you truthfully now, Paul, answered all the questions put to you?" Tunney calmly asked.

"I have answered all truthfully," Witzke responded.

"All that you volunteered are they true?" the special investigator inquired.

"All of them—I made only one untrue statement this morning and I rectified that this afternoon—that was about meeting Jahnke," said Witzke.

"Is there anything you want to volunteer that you forgot or that we forgot to ask you about?" questioned Tunney.

"I think I have practically told you everything I know," Witzke replied.

That the prisoner would consent to being questioned by Tunney at all seems inexplicable. As an imprisoned spy facing execution, Witzke obviously had nothing to gain from providing information to the U.S. military. During previous interrogations he had revealed no secrets to Byron Butcher, Major Barnes, or Captain Lipscomb and would remain close lipped about his wartime experiences in all future interviews. Witzke's willingness to answer questions posed by Tunney may have been less a reflection of his desire to assist the burly former policeman than of the consequences for *not* answering Tunney's questions.

In his autobiography *Velvet and Vinegar*, Major Norman Thwaites, a senior officer of the British Secret Intelligence Service stationed in New York City during the war, would later describe Tunney's March 1917 interrogation of two captured Hindu agents working for the Germans, Chakravarti and Sekunna:

> Arriving at the Criminal Court police headquarters, I found Colonel Nicholas Biddle, one of the police commissioners and head of military intelligence in New York, also in evening dress (having been dragged away from his evening meal), Guy Scull, and Inspector Tunney. Robert Nathan [of the British Indian Police] was also present.
>
> Then was played a remarkable scene. We assembled in a large room from which a door led to another. Behind a screen sat a wretched little Hindu [Chakravarti], his knees imprisoned between the mighty legs of Tunney, who,

with all the gentleness in the world, was inviting his guest to "come across" with the details of his part in the plot.

The little man was glib but evasive. On the other side of the screen we listened. Now and then Nathan would write a note on a scrap of paper which would be passed in to Tunney. These hints would indicate the line of questioning to take.

At midnight, however, we had obtained little useful information from the cautious and clever fellow. Tunney left the witness and joined us, mopping his brow . . .

When Sekunna came under Tunney's cross-examination things moved rapidly. "He came across clean and quick," as Tunney put it.

The transcripts from the first two days of Witzke's interrogation are recorded verbatim in question-and-answer format, eleven pages and twenty-five pages long, respectively. The results of the third day of Tunney's interrogation of Witzke are contained in a three-page summary document titled "Voluntary Statement of Lothar Witzke, Alias Pablo Waberski, Made After Refreshing His Memory." Witzke identified two German agents, "Siegel" (Adam Siegel) and "Rodriguez" (an alias used by Fred Herrmann), stating that "both worked for a captain of the North German-Lloyd Steamship Company." During this session, Witzke also provided an accurate description of Kurt Jahnke.

The summary from the final day of interrogation was simply titled "Voluntary Statement by Lothar Witzke, Alias Waberski." The prisoner was now able to identify the steamship captain as Frederick Hinsch. He informed Tunney that proof of his statements was contained in a notebook in Otto Paglasch's safe in Mexico City. A postscript at the bottom of the summary reads: "MEMORANDUM: Waberski is going to write a letter in German to Paglasch for the purpose of trying to secure possession of his memorandum book."

After four days of Tunney's third degree, Witzke had "come across" with a few valuable details, a hollow victory given that hostilities had ended ten months before.

The only enemy agent sentenced to death in the United States during World War I would escape the gallows with assistance from an unexpected source. Following the mutiny by black troops of the 24th Regiment at Fort Logan in August 1917, nineteen of the soldiers had been court-martialed and executed by hanging. The first thirteen soldiers were sent to the gallows quickly and secretly, allowing no time for a review or appeal of their sentences. When this became known, "President Woodrow Wilson gave orders that no such prisoner was to be executed [again] until he, personally, had reviewed the findings."

On November 2, 1918, Wilson received the record of the Witzke trial for review with sentence approved from U.S. Army major general DeRosey C. Cabell. Shortly thereafter "it was most strenuously urged by [government] officials in high authority that Witzke's offense was triable only in the civilian courts, and that the president ought not to confirm the sentence. On the mistaken supposition that he was a Russian national, it was argued that he was entitled to a jury trial under the constitution." Attorney General Thomas W. Gregory issued a secret opinion advising Wilson that Witzke, a civilian, should never have been tried by a military court-martial, but in federal court, noting that "Waberski is not a spy in the sense in which that word is used in the laws of war and if guilty of any offense is triable solely by the regular civilian criminal courts. If he could constitutionally be tried by court-martial, then it would logically follow that Congress could provide for the trial by military courts of any person, civilian or alien, accused of espionage or any other type of war crime, no matter where committed and no matter where such person was found and apprehended."

The court-martial record was then examined by an army board of review, which determined that the guilty verdict was justified but recommended that the sentence be commuted to confinement at hard labor. The Witzke trial record and review board finding were resubmitted to Wilson for judgment on May 20, 1919.

Some historians would claim that the attorney general's secret opinion strongly influenced the president's final decision. Or maybe it was the fact that by 1920 the world war was becoming a distant memory, making the execution of a spy a meaningless exercise. Perhaps Wilson was swayed by the fact that, although Witzke was guilty of being an enemy agent on a mission of death and destruction, it was equally certain that he was not guilty of the crime with which he had been charged, as described in the specification.

For whichever reason, on May 27, 1920, the president announced his decision:

> In the foregoing case of Lothar Witzke, alias Pablo Waberski, the sentence is confirmed and commuted to confinement at hard labor for the term of his natural life. As thus commuted the sentence will be carried into execution.
>
> Woodrow Wilson
> The White House

On June 16, Lothar Witzke was transferred to the U.S. penitentiary in Leavenworth, Kansas, becoming inmate number 15309. Confined at a time in penal history when "hard labor" meant exactly that, his life sentence at Leavenworth must have seemed to the agent scarcely better than a trip to the gallows. But Witzke's time behind bars would be relatively brief—and he would not forget the men who had put him there.

11

"Every Activity Is to Be Suspended . . ."

Lothar Witzke had disappeared without a trace.

By late February 1918, Jahnke was forced to accept the sad truth that his faithful lieutenant was either captured or dead. If the youth had been taken prisoner by the Americans and forced to talk, he knew a great deal about the spymaster's Mexico City operation. Jahnke vacated the house at Calle Colonia No. 4 and relocated his residence to Calle Chihuahua No. 167.

He left none too soon. Within days of his departure, Major Campbell's agents descended on Jahnke's former residence, but found nothing other than a few scraps of paper—newspaper wrappers with delivery labels addressed in the names of his various aliases, and a news clipping about a $20,000 fire at Eagle Pass, Texas, believed to have been caused by sabotage.

Aside from worries about his missing protégé, Jahnke had other concerns to deal with. In January 1918 a power struggle began for control of the German intelligence establishment in Mexico. His chief antagonist was germ warfare specialist Dr. Anton Dilger (code name "Delmar"), the confidential agent of the army's Abteilung III B. Angling to assume leadership of all espionage activities in Mexico and displace the navy's chief confidential agent, Jahnke, the germ doctor sent a report to the General Staff that Jahnke was not reliable and was unsuitable for intelligence work. In concert with Dilger, Captain Frederick Hinsch, organizer of prewar U.S. sabotage activity along the eastern seaboard, was also scheming to displace Jahnke as chief of naval sabotage operations.

Taking advantage of his strong relationship with Minister von Eckhardt, Jahnke outmaneuvered both of them.

In March, von Eckhardt wired Berlin: "Jahnke's work must not be interrupted and he is therefore receiving financial support through me. In consequence of very grave discoveries I request permission to [dismiss] Delmar and Hinsch from my Intelligence Service."

On April 29, Jahnke won a complete victory over his rivals when Berlin cabled the Madrid embassy where Dilger was visiting: "Please inform Delmar in reply to your telegrams 1073 and 1357 of March 26 and April 13 respectively that Jahnke has been made sole Naval Confidential Agent in Mexico."

His status as *Bevollmächtigter Geheimagent*, head of the espionage system for the American continent, confirmed, on May 28 Jahnke received new orders from his chief, Eugene Wilhelm, director of the German Naval Intelligence Service at Antwerp. Wilhelm instructed Jahnke that it was deemed highly desirable for a strike (mutiny) in the American army to be organized for the coming autumn. Secret operations in U.S. territorial possessions against Japanese merchant ships supplying raw materials and war goods were also to be undertaken, as well as operations against the Panama Canal. If the opportunity presented itself, vessels transporting corn from Australia to the United States should also be attacked. But the main targets would remain the U.S. mainland and the Panama Canal.

In his directive, Wilhelm framed the financial budget for Jahnke's organization and outlined the rewards he would receive for successful sabotage. Monthly expenses must not exceed one hundred thousand marks. If additional funds were required, the authorities in Berlin were to be contacted in advance before drawing monies. The bonuses paid for sabotage would be significant, and likely to further swell Jahnke's considerable wealth. For destroying Allied warships and trading ships, the spymaster would receive 20 percent of the value of the ship and cargo; for sabotage of all other objectives, the bonus would be paid in a lump sum not to exceed fifty thousand marks and would vary based on the importance and extent of the damage. The rewards would be distributed at the discretion of, and after investigation by, Minister von Eckhardt.

Throughout the spring and summer of 1918, while some of the greatest battles of the war were being fought on the western front, Jahnke continued to mount secret operations in support of a German victory. In June he was ordered to ready a *Stützpunkt* (base) for U-boats as soon as possible on the Mexican coast, "giving close attention to all details and making every possible preparation." The base was to be organized on the

Gulf of Mexico at a point not far from the traffic lane between southern U.S. ports and Yucatán, Cuba, and other islands in the Greater Antilles, near the U.S. border. In July, Jahnke informed Berlin that the Irish Secret Lodge in New York City had offered the services of its branch lodges in Argentina and Brazil for sabotage. In response he was advised "not to continue relations with those in Chile or Argentina, but the Brazil Lodge should direct its activities against allied warships and merchant vessels and important raw material industries, such as meat, manganese, mining and live cattle." In October, Jahnke cabled his superiors that he had arranged for a secret wireless station to be erected in Mexico City; his men were now working to establish communication with Grossfunkstelle Nauen, the powerful radio transmitter at Nauen.

On November 2, the German radio station in Mexico City received a brief, desultory wireless message from Nauen:

FOR JAHNKE:
EVERY ACTIVITY IS TO BE SUSPENDED AS SOON AS THE TRUCE HAS BEEN CONCEDED.

After the armistice was signed at Compiègne ending hostilities, Jahnke returned to Germany. In spite of his many wartime accomplishments, he remained reserved and retiring, declining any titles or decorations, and was known simply as "Herr Jahnke." In the years to come, the furtive spymaster would continue to operate in the shadows while serving a succession of disparate masters.

In 1921 Jahnke returned to Mexico, traveling on a passport issued in the name of "Albert E. Steffens" and well supplied with funds. Although ostensibly the secretary of a university professor named Hellman visiting Mexico to conduct agricultural research, Jahnke was suspected of plotting to foment unrest in the industrial and munitions centers of North America. When the U.S. embassy in Berlin started making inquiries concerning the agent's activities, the German government disowned him, and he was quietly ordered home.

During the 1920s, Jahnke developed a wide circle of influential friends throughout German officialdom. He became an adviser and political chief of the Black Reichswehr, the secret paramilitary formation created to circumvent the restrictions of the Treaty of Versailles, which conducted sabotage in the French-occupied Ruhr and political murders in Germany. Jahnke was later reported to be the secretary of the Diplomatic Information Bureau of Gustav Stresemann, onetime chancellor and foreign minister of the Weimar Republic. By the time of the Locarno Conference, he was also working as an agent of the Fourth Department of the Soviet Commissariat for War, the secret military intelligence service, supplying information to the Russians as well.

In 1927, during a period of close economic and military cooperation between the Soviet Union and Weimar Germany, Foreign Minister Stresemann became concerned that the Soviet ambassador in Berlin lacked sufficient authority to negotiate important matters and decided to make a personal visit to Stalin in Moscow. Confidential preparations for the journey were underway when Jahnke became aware of the trip and informed the Soviets. As a result, the visit was canceled, and Stresemann went to Locarno instead of Moscow. It was an action by the enigmatic spymaster that had significant consequences, ensuring that the secret flow of Russian arms to the German military continued unabated.

Jahnke's life was devoted to sabotage and espionage, and it is therefore remarkable that from 1926 to 1928 the spymaster served as a representative in the Prussian Diet (parliament), helping to make laws for the dominant state in the Weimar Republic.

With the death of Weimar statesman Gustav Stresemann in October 1929, Jahnke strengthened his connections to the rising political force in Germany—the Nazi Party. Shortly after Hitler came to power, Jahnke joined with SA *obergruppenführer* Franz von Pfeffer, the founder of the Sturmabteilung "brown shirts," to organize an information bureau in the Reich Chancellery for acquiring military, political, and economic information from abroad. Known as Büro I or the "Jahnke Büro," the department was established under the direction of Deputy Führer Rudolph Hess with a budget of 450,000 reichsmarks. Jahnke personally selected the personnel of the new organization, which collected information primarily from France and the Low Countries, but also received reports from sources in the United Kingdom, Ireland, the United States, and as far afield as Japan and China, where Jahnke had developed a friendship with the powerful Soong family. His sources "were high-level foreign politicians, civil servants, etc., or alternatively members of disaffected groups, e.g. Welsh, Breton, Flemish nationalists, or pro-German fascist organizations." The Jahnke Büro produced an intelligence summary that was distributed on a regular basis to the deputy führer, who forwarded the secret reports to Hitler, the Foreign Ministry, and the Abwehr, Germany's military intelligence service.

The official location of Jahnke's spy agency was Wilhelmstrasse 64, the ministry building of Rudolph Hess, but its actual headquarters was in an office at Jahnke's private residence, Sedanstrasse 26, Steglitz, Berlin. Here

Jahnke maintained an extensive registry of secret files in two rooms on the ground floor. When not at his home in Berlin, the wealthy intelligence adviser resided at a magnificent country estate that he owned, situated among the forests and lakes of the Pomeranian coastal plain. Although there was no electric security fence surrounding the property as in Mexico, several big cats that Jahnke kept as pets were on the grounds.

In September 1939, a consolidation of intelligence departments occurred that resulted in the creation of the Reichssicherheitshauptamt, the Main Security Office, and the Jahnke Büro was dissolved by a personal directive of Adolf Hitler. A few days after his dismissal, Jahnke was contacted by the sinister Reinhard Heydrich and invited to join the Sicherheitsdienst (SD) security service of Reichsführer Heinrich Himmler as adviser to Amt VI, the foreign intelligence service. Jahnke would continue to ply his trade in the SD, gathering information from around the world for his new boss, SS-Sturmbannführer Walter Schellenberg, the thirty-year-old head of counterespionage.

Schellenberg relied on Jahnke as an "old hand" in intelligence matters, seeking his counsel on foreign operations and international developments. Jahnke confided to the spy chief that the main purpose of a secret service was to act as a *käseglocke*, the traditional German glass cover placed over cheese for protection against rats and other vermin. Perhaps influenced by his past experience with Altendorf and Gleaves, Jahnke also advised his superior that "the full value of a secret service always depended on the number and the standard [capabilities] of its double agents."

Schellenberg was impressed by Jahnke, particularly after reading his secret service personnel file—three crates of them. "Politically he was interested only in questions of major importance. [By the late 1930s] Jahnke was a big heavy man with the thick skull of a Pomeranian peasant, and when he sat opposite you, impassive, with his eyes half closed, he gave an impression of reticence and cunning."

Jahnke became a senior adviser to the Nazi leadership on foreign intelligence, if not always trusted by them. He was considered an unscrupulous agent with uncertain loyalties. When Heydrich received information from a White Russian general that Soviet marshal Tukhachevsky was plotting with the German General Staff to overthrow Stalin, the SS leader immediately grasped its importance as a means to create infighting among the Soviets themselves. Jahnke disagreed, believing that the general was passing Soviet disinformation to arouse Heydrich's suspicions against the German General Staff. Heydrich was not convinced by Jahnke's argument and, with his suspicions of Jahnke now aroused, placed him under house arrest for three months.

In late 1941, German secret service officials discovered that Japan was planning to take military action, but were uncertain what direction she would take with regard to Russia, the United States, and China. At this critical moment, Schellenberg managed to engineer Jahnke's return to Amt VI to help uncover the Japanese strategy. Although Adolf Hitler knew Jahnke personally, "Jahnke was persona non grata with Hitler, who suspected him of being a British agent in disguise. . . . Both Himmler and Heydrich mistrusted him and had a great aversion toward him. They had fought him ruthlessly—for their own purposes—and had almost brought about his downfall." With considerable difficulty, Schellenberg obtained agreement from Heydrich regarding Jahnke's reemployment, and the spymaster was dispatched to Switzerland to gather information from his contacts on Japanese intentions.

At the end of October, Jahnke delivered a report to Schellenberg from the Japanese secret service, confirmed by his sources, that Prime Minister Hideki Tojo thought President Roosevelt would never yield in negotiations aimed at ending Japanese aggression in Asia, and therefore it was to be assumed that a decision to strike against America would be taken. Schellenberg would recall:

> Hitler at first remained skeptical about our reports until at last, in the middle of November, at his wish I sent a message through Jahnke to the Japanese secret service, saying that Germany was anxious to secure Japanese participation in the war, no matter what its nature or direction. I believe that this encouragement helped to influence Japanese policy.

On December 7 the Japanese navy attacked Pearl Harbor.

As the war progressed, Jahnke's star fell into decline. In March 1942 the aging spymaster learned that the Japanese intended to work toward bringing about a compromise peace between Germany and the Soviet Union. Believing that a separate agreement with Stalin was a real possibility, Jahnke tried to have the proposal considered at the highest levels of the Nazi hierarchy, but the idea was officially rebuffed. Jahnke's contacts in the Chinese secret service proposed that Germany assist in brokering a separate peace between Japan and China. To explore this possibility, Jahnke traveled to Switzerland to meet with his Chinese contacts. While he was away, Schellenberg received an astounding report which contained evidence that Jahnke was in fact a top British agent and that his real purpose in going to Switzerland was to receive orders from his British masters. Schellenberg had Jahnke placed under surveillance, and the chief of the

Gestapo, Heinrich Müller, attempted to have him arrested for treason. It was only the network of contacts that Jahnke had developed around the world, of great future value to the crumbling regime, that kept him alive. Now in exile, Jahnke continued to receive a monthly salary of two thousand reichsmarks, use of a car, and special concessions like gasoline that were being rationed due to the war. In 1943, Jahnke's Berlin residence was destroyed in an air raid, and he retreated to his estate in the country where he led a remote and solitary existence. Ever the schemer, he confided to a former associate that "he intended to let himself be overrun by the Russians and that he had connections to [Minister of Foreign Affairs] Molotov."

After the Soviet occupation of Pomerania in the spring of 1945, Jahnke could no longer be found. Some said he had been taken prisoner by the advancing Russians; others held that the spymaster had been executed by the Soviet counterintelligence service, SMERSH.

The only thing known for certain is that Jahnke was never heard from again.

Without warning, Leavenworth inmate number 15309 suddenly stopped following the rules.

For almost three years, Lothar Witzke had obeyed prison regulations with military precision, in a manner befitting the naval officer that he was. Even Warden Biddle took note of his exemplary conduct when, after an explosion wrecked the prison boiler room in July 1921, Witzke rushed into the steam-filled chamber in response to cries for help and, at serious risk to himself, helped save the lives of other prisoners.

Then on April 14, 1923, Witzke committed his first act of disobedience, one of the guards noting in his prison record:

> This man never shows himself for count. I have to hunt him up myself. This evening I had to count three times. When I threatened to report him he told me that my reporting him would be of no consequence to him. Reprimanded.

The reason for Witzke's sudden indifference to authority soon became clear: they were getting him out.

The German government had not forgotten their captured agent and for years had been exerting pressure through diplomatic channels to obtain his release as the last prisoner of war. It was no matter that on January 17, 1921, after months of agitation by German officials, the acting judge advocate general of the U.S. Army, E. A. Kreger, had reviewed the trial record of the Witzke court-martial and denied clemency. In November

1922, Baron Hans George Hermann von Plessen, a retired field marshal posted to the embassy in Washington, launched a new appeal for Witzke's release. Five months later, the German ambassador, Dr. Otto Wiedfeldt, made a personal visit to General Bethel, the judge advocate general, to intercede on Witzke's behalf. The next day the ambassador sent Bethel a letter imploring that:

> Other countries, including Germany, have since released all their prisoners of war and among them those who were sentenced for the offense of espionage. It would therefore do much to pacify public opinion in my country and would be considered a special act of grace by my government, if the United States of America, as France did a few months ago, were now also to set free their last prisoner of war. I know this would be much appreciated in my country, for the case of Lothar Witzke . . . has not only attracted the attention of public opinion, but has also frequently been discussed in the German Reichstag.

On September 26, the judge advocate general sent a communiqué to the adjutant general recommending that Witzke be released as a matter of policy, since England had freed all remaining German prisoners of war in 1920, and the previous January the French had done likewise. On November 22, 1923, President Coolidge pardoned Witzke on the understanding that he would leave the country immediately and never return.

On the day before Thanksgiving 1923, Witzke walked out of Leavenworth penitentiary into the bright Kansas sunshine, a free man once again. He was twenty-eight years old and had spent the last six of those years behind bars. The German consul in Kansas City, Henry Wilde, sent to escort Witzke from Leavenworth, inquired before the crowd of gathered reporters: "Prison life would not be so bad if they did not take away your liberty, would it?"

"No," responded the former agent, "but when they take that away, they take it all."

"I'm glad to be going home to my family—or what's left of it," he continued. "I'll have to find a job first thing. The only trade I have is engineer, which I learned at Leavenworth."

The consul provided Witzke with a new set of clothes and money to travel to New York City, where he booked passage on the Hamburg-America liner *Albert Ballin* for his return to Germany. In Berlin he was received by Admiral Paul Behncke who bestowed the former agent with the Iron Cross, First and Second Class, for "valuable services in time of war."

The Weimar Republic that Witzke returned to was a very different place than the Germany he had left a decade before. Although the economy had recovered from the severe hyperinflation of 1921–1923, when basic staples like bread or eggs cost *billions* of marks, the proud Kaiserreich had been supplanted by a centrist government that to veterans like Witzke appeared servile to the victorious Allied powers. One acquaintance noted, "As he [Witzke] described it he said that he and others of the old regime do not recognize this government as representing Germany at all."

For a time the ex–naval officer served in the Black Reichswehr, the surreptitious army organized in violation of the Treaty of Versailles, and then for six months carried out secret assignments for Jahnke's intelligence organization. In the spring of 1925, Witzke returned to Mexico City and took a job with the Ford Motor Company. His reasons for going back to Mexico remain unclear, but at least in part he hoped to settle accounts with the men who had betrayed him seven years before.

By 1934 Witzke was in Hankow, China, managing operations for the Hamburg-Amerika shipping line. From an elevated platform on the Yangtze River, the thirty-nine-year-old Witzke could occasionally be seen barking orders into a megaphone as he guided arriving German freighters to their moorings. Most probably the job was a cover for espionage work he was performing for the Abwehr, the German military intelligence service, soon to be led by a lieutenant (now admiral) that he had served under aboard the *Dresden*, Wilhelm Canaris.

When the Second World War began, Witzke was back in Europe on active duty with the Abwehr, sometimes clad in a naval uniform with a single stripe, at other times in civilian clothes. He was reported to be a member of Abwehrabteilung II, a special forces unit that had been established to perform sabotage and espionage missions behind enemy lines. The most important of the Abt II stations on the northern coast of occupied France was Oberleitstelle Brest, engaged in the training, equipment, and transport of spies and saboteurs being sent to the United Kingdom. British intelligence sources (Abwehr defectors) reported that the Brest contingent was commanded by a naval *korvettenkapitän* named Scheidewind, ably assisted by his adjutant, Lieutenant Lothar Witzke, who assembled a small fleet of fishing smacks for use in infiltrating agents across the English Channel. In German radio traffic intercepted by the British, Witzke appeared under the code name "Charlie." He was said to have dispatched multiple spy missions to England during 1940–1941, taking an active role in recruiting the agents that were sent. While awaiting transfer to North Africa in 1942, Witzke was spotted in Athens by SIS informants, escorting a sabotage party to a transport boat. Two years later the Abwehr was reorganized, and Witzke likely transferred to the Sicherheitsdienst or to an army combat unit.

When the war ended, Witzke was again taken prisoner. For over a year, from November 30, 1945, to December 23, 1946, he was interned in an Allied POW camp. Two years after his release from captivity, like Jahnke before him, Witzke found a place in politics. As a candidate of the German Party, the former saboteur-assassin was elected to a seat in the Hamburg parliament that he held from 1949 to 1952.

Witzke served in the Hamburg legislature at the height of the Cold War, when Western intelligence services were increasingly concerned about agents and assets of the former German spy agencies being employed in the service of the Soviets. Jahnke had established a worldwide network of high-level informants and then disappeared into the Russian zone of occupation. British and American intelligence began to wonder whether Jahnke might now be running a spy network in the service of the Soviets.

In an effort to answer this question, in 1952 the British MI5 German station interviewed one of Jahnke's oldest associates, Lothar Witzke. As in all prior interrogations (except the session conducted by Tunney), Witzke provided little information. The MI5 case officer noted: "No success was achieved by direct questioning of Witzke. He invariably replied that he had not been sufficiently in Jahnke's confidence to know the answer, gave generally vague replies, or refused to answer." But the former agent did offer one insight into the possibility that Jahnke had defected to the Soviet Union: "Jahnke never made any secret of his desire for a Russo-German entente, being in this a follower of Bismarck. Witzke ascribed this partly to the fact that Jahnke was an East Prussian born in Posen [as was, of course, Witzke himself]."

The interview with MI5 would be Lothar Witzke's final interrogation. On January 6, 1962, the former agent died at the age of sixty-six in Hamburg, Germany.

Throughout a career in clandestine service that took him around the world, Witzke never forgot the mission to Nogales or the Allied agents who thwarted the German plot and nearly sent him to the gallows. A decade after being captured on Morley Avenue, lawyers representing the Lehigh Valley Railroad, owners of Black Tom Island, the munitions terminal sabotaged in 1916, located the former agent in Maracaibo, Venezuela. Characteristically, Witzke refused to provide any information about the secret missions he had undertaken for Germany during the war, but he did share his sentiments toward his companions on the fateful journey to the border.

In a memorandum dated January 13, 1929, the attorneys recorded:

Witzke stated that he succeeded in his work because he was "sufficiently ruthless to get everything out of the way that interfered with what I wanted to do." He discussed having had Altendorf at the point of his pistol on one occasion for a considerable time and expressed regret that he had not put him out of the way then. When Altendorf was mentioned Witzke's eyes flashed fire and he gave every indication that he intended to try and find him. He also indicated that he had gone to Mexico after getting out of prison for the purpose, among others, of finding Gleaves. He said that it was a curious thing that Gleaves disappeared from Mexico when he got there and that he could not find him anywhere.

William Gleaves left British naval intelligence shortly after the Armistice. By 1927 he was established as a hotelier in Mexico City, the owner and operator of the Casa Huesped hotel, the "Guest House" at Calle Estaciones No. 12. Gleaves had survived his double life as a German agent—and Witzke's retribution.

Dr. Paul Bernardo Altendorf, the man Witzke had threatened to put in the cemetery with the many other people he had laid there if he ever betrayed him, returned to duty following the arrest in Nogales. Concerned that a large number of German agents were reported to be heading for the United States, an order came from military intelligence headquarters in Washington for Altendorf to cross into Mexico once again. On the night of March 11, 1918, shepherded by U.S. customs officials, Agent A-1 slipped past the border guards into Nogales, Sonora, and caught a passenger train headed south.

In the months that followed, the master spy would achieve a remarkable series of intelligence coups. At the port of Mazatlán, Altendorf learned that the Germans were planning to acquire a salvaged Mexican gunboat, the *Morelos*, for use as a submarine tender. He thwarted the scheme by convincing the ship's owner that the vessel was about to be confiscated by the Mexican government and induced him to sell it to an American firm instead. Still recognized as a loyal comrade by the Germans, Altendorf made the acquaintance of a number of enemy operatives, including a Spaniard named Salvary, recruited to infect cattle in the American southwest with germ cultures, and Carl Jacobsen, the saboteur from whom Consul Chapman obtained incendiary pencils, and alerted U.S. military intelligence to their danger. In Tepic, Altendorf met a German engineer named Gaedke and discovered a secret wireless station built to communicate with U-boats in the Gulf of Mexico.

But soon the double agent's cover was wearing thin. Warned by the proprietor of his hotel that "the Germans are after you," Altendorf once again disguised himself as a Mexican and beat a hasty retreat to Nogales, one step ahead of his pursuers, by hiding in the caboose of a passenger train.

After providing testimony at Witzke's court-martial, Altendorf asked Major Barnes, department intelligence officer at Fort Sam Houston, for a new assignment. Barnes told him to "look around San Antonio and see what you can find to do." Forty-eight hours later, Altendorf was enrolled as a member of the Tannhauser Halle, the leading German club in the city, and began to make himself familiar with suspected enemy agents in the area.

Among these was Dr. Ludwig Heinrich Reuter, a German chemist who had studied at Heidelberg and Erlangen Universities before serving in the 2nd Bavarian Army Corps. Based on reports of Reuter's suspicious activity—such as making frequent trips below the border and directing a Mexican employee to carry secret messages to unknown contacts there—military intelligence had kept the San Antonio resident under surveillance for over a year, but observed nothing that justified his arrest.

In early October, Bureau of Investigation special agent William Neunhoffer, accompanied by a military intelligence sergeant named John Perez, paid a visit to Reuter's home while he was away and installed a dictograph, a primitive eavesdropping device that captured voices and sounds in a room and transmitted them over wire to a remote location. The two men then took up positions in an adjoining flat where German-speaking Neunhoffer held a receiver to his ear, prepared to dictate any conversations overheard to Perez who would act as a transcriber.

A short time later, Dr. Altendorf knocked on Reuter's door at 1919 San Pedro Avenue and was received by a man in his early forties, barely five feet two inches tall, with a kaiser mustache.

"My name is Dr. Amagini," said Altendorf in German.

"My name is Ludwig Reuter," Reuter casually replied, apparently expecting a caller. "Who sent you to me?"

"I was sent by Rabe, also by Captain Devaetz. Mr. Krisch also told me about you. You may have confidence in me. You may speak to me."

Reuter ushered "Dr. Amagini" inside, and as the two men became comfortable in each other's company, their discussion turned to covert activity, with each statement captured by Neunhoffer and Perez in the flat nearby.

"I am very glad I have found a respectable friend after a long time," said Reuter. "I received letters in the name of Mr. Neumann from Mexico, but lately I haven't received any. They must have stopped them at the censor's office."

"Do you know Mr. Jahnke?" asked Altendorf.

"Oh, I know Jahnke," Reuter responded. "This is the man that knows about chemical work. He is a marine officer."

"Do you know Pablo Kettenbach?"

"Oh, yes, of course. I want to go to [Nuevo] Laredo, but I am sure if I go as I am now, they will have an officer behind me who will arrest me. I was thinking of disguising myself."

"If you want to disguise yourself, I will take you down to Brownsville and there you may make arrangements with Vice Consul Garse [for papers to cross into Mexico]," said Altendorf.

"I am to receive letters here under the name of Sanchez. . . . They don't know I am going under assumed names. Do you think they found out anything about Von Papen?"

"I don't think so," Altendorf replied.

"I hope not, for I am mixed up with it. I prepared the chemical stuff," said Reuter. "The submarines haven't worked well lately."

"No, they haven't worked well," said Altendorf.

"We want the American soldiers to get across and then we will cut off their provisions."

Following this initial encounter, Altendorf met Dr. Reuter at his home on two subsequent occasions, each visit drawing out more information about his activities in the United States and each conversation carefully transcribed by a German-speaking agent at a dictograph receiver. Reuter's assignment had been to spread German propaganda in the United States and secure legislation to prevent passengers from traveling on ships to Europe. The Germans planned to win the war through unrestricted submarine warfare, and according to Reuter, "the seriousness of such a course would be lessened by the absence of passengers." Reuter was directed to manipulate U.S. politicians deemed "German-friendly" to enact legislation that would keep meat and foodstuffs at home rather than being shipped to feed Allied soldiers overseas. The money to fund his efforts was being furnished by a man named Bruhn; for additional funds he relied on a German consul in Mexico named Burchard. In 1915 Reuter had worked for von Papen and received $2,000 from the military attaché to manufacture explosives that were used for sabotage in New Jersey. The following year, Reuter had organized a twenty-thousand-strong German committee in Detroit, but came under suspicion and fled to Texas. The enemy agent confided to Altendorf that "he did not fear detectives for the reason that he did not have a scrap of paper on him to show what he had been doing; the furnace in his room had been busy night and day. Everything had been destroyed and he would soon be in Mexico."

On the evening of October 8, 1918, plans were in place for Reuter to cross the border into Mexico guided by "Dr. Amagini," who had provided the chemist with a suitable disguise. Captain E. V. Spence, a military intelligence officer at Fort Sam Houston, described Reuter's subsequent arrest in a report to his superiors:

At 9 P.M. writer in company with Mr. William Neunhoffer, agent of the Department of Justice, went to Kay Depot and at 10 o'clock a large service car arrived at the station in which there were two men, one our informant A-1, and the other, the subject, dressed in a dark suit, an extra-large white hat, glasses, and a black beard. Instead of entering the station they went to the rear of the building and entered a Pullman car on the S. A. U. & G. train. At 10:30 writer, accompanied by Justice Department agent, entered the train where we found agent A-1 and subject.

A-1 was questioned and stated that he was a Mexican, going to Mexico. Subject stated that his name was Mason, that he was going to Brownsville, and that he had come from New York. Handcuffs were placed on both subject and informant A-1, and they were taken to the Department of Justice office and questioned, where subject gave his name as Ludwig Reuter. He made no mention at this time of his false beard. Both men were then removed to the Fort Sam Houston guard house. While on the way, subject took out his handkerchief to mop his face and unconsciously wiped his beard off. When questioned about how quickly he took a shave, he answered, "yes, my head sure hurts me."

Altendorf later related that the officer who arrested Reuter "could hardly control his laughter long enough to attend to business." Like other German operatives the doctor-spy had crossed paths with in Mexico—Paglasch, Jahnke, and Gaedke—Reuter was certain that Altendorf was a dedicated German agent. Following his arrest, the chemist even offered to assist the government in obtaining information from Altendorf in exchange for being released! Instead, agent Ludwig Heinrich Reuter was escorted under warrant to the army internment camp at Fort Oglethorpe, Georgia.

Dr. Amagini next made the acquaintance of Count Saint Pierre Fremonte Rodynko, a former lieutenant of horse artillery in the Austro-Hungarian army who for the past year had been under surveillance by the U.S. Secret Service. After convincing Rodynko that he was a German spy and telling the count that secret business could not be discussed in the street, Altendorf invited him to his room at the Travis Club where a dictograph had been installed with wires leading to a room in which an intelligence officer and two sergeants sat waiting. During the conversation that followed, the suspect informed Dr. Amagini that he had studied medicine and chemistry in Europe, mentioning that "when he had been in the War School in the Austrian Army he had studied how a big army can be destroyed by sending microbes or germs through spies to the armies of the enemy, and had studied how many germs would be required to affect five hundred thousand, or a million soldiers; he had studied how they might be disorganized through this process in case the enemy could not be beaten by arms. At the same time he had studied on the immunity of his own army from contact with these germs." These comments, along with other indiscretions about past intelligence work, convinced the authorities that Count Rodynko was a dangerous menace. Trapped (or entrapped) by his own words, Saint Pierre Fremonte Rodynko was placed under arrest and interned as an alien enemy at Fort Oglethorpe, Georgia.

At war's end, the U.S. Army Military Intelligence Section was drastically reduced in size. Altendorf attempted to obtain a position in the military intelligence "Corps of Interpreters" but was informed that "in accordance with the present ruling of the War Department, no transfers to the Corps of Interpreters are now being made." His superiors tried to retain him for a last secret mission, but their efforts were unsuccessful and Altendorf was demobilized in April 1919.

Finding himself unemployed in the United States, with limited prospects and no money in the bank, the former agent decided to cash in on a ready asset—his life story. Altendorf accepted an offer from the McClure Newspaper Syndicate for the rights to a personal account of his wartime adventures. Published as "On Secret Service in Mexico," Altendorf's memoir was syndicated as a thirty-installment series in newspapers across the country and detailed his experiences as a secret agent from his first arrival in Mexico to his demobilization after the armistice. It was the first time that the American public learned of Kurt Jahnke's espionage network or became aware that a twenty-two-year-old German spy named Lothar Witzke had been captured in Nogales and was behind bars at a military prison in Texas. Although there were no laws in 1919 to prevent someone outside the government from revealing secret operations, by publishing his story Altendorf burned his bridges to former colleagues in military intelligence.

The newspaper publicity made Altendorf a national figure, and he was invited to numerous speaking engagements. Despite his newfound fame, within a year the money received from the newspaper syndicate was running low. He had buried $14,800 on the west coast of Mexico during the war, but he had also left behind a score of enemies who would make any attempt to retrieve the hidden fortune a risky proposition. With few options available, Altendorf decided to take his chances and return to Mexico.

"I was hard up for money and being engaged to get married, I wanted this money very badly," the doctor later recalled. It was a decision he would come to regret.

In August 1920, Altendorf crossed the border at Nuevo Laredo and took a train to Mexico City. He went to the National Palace hoping to meet with President de la Huerta and obtain assistance in recovering the buried cash, but was instead ushered into the office of General Plutarco Elías Calles, now the powerful minister of war and marine. Calles had not forgotten the onetime officer on his staff who had tricked him into dismissing the loyal Major Schwierz and had revealed the secret mission of Lothar Witzke to the *norteamericanos* before deserting from the Mexican army. When Altendorf held out his hand, the general turned away and barked an order to an armed detail of Yaqui soldiers. They were to deliver the traitor to Santiago Tlatelolco prison. If he attempted to escape, they were to open fire. Altendorf asked for a chance to explain, but Calles refused to listen, responding sharply: "Keep quiet and do not say one more word—obey orders and go."

At Santiago prison the former agent was placed in a cell with an iron bed and no mattress. A barred window looked out onto a courtyard. After a night of fitful sleep, Altendorf watched as two prisoners were brought to the courtyard wall and shot. For over a week he remained incommunicado in the dank prison cell, threatened and browbeaten, wondering when his turn would come to be taken to the wall. On his ninth day in the lockup, without notice, two army officers appeared—Colonel Mendoza and Major Jiménez—who informed him that President de la Huerta had ordered him deported from Mexico as a "pernicious foreigner." The officers had been dispatched to escort him to Juárez where he would be put across the line. Not wanting trouble with the Americans for executing their spy, General Calles had decided to have him sent home instead.

After a two-day train ride, they reached the border station at Juárez where Altendorf encountered a new problem. Because the former agent had been born in Austria, he was considered an alien enemy, and the immigration officials refused him entry into the United States. Colonel Mendoza sent a wire to Mexico City explaining the situation and requested further instructions. He received an ominous reply: "Bring Altendorf back to Mexico City at once." It took little imagination to predict what awaited the prisoner on his return, and Altendorf began to plan his escape.

That night at the hotel room the men were sharing, Mendoza and Jiménez started drinking heavily. Altendorf watched the progress of their revelry, and when they were fully inebriated he slipped silently past his slumbering guard into the darkened street. He managed to obtain a horse bridle and then found a horse, which he mounted bareback and galloped off into the night toward the border. At the bank of the Rio Grande, Altendorf abandoned the horse and swam across to safety, the second time in as many years that he had escaped from Mexico into the United States.

On the morning of September 16, 1920, a horse-drawn delivery wagon moved slowly through the financial district of New York City and came to a stop in front of the J. P. Morgan bank at 23 Wall Street. The driver exited the vehicle and hurried off, apparently to meet with a customer. Minutes later, a fifty-pound charge of blasting gelatin detonated, blowing the horse and wagon to pieces. The financial district was transformed into a scene of catastrophic devastation. Hundreds of office windows were shattered by the blast, sending a torrent of glass shards raining down onto the street below, and a parked car was overturned that immediately burst into flames. Thirty-eight people were killed and over a hundred injured by flying debris. Leaflets found in a nearby mailbox emblazoned with a warning from "American Anarchist Fighters" to "free the political prisoners or it will be death to you all" suggested that radical anarchists were responsible for the deadly attack.

Investigations into the bombing were launched by the Justice Department's Bureau of Investigation, the New York City Police, the fire department, and several insurance companies. One of those searching for answers was William J. Burns, the famed president of the Burns International Detective Agency, who was engaged by the American Bankers Association to solve the crime. One of Burns's informants on anarchist activities, a long-time radical named Wolfe Lindenfeld, reported that the perpetrators of the deadly outrage had fled to Europe.

In March 1921, Burns sent his informant across the Atlantic to find them. Lindenfeld toured the continent attending communist gatherings to obtain information and then disappeared without a trace. To make matters worse, Burns discovered that Lindenfeld was an active communist who had possibly been involved in the Wall Street bombing himself.

To locate his missing informant, Burns dispatched a trusted investigator to Europe: Dr. Paul B. Altendorf. Shortly after fleeing Mexico, Altendorf had moved to New York City and become an operative with the Burns Agency at a salary of eight dollars per day. To establish his cover for the mission, Altendorf made the acquaintance of Isaac Hourwich, a legal adviser to the Soviet government in the United States, and enrolled in a U.S.-based communist front organization. Fully equipped with credentials that identified him as a bona fide Marxist, Burns's new operative departed for Poland.

After arriving in his homeland, Altendorf made little headway in the search for Lindenfeld, while his contact with communist intermediaries resulted in the doctor being detained by Polish authorities for questioning. He misrepresented himself as being on an official mission for the U.S. government, which caused further trouble with the American embassy. Altendorf eventually joined forces with a Justice Department agent named Silvester Cosgrove, and together the pair were able to track down Lindenfeld. The informant claimed that although he had not been involved in the bombing himself, he knew the full story. Lindenfeld turned state's evidence and provided a ten-thousand-word sworn statement that revealed a mass of details about the crime, even naming the principals involved.

With the capture of Wolfe Lindenfeld, Altendorf once again became a national hero, hailed in newspapers as the "wartime super-spy" who had helped identify the culprits behind the dastardly attack. Then the case took an unexpected turn when Lindenfeld was exposed as a fraud—his confession had been a total fabrication. The informant had no knowledge of the Wall Street bombing, and his false testimony left the investigators with little evidence and no suspects. Overnight William J. Burns became a national laughingstock, and the public career of Paul Bernardo Altendorf came to an end.

During the world war, Dr. Altendorf had been a legend in American military intelligence. But less than two years later, after revealing secret operations in his memoirs, being imprisoned in Mexico, and finally his participation in the Lindenfeld fiasco, Altendorf's reputation was forever ruined.

In September 1928, a New York promoter named Hyman Epstein offered to pay the former agent $150,000, if he appeared to claim it "as a reward for services Altendorf rendered him five years ago." According to Epstein, "unless the doctor returns within the next five or six weeks, the fortune . . . will be lost to him forever." Altendorf wisely chose not to surface and claim the promoter's "reward." The roving adventurer remained where he was, consorting with a gang of Prohibition rumrunners in Cuba.

After delivering Witzke to the Fort Sam Houston prison in February 1918, Byron S. Butcher continued to lead counterespionage fieldwork for the military intelligence office at Nogales. Clandestine operations along the border had not ended following Waberski's "disappearance." Many enemy agents remained on the loose, including the dangerous Dietz and Schmidt, and sources had revealed that a general movement of German operatives from Mexico to the United States was underway for the purpose of creating civil and labor disturbances in the southwest.

Major Barnes warned of the danger in an urgent memo to intelligence officers issued on March 14:

> A conference was expected to be held in Piedras Negras between Germans and IWW's from the states of Texas, Oklahoma, and New Mexico, sometime during February and March. A careful watch should be kept for this and it may be possible to get on the track of some of their activities. Any persons expected of being IWW's should be carefully covered and every possible effort made to get on the track of any information which might lead to the discovery of some of these German and IWW plots.

At the end of March, Butcher and William Haley, a special agent of the War Trade Board, departed from Nogales on an extended road trip across the Southwest to investigate the potential for war production being disrupted by "certain IWW agitators and foreign elements." Reports of the journey openly published in local newspapers during this simpler time noted that the two government agents were accompanied on part of the trip by General Álvaro Obregón, who visited Alexander Baird, the British consul in Douglas, Arizona, obtaining permission to export government-controlled jute sacks from the United States to Sonora. The consul was on excellent terms with Butcher and readily agreed to Obregón's request to endorse bills of lading for the sacks, provided they were later reexported back to the United States with garbanzo beans from Mexico.

In the years since their first meeting at the height of the Mexican Revolution, Butcher and Obregón had become close friends and associates. The general was now one of the most powerful men in Mexico and would soon be elected the country's president; his agricultural enterprises made him one of the largest vegetable growers in the land. Butcher looked upon Obregón not only as a stalwart friend, but as a path to future prosperity. There were few favors that he would not perform, or missions that he would not undertake, for the general.

The friendship between the two men was viewed with concern by Butcher's superiors in military intelligence. Although the former newsman's access to the influential leader could be of great assistance to counterespionage activities in Mexico—a country in which the U.S. government had been unwelcome since the incursion by Pershing's punitive expedition two years before—an intelligence officer in charge of secret operations maintaining a close personal relationship with a Mexican general was also seen as a potential liability.

The situation came to a head in June 1918. To counter German intrigues, Butcher periodically submitted articles to U.S. newspapers and news agencies that exposed enemy plans or provided misleading "disinformation." The previous August he had wired a dispatch from the local Western Union office to the Associated Press in Chicago that included a quote from Obregón which stated: "General Pershing was making a big mistake if he assumed that invading Germany would be like invading Mexico." Perhaps intended as advice for a fellow general, in the charged atmosphere of the day the statement was perceived as "disloyal" and harmful to the war effort. As soon as the wire reached military censorship in Nogales, it was suppressed. When Butcher learned what had transpired, he was incensed and angrily demanded that the military censor at Nogales allow him access to his files to see what other dispatches might have been held back. After the censor was dismissed in March 1918, the man filed a grievance that brought attention to bear on Butcher's dispatch from Obregón.

The senior intelligence officers of the Southern Department, subordinate in rank to General Pershing, were uneasy about this latest development. Their concern heightened when a trip Butcher made to Washington on official business (his application for an army commission) appeared to have a secondary motive. Major Barnes observed that the visit was "probably for the further purpose of rendering some assistance to General Álvaro Obregón who is extensively engaged in various business enterprises in Sonora, Mexico. It is assumed that his assistance to General Obregon was in connection with getting certain export licenses."

Hoping to limit Butcher's contact with Obregón, Barnes transferred the special agent from the military intelligence office at Nogales to the office in El Paso, 340 miles distant. Butcher responded by resigning from the military intelligence branch—and taking a position as a commercial agent for General Obregón. In his new role he would be responsible for marketing the chickpea harvest grown on the general's farms and ranches in Sonora to buyers in the United States.

After Butcher's decision to step down became public, the *Nogales Border Vidette* informed its readership:

> Byron S. Butcher, the well-known, efficient military intelligence officer for the United States government at this place, has resigned to accept a more lucrative position in General Obregón's brokerage and commission office. Byron is a high-class man and General Obregón is fortunate in securing his services. He'll make good in any responsible position of trust.

The job at the general's commission house proved only temporary, and seven months later Butcher accepted a better opportunity with the American Graphite Company as a salesman representing the firm's products to customers in Central and South America. In a note about his new position sent to Obregón, whom he respected and admired, Butcher reassured the general:

> The only stipulation I have with the graphite company is that I am at liberty to go with you provided you should at any time need me or any time I may be of assistance to you. In event of such an occurrence, mi general, I want you to feel at liberty to call upon me at any place and at any time—I am always at your service.

The call for assistance from his *compañero* would come sooner than expected. In 1920, Álvaro Obregón was elected president of Mexico and was immediately confronted with a major problem. Before business could be conducted between the United States and Mexico, the U.S. government would first have to recognize the Obregón administration as the legitimate government of Mexico. But, concerned about provisions in the Mexican constitution that placed restrictions on foreign ownership of land and resources, the Harding administration wanted Obregón to sign a "Treaty of Amity and Commerce" that guaranteed foreign ownership rights before providing recognition. Such an action would force Obregón to repudiate articles of the constitution, a very unpopular move at home.

To present the Mexican position to the U.S. government, the new president sent a three-member delegation to Washington. One of his personal representatives was Byron S. Butcher, former U.S. Army military intelligence agent. A decade earlier, Butcher was living a rough-and-tumble existence as a newsman in the mining camps of northern Sonora; now he was negotiating with officials at the highest level of the U.S. administration. The matter of recognition would later be resolved at the Bucarelli Conference of 1923, but the bond between Obregón and Butcher would continue to grow.

In the late 1920s, Butcher returned to the general's payroll as a manager with the Yaqui Distributing Company, the firm that marketed and distributed produce grown on Obregón's three estates, which covered thirty-three thousand acres of land on the west coast of Mexico. In addition to his agricultural holdings, the general also had interests in flour and rice mills, fish canneries, fruit orchards, and livestock. When a successor company to

Yaqui Distributing was established called Obregón & Company, Butcher would be named one of the stockholders.

The former intelligence agent's path to financial success seemed assured. Then on July 17, 1928, while Butcher was in New York City tending to distribution arrangements for a large shipment of fruit and vegetables to the United States, fate took a hand.

On that day, Álvaro Obregón was at a restaurant in Mexico City, attending a banquet in celebration of his being elected president of Mexico for a second time. Seated at the place of honor beneath a bouquet of flowers, the general was conversing with other dignitaries when a young man with a pencil and sketch pad began to make his way along the banquet table drawing caricatures of the officials. He was a talented artist, and his work generated lively comments from the guests whose images he had sketched. When he reached Obregón, the new president smiled and leaned forward to look at his caricature. The artist instantly transferred the drawing pad into his left hand and with his right withdrew an automatic pistol and fired three shots into Obregón's face, then paused several seconds and fired two more. With eyes open wide in surprise, the president-elect fell onto the table dead. His twenty-six-year-old assassin, León Toral, angered by government policies restricting religion, was quickly apprehended. Toral would be executed by firing squad in 1929.

The assassination of Álvaro Obregón not only ended the life of one of the legendary figures of the Mexican Revolution; it closed the door to any future opportunities that Butcher's long association with the general might have prompted. Following the president's death, Butcher became manager of the Nogales office of Obregón & Company, but the business suffered after the Wall Street crash and he departed a short time later. Butcher struggled through the hard years of the Depression, brokering carlots of produce from the west coast of Mexico to earn a living, and by 1940 he was out of work.

His situation improved with the buildup in U.S. defense production at the outbreak of the Second World War. In 1942, at the age of fifty-six, the former intelligence officer secured a high-paying job at the Consolidated Steel Corporation's Orange, Texas, shipyard. Located on the southeastern Texas border near the Gulf of Mexico, the Orange shipyard received huge government contracts to build warships for the U.S. Navy and at its peak supported a workforce of twenty thousand employees. Throughout the war, while Jahnke performed secret missions for the Sicherheitsdienst security service of Heinrich Himmler, and Witzke dispatched spies and saboteurs to operate behind Allied lines, Butcher was at work in the Texas shipyard, helping to build destroyers, destroyer escorts, and landing craft for the U.S. Navy.

In 1950 Byron Butcher retired and with his wife Augusta moved to her hometown of San Antonio, Texas. Six years later Byron S. Butcher died of cancer in San Antonio at the age of seventy.

Time is not kind to heroes.

On the State of Texas death certificate for Butcher, the question, "Was Deceased Ever in U.S. Armed Forces?" is answered "unknown." An obituary published in the *San Antonio Express* on the day of his funeral states that Butcher was survived by his wife, two sisters-in-law, and a brother-in-law; there is no mention of any past accomplishments.

Today Byron Butcher rests in an untended grave at a small cemetery in San Antonio, where situated among scattered twigs, sticks, and leaves, a small rectangular granite marker in the ground reads simply:

BYRON S. BUTCHER
1885–1956

Like Paul Bernardo Altendorf and William Gleaves, Byron Butcher has faded into obscurity. There is no memorial for the man who walked down a dusty Nogales street and shoved a revolver into the back of an enemy agent bent on unleashing a wave of death and destruction, apprehending the assassin who had come to kill him; or for the doctor-spy who maintained a false cover while accompanying an adversary across 1,500 miles of Mexican territory, risking instant death if his true allegiance was revealed; or for the black man who faithfully served the Allied cause at a time of racial injustice, even riding the exposed "cowcatcher" on front of a speeding locomotive during a bandit attack to expose the German espionage network.

This book is their story.

Notes

CHAPTER I

1 **The hurricane was building in intensity:** Albert Pagels, *Mein Leben* (Berlin: Verlag Scherl, 1940), 91–92; Calafate, "Concealing the Dresden," *Blackwood's Magazine* 237 (January 1935): 128–29.

1 **Albert Pagels was a thirty-six-year-old:** Pagels, *Mein Leben*, 5, 13–33, 63–68; Calafate, "Concealing the Dresden," 133.

2 **On the stormy afternoon:** Pagels, *Mein Leben*, 91.

2 **The East Asia Squadron:** Nick Hewitt, *The Kaiser's Pirates* (New York: Skyhorse, 2013), 16–17, 66–70.

2 **The Kreuzergeschwader was led:** Hewitt, *The Kaiser's Pirates*, 16, 98–105, 109–10; Chris Sams, *German Raiders of the First World War* (Croydon [UK]: Fonthill Media, 2015), 32–33 106, 112–13.

3 **At Punta Arenas on December 6:** Calafate, "Concealing the Dresden," 133–34.

3 **Stubenrauch and the three marine officials:** Calafate, "Concealing the Dresden," 133.

3 **"My dear Pagels, can you go out to sea":** Pagels, *Mein Leben*, 91.

3 **"I jumped out of bed":** Pagels, *Mein Leben*, 91.

3 **At the German consulate:** Pagels, *Mein Leben*, 91–92; Calafate, "Concealing the Dresden," 134.

3 **"soaked and shivering":** Pagels, *Mein Leben*, 91.

4 **As they approached the Cockburn Channel:** Pagels, *Mein Leben*, 92; Calafate, "Concealing the Dresden," 134–35.

4 **On December 9:** Pagels, *Mein Leben*, 92; Calafate, "Concealing the Dresden," 135.

4 Information on Pagel's visit to the *Amasis* from: Pagels, *Mein Leben*, 92–93; Calafate, "Concealing the Dresden," 135.

4 **The morning before Pagels's fishing boat:** Hewitt, *The Kaiser's Pirates*, 121–22; Sams, *German Raiders of the First World War*, 125–26.

4 **The British warships fired up:** Hewitt, *The Kaiser's Pirates*, 123–41; Sams, *German Raiders of the First World War*, 127–36.

5 **The only ships of the Kreuzergeschwader:** Sams, *German Raiders of the First World War*, 133.

5 **Downhearted at having arrived:** Pagels, *Mein Leben*, 93, 100; Calafate, "Concealing the Dresden," 135–36.

5 **The indefatigable seal trapper:** Calafate, "Concealing the Dresden," 136.

5 **On his last visit:** Pagels, *Mein Leben*, 101; Calafate, "Concealing the Dresden," 136.

6 **"This time I was not forty-eight":** Pagels, *Mein Leben*, 93, 101.

6 **After leading the *Dresden*:** Pagels, *Mein Leben*, 101–2; Calafate, "Concealing the Dresden," 136–37.

6 **On his return voyage:** Pagels, *Mein Leben*, 102.

6 **Safe in its remote hideaway:** Pagels, *Mein Leben*, 102.

6 **"a cut flower in a vase":** Winston S. Churchill, *The World Crisis*, vol. 1, *1911–1914* (London: Thornton Butterworth, 1923), 295.

7 **In late December the outlook:** Pagels, *Mein Leben*, 102–3; Calafate, "Concealing the Dresden," 137–38.

7 **The *Sierra Cordoba* was met:** Pagels, *Mein Leben*, 103–4; Calafate, "Concealing the Dresden," 138.

7 **With the *Elfriede*'s engine:** Pagels, *Mein Leben*, 105; Calafate, "Concealing the Dresden," 139.

8 **I was caught in a bad trap:** Pagels, *Mein Leben*, 105.

8 **Deciding that it was too dangerous:** Pagels, *Mein Leben*, 107; Calafate, "Concealing the Dresden," 140.

8 **Once the coast was clear:** Pagels, *Mein Leben*, 108; Calafate, "Concealing the Dresden," 140.

8 **The voyage to the liner's hideaway:** Pagels, *Mein Leben*, 108; Calafate, "Concealing the Dresden," 141–42.

8 **"Schaeffer was shocked at Lüdecke's order":** Calafate, "Concealing the Dresden," 142.

8 **The *Elfriede* was hauled aboard:** Pagels, *Mein Leben*, 109–10; Calafate, "Concealing the Dresden," 142.

9 **The most difficult obstacle:** Pagels, *Mein Leben*, 110–11; Calafate, "Concealing the Dresden," 142–43.

9 **The *Dresden*'s coal bunkers were filled:** Pagels, *Mein Leben*, 112–16; Calafate, "Concealing the Dresden," 143.

9 **In recognition of the perilous missions:** Calafate, "Concealing the Dresden," 144.

9 **On February 14, 1915:** Pagels, *Mein Leben*, 119–20; Hewitt, *The Kaiser's Pirates*, 152–53.

9 **On March 8, the *Dresden*:** Pagels, *Mein Leben*, 120; Hewitt, *The Kaiser's Pirates*, 152–53.

10 **At this point the luck:** John Humphrey, *German Surface Raider Warfare* (London: Leonaur, 2017), 18; Hewitt, *The Kaiser's Pirates*, 154.

10 **The British cruisers opened fire:** Hewitt, *The Kaiser's Pirates*, 155; Sams, *German Raiders of the First World War*, 167; Michael Mueller, *Nazi Spymaster* (New York: Skyhorse, 2017), 17–18.

10 **Lüdecke dispatched his adjutant:** Mueller, *Nazi Spymaster*, 18; Hewitt, *The Kaiser's Pirates*, 156.

10 **The injured survivors:** Hewitt, *The Kaiser's Pirates*, 156–57; Mueller, *Nazi Spymaster*, 19.

11 **"The officers used to rant":** C. P. Christensen, *Letzte Kaperfahrt nach Quirinquina* (Berlin: Drei Masken Verlag, A.G., 1936), 214.

11 **Among the first to depart:** Mueller, *Nazi Spymaster*, 19–20; Sams, *German Raiders of the First World War*, 168.

11 **An even more daring escape:** Sams, *German Raiders of the First World War*, 168–69.

11 **Lothar Witzke was born:** "SECRET extract P.F. 601,803," National Archives (UK) Kew, Richmond, MI6 Security Service (PF Series) Files, 23 Aug 1918–01 Oct 1945, Witzke, Lothar, Reference KV2/2296, 19; "Statement of Lothar Witzke of September 16, 1919, in His Examination by Capt. Thomas J. Tunney," U.S. National Archives and Records Administration (hereafter cited as NARA), RG76, Mixed Claims Commission (hereafter cited as MCC), United States and Germany 1922–1939, Printed United States Exhibits, Exhibit 24, 55–56; Captain Henry Landau, *The Enemy Within* (New York City: Putnam, 1937), 34–35.

12 **The war automatically transferred:** "Spy," *American Foreign Service Journal* 11, no. 11 (November 1934): 581.

12 **"a slight crippling effect":** "Physicians Examination of Prisoners, Lothar Witzke," undated, NARA, Inmate File of Lothar Witzke (aka Luther Witzke, aka Lather Witcke), RG129, Records of the Bureau of Prisons 1870–2009, Series Inmate Case Files, 7/31/1895–11/5/1957, 23.

12 **"well-built, athletic young fellow":** Landau, *The Enemy Within*, 35.

12 **"a very likeable boy":** "Unofficial Memorandum of Additional Facts Disclosed by Lothar Witzke," January 13, 1929, NARA, RG76, MCC, United States and Germany 1922–1939, Printed United States Exhibits, Annex A to Exhibit 630, 2817.

12 **"Broad shouldered and strong":** "Personal Characteristics of Lieutenant Lothar Witzke, File No. PF 601,803," National Archives (UK) Kew, Rich-

mond, MI6 Security Service (PF Series) Files, 23 Aug 1918–01 Oct 1945, Witzke, Lothar, Reference KV2/2296, 5.

12 **Our usefulness in Chile thus ended:** "Spy," *American Foreign Service Journal* 11, no. 11 (November 1934): 582.

13 **Bopp proposed an alternative:** "Continuation of the Examination of Pablo Waberski," NARA, RG76, MCC, United States and Germany 1922–1939, Printed United States Exhibits, Exhibit 24, 66.

13 **"I was getting tired":** "Statement of Lothar Witzke of September 16, 1919, in His Examination by Capt. Thomas J. Tunney," NARA, RG76, MCC, United States and Germany 1922–1939, Printed United States Exhibits, Exhibit 24, 59; Landau, *The Enemy Within*, 35.

13 **Consul Bopp sympathized:** Chad Millman, *The Detonators* (New York: Little, Brown, 2006), 80.

CHAPTER 2

15 **Kurt Jahnke was a frequent visitor:** Report by Don S. Rathbun, "Mare Island Explosion of July 9, 1917," March 29, 1918, NARA, M1085, Investigating Case Files of the Bureau of Investigation 1908–1922, Roll boi_german_257-850_0069, Case No. 8000-10626, 95; "Special Border Report from Captain Joel A. Lipscomb," February 7, 1918, NARA, RG76, MCC, United States and Germany 1922–1939, Printed United States Exhibits, Exhibit 227, 620.

15 **"but could not wear them well":** Letter to Mr. Vessey from D. Mellard re: interview of Augusta Kell-Pfeffer, September 17, 1941, National Archives (UK) Kew, Richmond, MI6 Security Service (PF Series) Files, 23 Aug 1918–01 Oct 1945, Jahnke, Kurt, Reference KV2/755.

15 **Born on February 17, 1882:** "Extract from Kurt Salzmann's Diary," January 7, 1941, National Archives (UK) Kew, Richmond, MI6 Security Service (PF Series) Files, 23 Aug 1918–01 Oct 1945, Jahnke, Kurt, Reference KV2/755; "Biography of Kurt Jahnke," undated, National Archives (UK) Kew, Richmond, MI6 Security Service (PF Series) Files, 23 Aug 1918–01 Oct 1945, Jahnke, Kurt, Reference KV2/755.

15 **Little is known of his early life:** "U.S. Marine Corps Muster Rolls 1798–1958," NARA, RG127, Records of the U.S. Marine Corps, Kurt A. Jahnke, T977, Roll 0067, 59, 216, 364; Roll 0068, 66; Roll 0071, 526; Roll 0072, 57.

16 **Following his service with the Marines:** Copy of translation of report by Walter Schellenberg, Head of Amt VI of RSHA, on Herr Jahnke and his activities (Nr. 95a), August 23, 1945, National Archives (UK) Kew, Richmond, MI6 Security Service (PF Series) Files, 23 Aug 1918–01 Oct 1945, Jahnke, Kurt, Reference KV2/755, 2.

16　**While living in San Francisco:** Copy of translation of report by Walter Schellenberg, Head of Amt VI of RSHA, on Herr Jahnke and his activities (Nr. 95a), August 23, 1945, National Archives (UK) Kew, Jahnke, Kurt, Reference KV2/755, 2; Walter Schellenberg, *The Labyrinth* (New York: Harper and Brothers, 1956), 23–24.

16　**"So grateful were the Chinese":** Schellenberg, *The Labyrinth*, 24.

16　**When Lothar Witzke met Jahnke:** Landau, *The Enemy Within*, 34, 214–15.

17　**The munitions factories of Europe:** Captain Franz von Rintelen, *The Dark Invader* (New York: Macmillan, 1933), 62–68.

17　**"it was a spectre, an intangible phantom":** von Rintelen, *The Dark Invader*, 67.

18　**On January 15, 1915, German army councilor:** "German Spies in America," *Liberty Magazine*, February 21, 1931, 8.

18　**On November 28, 1914, a circular:** "German Spies in America," *Liberty Magazine*, February 21, 1931, 9.

18　**The importance of these directives:** John Price Jones and Paul Merrick Hollister, *The German Secret Service in America 1914–1918* (Boston: Small, Maynard & Company, 1918), 4–17, 31–39; Landau, *The Enemy Within*, 4–7, 42–44, 102.

19　**"prevent or delay the exportation":** Heribert von Feilitzsch, *The Secret War on the United States in 1915* (Amissville: Henselstone Verlag, 2015), 75.

19　**Koenig "had arms like an ape":** Jones and Hollister, *The German Secret Service in America*, 74.

19　**In 1914 there had been few fires:** Bill Mills, *The League* (New York: Skyhorse, 2013), 41–42, 45.

20　**For a solution to destroying Allied munitions ships:** von Feilitzsch, *The Secret War on the United States*, 21; "Interview with Walter T. Scheele," Washington, March 23, 1918, NARA, M1085, Investigating Case Files of the Bureau of Investigation 1908–1922, Roll boi_german_257-850_0069, Case No. 8000-925, 135–36.

20　**The solution that Dr. Scheele devised:** "Synopsis Walter Theodore von Scheele," June 1, 1918, NARA, M1085, Investigating Case Files of the Bureau of Investigation 1908–1922, Roll boi_german_257-850_0069, Case No. 8000-925, 55–56; "Interview with Walter T. Scheele," Washington, March 23, 1918, NARA, M1085, Investigating Case Files of the Bureau of Investigation 1908–1922, Roll boi_german_257-850_0069, Case No. 8000-925, 153–71; von Rintelen, *The Dark Invader*, 104–7; "Statement of Ernst Becker," undated, NARA, M1085, Investigating Case Files of the Bureau of Investigation 1908–1922, Roll boi_german_257-850_0069, Case No. 8000-925, 444.

21　**Dr. Scheele's "cigars" provided:** "Synopsis Walter Theodore von Scheele," June 1, 1918, NARA, M1085, Investigating Case Files of the Bureau of Investigation 1908–1922, Roll boi_german_257-850_0069, Case No. 8000-925, 56;

von Feilitzsch, *The Secret War on the United States*, 88–89; Jones and Hollister, *The German Secret Service in America*, 160–62; Landau, *The Enemy Within*, 305–7.

22 **The port at Marseille:** "Nine Bombs on One Ship," *Washington Post*, July 11, 1915, 3; "Nine Bombs on Vessel," *Topeka State Journal*, July 10, 1915, 2; "Find Nine Bombs on Kirkoswald," *South Bend News-Times*, July 10, 1915, 1.

22 **After analyzing the bomb casings:** Thomas J. Tunney, *Throttled!* (Boston: Small, Maynard & Company, 1919), 129–30.

22 Information on the solution of the incendiary ship bombs case (Dr. Scheele's "cigars") by New York City Police comes from: Tunney, *Throttled!*, 126–80.

22 **"Our study disclosed":** Tunney, *Throttled!*, 130.

23 **"Just about the time":** Tunney, *Throttled!*, 238; Landau, *The Enemy Within*, 38.

23 **"I was his superintendent":** Tunney, *Throttled!*, 161.

24 **"Just you wait":** Tunney, *Throttled!*, 162.

24 **In October 1915, Lewis J. Smith:** Landau, *The Enemy Within*, 25–26.

25 **For months the Justice Department:** Landau, *The Enemy Within*, 26–27.

25 **"violations of the Federal Criminal Statutes":** Landau, *The Enemy Within*, 26–27.

25 **In New York, Tunney's bomb squad:** Jules Witcover, *Sabotage at Black Tom* (Chapel Hill, NC: Algonquin Books of Chapel Hill, 1989), 67–68, 127–28; Jones and Hollister, *The German Secret Service in America*, 221.

25 **By 1915, Jahnke had graduated:** Richard R. Doerries, "Tracing Kurt Jahnke: Aspects of the Study of German Intelligence," in *Historians and Archivists*, ed. George O. Kent (Fairfax, VA: George Mason University Press, 1991), 31.

25 **"My youthful appearance":** "Spy," *American Foreign Service Journal* 11, no. 11 (November 1934): 582.

26 **Jahnke refined the process of sabotage:** Reinhard R. Doerries, *Diplomaten und Agenten* (Heidelberg: Universitätverlag C. Winter, 2001), 35; *Crocker Langley Directory 1916*, Jahnke, 994 (accessed via www.fold3.com, city directories); Landau, *The Enemy Within*, 213, 214.

26 **A full roster of the sabotage missions:** Report by Don S. Rathbun, "Mare Island Explosion of July 9, 1917," March 29, 1918, NARA, M1085, Investigating Case Files of the Bureau of Investigation 1908–1922, Roll boi_german_257-850_0069, Case No. 8000-10626, 95.

26 **"In addition to their work":** Landau, *The Enemy Within*, 35.

26 **In an unguarded moment:** Paul Bernardo Altendorf, "On Secret Service in Mexico," *El Paso Herald*, November 5, 1919, 1; Paul Bernardo Altendorf, "U.S. Agent Is Ordered to Join Mission to Arrange Mexican-German Invasion of U.S.," *El Paso Herald*, November 22, 1919, 1; "Letter Dated January 15, 1921 from the Acting Judge Advocate General to the Adjutant General," NARA, RG76, MCC, United States and Germany 1922–1939, Printed United

States Exhibits, Exhibit 157, 507–8; Testimony of Paul B. Altendorf, August 16 and 17, 1918, NARA, RG76, MCC, United States and Germany 1922–1939, Printed United States Exhibits, Exhibit 321, 965, 978; Landau, *The Enemy Within*, 102.

27 **The SS *Minnesota* was the largest ocean liner:** "Minnesota, Largest Going to Orient, to Enter Atlantic Trade," *Princeton (MN) Union*, October 7, 1915, 7; "Shippers Divided on Traffic Effect of Seaman's Law," *Minneapolis Star Tribune*, November 5, 1915, 10; "Quits the Oriental Trade," *Brainerd (MN) Daily Dispatch*, November 16, 1915, 1.

27 **To remain profitable:** "Quits the Oriental Trade," *Brainerd (MN) Daily Dispatch*, November 16, 1915, 1.

27 **In order to raise a crew:** Letter from J. H. Carroll to Justice Department, December 6, 1915, NARA, M1085, Investigating Case Files of the Bureau of Investigation 1908–1922, Roll boi_german_257-850_0059, Case No. og-204, 11; Report by E. M. Blanford, "RE: S/S Minnesota," December 14, 1915, NARA, M1085, Investigating Case Files of the Bureau of Investigation 1908–1922, Roll boi_german_257-850_0059, Case No. og-204, 27.

27 **"It is apparent that there is no trouble":** Letter from J. H. Carroll to Justice Department, December 6, 1915, 11.

27 **At San Pedro I [had] joined:** "Spy," *American Foreign Service Journal* 11, no. 11 (November 1934): 582.

28 **On November 14, 1915, the SS *Minnesota*:** Letter from J. H. Carroll to Justice Department, December 6, 1915, 11.

28 **Four days later:** Letter from J. H. Carroll to Justice Department, December 6, 1915, 11–12; Report by Don S. Rathbun, "IN RE: Steamer Minnesota," December 13, 1915, NARA, M1085, Investigating Case Files of the Bureau of Investigation 1908–1922, Roll boi_german_257-850_0059, Case No. og-204, 23–24.

28 **"he did not expect to return":** Letter from J. H. Carroll to Justice Department, December 6, 1915, 11; Report by Don S. Rathbun, "IN RE: Steamer Minnesota," December 13, 1915, 22; Report by Don S. Rathbun, "IN RE: Steamer Minnesota," December 16, 1915, NARA, M1085, Investigating Case Files of the Bureau of Investigation 1908–1922, Roll boi_german_257-850_0059, Case No. og-204, 46.

28 **The *Minnesota* was equipped:** Report by E. M. Blanford, "RE: S/S Minnesota," December 14, 1915, 27; Letter from J. H. Carroll to Justice Department, December 6, 1915, 12.

28 **"Now 653 miles from San Francisco":** Letter from J. H. Carroll to Justice Department, December 6, 1915, 12.

29 **National wire services:** "Plotters May Have Used Chemicals," *Victoria (BC) Daily Times*, December 6, 1915, 1.

29 **Concerned that the liner:** Letter from J. H. Carroll to Justice Department, December 6, 1915, 11–13; Report by Tom Howick, "IN RE: Steamer Minne-

sota; Probable Neutrality Matter," December 9, 1915, NARA, M1085, Investigating Case Files of the Bureau of Investigation 1908–1922, Roll boi_german_257-850_0059, Case No. og-204, 20.

30 **Special Agent Tom Howick called:** Report by Tom Howick, "IN RE: Steamer Minnesota; Probable Neutrality Matter," December 9, 1915, 20–22; Report by Tom Howick, "IN RE: Steamer Minnesota; Probable Neutrality Matter," December 13, 1915, NARA, M1085, Investigating Case Files of the Bureau of Investigation 1908–1922, Roll boi_german_257-850_0059, Case No. og-204, 33.

30 **"was well aware of the Anderson woman":** Report by Tom Howick, "IN RE: Steamer Minnesota; Probable Neutrality Matter," December 10, 1915, NARA, M1085, Investigating Case Files of the Bureau of Investigation 1908–1922, Roll boi_german_257-850_0059, Case No. og-204, 42.

30 **"from a friend of the Martin woman":** Report by Tom Howick, "IN RE: Steamer Minnesota; Probable Neutrality Matter," December 13, 1915, 45.

30 **"it now appears that":** Report by Tom Howick, "IN RE: Steamer Minnesota; Probable Neutrality Matter," December 13, 1915, 45.

30 **Agent Howick next obtained:** Report by Tom Howick, "IN RE: Steamer Minnesota; Probable Neutrality Matter," December 10, 1915, 35–40.

30 **Special Agent E. M. Blanford:** Report by E. M. Blanford, "RE: S/S Minnesota," December 14, 1915, 26–27, 29; Report by Don S. Rathbun, "IN RE: Steamer Minnesota," December 17, 1915, NARA, M1085, Investigating Case Files of the Bureau of Investigation 1908–1922, Roll boi_german_257-850_0059, Case No. og-204, 55.

31 **"Unable to discover anything which":** Report by Don S. Rathbun, "IN RE: Steamer Minnesota," December 16, 1915, NARA, M1085, Investigating Case Files of the Bureau of Investigation 1908–1922, Roll boi_german_257-850_0059, Case No. og-204, 46.

31 **"there was a little 'crew talk'":** Report by Don S. Rathbun, "IN RE: Steamer Minnesota," December 16, 1915, 47.

31 **"in the course of time the interior":** Report by Don S. Rathbun, "IN RE: Steamer Minnesota," December 16, 1915, 47.

31 **"the failure of the ship's boilers":** "Steamship Minnesota Mechanically Unsound," *Minneapolis Star Tribune*, December 16, 1915, 2.

32 **Throughout 1916, a pivotal year:** "Steamship Minnesota Leaves for London," *Minneapolis Star Tribune*, February 16, 1917, 2.

32 **Martha Held's neighbors were convinced:** Millman, *The Detonators*, 10–11; Landau, *The Enemy Within*, 145–46; "German Spies in America," *Liberty Magazine*, March 14, 1931, 51–52.

32 **"The china and silver would be removed":** "German Spies in America," *Liberty Magazine*, March 14, 1931, 52.

32 **One of the young women:** Millman, *The Detonators*, 88–89; Landau, *The Enemy Within*, 145–48; "German Spies in America," *Liberty Magazine*, March 14, 1931, 52–53.

32 **Named for its tomcat shape:** Landau, *The Enemy Within*, 77–78.

33 **The facility was protected by:** "German Spies in America," *Liberty Magazine*, April 4, 1931, 54; Landau, *The Enemy Within*, 78, 84, 142.

33 **At ten o'clock on the evening:** "German Spies in America," *Liberty Magazine*, April 4, 1931, 54; Landau, *The Enemy Within*, 78–79.

33 **In the upper bay:** Millman, *The Detonators*, 90; Landau, *The Enemy Within*, 78, 84; Witcover, *Sabotage at Black Tom*, 161.

34 **Developed by Abteilung III B:** Report by Charles E. Breniman, "IN RE: Pencil in Glass Tube Containing Chemicals Used by Enemy Aliens to Destroy Works of Entente Allies," April 26, 1918, NARA, M1085, Investigating Case Files of the Bureau of Investigation 1908–1922, Roll boi_german_257-850_0069, Case No. 8000-196474, 1–4; Report by H. B. Mock, "IN RE: Carl Jacobsen: Alleged Alien Enemy and Espionage Act Violation Investigation," May 11, 1918, NARA, M1085, Investigating Case Files of the Bureau of Investigation 1908–1922, Roll 645, Roll boi_german_257-850_0103, Case No. 8000-233186, 10–15.

34 **Around midnight the saboteurs:** Millman, *The Detonators*, 90; Landau, *The Enemy Within*, 79.

34 **Somewhere in the darkened yard:** Witcover, *Sabotage at Black Tom*, 160–62; Landau, *The Enemy Within*, 81–84.

35 **At 12:45 a.m., a Dougherty watchman:** Landau, *The Enemy Within*, 79.

35 **Out on the open water:** For TNT velocity of detonation, see Tenney L. Davis, *The Chemistry of Powder and Explosives* (Las Vegas, NV: Angriff Press, 1943), 139–40; "Special Border Report from Captain Joel A. Lipscomb," February 7, 1918, NARA, RG76, MCC, United States and Germany 1922–1939, Printed United States Exhibits, Exhibit 227, 619, 621; "Special Border Report from Captain Joel A. Lipscomb," February 2, 1918, NARA, RG76, MCC, United States and Germany 1922–1939, Printed United States Exhibits, Exhibit 228, 619–20; Testimony of Paul B. Altendorf, NARA, RG76, MCC, United States and Germany 1922–1939, Printed United States Exhibits, Exhibit 321, 965.

35 **The explosion of the *Johnson 17*:** "Munitions Explosion in New York Harbor," *Kingston (NY) Daily Freeman*, July 31, 1916, 1; "Munition Explosions Cause Loss of $20 Million," *New York Times*, July 31, 1916, 2, 4; Landau, *The Enemy Within*, 79.

35 **Miraculously only five people:** Millman, *The Detonators*, 94; "Munition Explosions Cause Loss of $20 Million," *New York Times*, July 31, 1916, 1–2.

35 **The smoke had not cleared:** "Railroad Heads to Be Arrested for Explosion," *New York Times*, July 31, 1916, 1.

36   **Lawyers working for the owners:** Landau, *The Enemy Within*, 213, 215.

36   **By 1916, rumors about Jahnke's:** Millman, *The Detonators*, 81–82; Richard B. Spence, "K. A. Jahnke and the German Sabotage Campaign in the U.S. and Mexico, 1914–1918," *The Historian*, Fall 1996, 97, 99; Landau, *The Enemy Within*, 34; "K. A. Jahnke, Report on Activities in the United States and Mexico," undated, National Archives (UK) Kew, Richmond, MI6 Security Service (PF Series) Files, 23 Aug 1918–01 Oct 1945, Jahnke, Kurt, Reference KV2/755, 1.

37   **Seventeen months after Jahnke:** "Non-statistical Manifests and Statistical Index Cards of Aliens Arriving at Laredo, Texas, May 1903–November 1929," NARA, RG85, Roll No. 109, Image 4944, "Pablo Waberski," 1.

37   **After being granted entry:** "World War 1 Draft Registration Cards, 1917–1918," NARA, M1509, Image 3, "Pablo Waberski," 1–2; Testimony of Byron S. Butcher, August 17, 1918, NARA, RG76, MCC, United States and Germany 1922–1939, Printed United States Exhibits, Exhibit 321, 1053–55.

37   **One quiet night in late June 1917:** "Secret Probe in Blast Is Rushed by U.S. Sleuths," *San Francisco Examiner*, July 10, 1917, 1; "6 Dead 38 Injured at Mare Island," *Sausalito News*, July 14, 1917, 1.

38   **Monday, July 9, began like any other:** "Many Injured as Blast Wrecks Magazine Stations," *Sacramento Bee*, July 9, 1917, 1; Mare Island Explosion—Six Persons Killed at Navy Yard and Many Wounded," *Colorado Herald Democrat*, July 10, 1917, 1; "Explosion Kills Six in Mare Island Yard," *New York Times*, July 10, 1917, 16.

38   **The family's routine continued:** "Powder Magazine Blows Up, Bay Cities Shaken," *Tulare (CA) Advance Register*, July 9, 1917, 1; "Many Injured as Blast Wrecks Magazine Stations," *Sacramento Bee*, July 9, 1917, 1; "Explosion Kills Six in Mare Island Yard," *New York Times*, July 10, 1917, 16.

38   **The black powder storehouse:** "Explosion in a Navy Yard," *Atchison (KS) Daily Globe*, July 9, 1917, 1; "The Streets of Vallejo Are Glittering Scrap Heaps," *San Francisco Examiner*, July 10, 1917, 2.

39   **Captain Harry George, the commandant:** "Many Injured as Blast Wrecks Magazine Stations," *Sacramento Bee*, July 9, 1917, 5; "Explosion Kills Six in Mare Island Yard," *New York Times*, July 10, 1917, 16.

39   **"blackpowder would not blow up":** "The Streets of Vallejo Are Glittering Scrap Heaps," *San Francisco Examiner*, July 10, 1917, 2.

39   **The naval investigation revealed:** Report from Don S. Rathbun to A. Bruce Bielaski, "IN RE: Mare Island Explosion of July 9, 1917," September 4, 1917, NARA, M1085, Investigating Case Files of the Bureau of Investigation 1908–1922, Roll boi_german_257-850_0081, Case No. 8000-10626, 60–64.

39   **Miss Julia Daly told the naval board:** Report from Don S. Rathbun to A. Bruce Bielaski, "IN RE: Mare Island Explosion of July 9, 1917," July 23, 1917, NARA, M1085, Investigating Case Files of the Bureau of Investigation 1908–1922, Roll boi_german_257-850_0081, Case No. 8000-10626, 15; Report from

Don S. Rathbun to A. Bruce Bielaski, "IN RE: Mare Island Explosion of July 9, 1917," September 4, 1917, NARA, M1085, Investigating Case Files of the Bureau of Investigation 1908–1922, Roll boi_german_257-850_0081, Case No. 8000-10626, 65.

40 **"had never appeared to read this paper":** Report from Don S. Rathbun to A. Bruce Bielaski, "IN RE: Mare Island Explosion of July 9, 1917," September 4, 1917, NARA, M1085, Investigating Case Files of the Bureau of Investigation 1908–1922, Roll boi_german_257-850_0081, Case No. 8000-10626, 65.

40 **Mrs. Schmertman of South Vallejo:** Report from Don S. Rathbun to A. Bruce Bielaski, "IN RE: Mare Island Explosion of July 9, 1917," September 4, 1917, NARA, M1085, Investigating Case Files of the Bureau of Investigation 1908–1922, Roll boi_german_257-850_0081, Case No. 8000-10626, 65–67.

40 **"I went on the side of the hill":** Report from W. G. McMillian, "IN RE: Mare Island Explosion of July 9, 1917," September 25, 1917, NARA, M1085, Investigating Case Files of the Bureau of Investigation 1908–1922, Roll boi_german_257-850_0081, Case No. 8000-10626, 83.

40 **Investigators found a piece of a clock:** "Portion of Clock Is Found on the Scene," *San Francisco Chronicle*, July 12, 1917, 1; "Plot Suspect Seized on Mare Island," *San Francisco Examiner*, July 12, 1917, 1.

41 **"I was lying [in bed]":** Testimony of Paul B. Altendorf, NARA, RG76, MCC, United States and Germany 1922–1939, Printed United States Exhibits, Exhibit 321, 977; "Special Border Report from Captain Joel A. Lipscomb, Titled: Foreigners German Activity," February 2, 1918, NARA, MID 10541-268, 64.

41 **The MacKenzie family was laid to rest:** "Family, Victim of Mare Island Blast, Is Buried," *San Francisco Examiner*, July 12, 1917, 4.

41 **On August 26, 1917, six weeks after:** Information on the encounters between military intelligence special agent "G. C." and Kurt Jahnke from: Memorandum from Captain Walter S. Volkmar to Intelligence Officer, Headquarters Third District, "Subject: Report—German Activities in the U.S. and Mexico," August 28, 1917, NARA, RG76, Box 5, 1–4.

CHAPTER 3

43 **The German agents crossed the border:** Landau, *The Enemy Within*, 112; Robert Koenig, *The Fourth Horseman* (New York: Public Affairs, 2006), 221.

43 **Self-governed nations do not:** "President Wilson's Declaration of War Message to Congress, April 2, 1917," NARA, RG46, Records of the United States Senate, Journals and Minute Books 1797–1968, NAI 2668825.

44 **With the United States on a war footing:** Mills, *The League*, 23, 37.

44 **"If you can't go to the trenches":** "To Win This War We Must Jail German Spies" (advertisement), *Needlecraft*, January 1918, 22.

44   **"To win this war we must":** "To Win This War We Must Jail German Spies,"
     22.

44   **The flight of German spies:** Landau, *The Enemy Within*, 112; Witcover,
     Sabotage at Black Tom, 209–10.

45   **The warm relationship:** Information on Fletcher's reception from: "Ger-
     man Efforts in Mexico," *World's Work: A History of Our Time* 35 (December
     1917): 214.

45   **Once established in Mexico City:** Friedrich Katz, *The Secret War in
     Mexico* (Chicago: University of Chicago Press, 1981), 396–97; Testimony of
     Major R. M. Campbell, August 17, 1918, NARA, RG76, MCC, United States
     and Germany 1922–1939, Printed United States Exhibits, Exhibit 321, 1032;
     Richard R. Doerries, "Tracing Kurt Jahnke: Aspects of the Study of German
     Intelligence," in *Historians and Archivists*, ed. George O. Kent (Fairfax, VA:
     George Mason University Press, 1991), 31.

46   **"only through concert with Germany":** "Special Border Report from Cap-
     tain Joel A. Lipscomb," February 7, 1918, NARA, RG76, MCC, United States
     and Germany 1922–1939, Printed United States Exhibits, Exhibit 227, 622.

46   **"Jahnke was as big a man":** "Special Border Report from Captain Joel A.
     Lipscomb," February 7, 1918, NARA, RG76, MCC, United States and Ger-
     many 1922–1939, Printed United States Exhibits, Exhibit 227, 622.

46   **Already a man of great wealth:** "Special Border Report from Captain
     Joel A. Lipscomb," February 7, 1918, NARA, RG76, MCC, United States
     and Germany 1922–1939, Printed United States Exhibits, Exhibit 227,
     620, 621; "Summary for Captain Keppel," unsigned, undated, NARA,
     MID 10541-268, 1; Affidavit of Alfred Edward Woodley Mason, February
     15, 1929, NARA, RG76, MCC, United States and Germany 1922–1939,
     Printed United States Exhibits, Exhibit 625, 2758; Richard B. Spence,
     "K. A. Jahnke and the German Sabotage Campaign in the U.S. and Mexico,
     1914–1918," *The Historian*, 107.

46   **The Hotel Juarez was the central:** Report from W. C. Stillson, "In re:
     Jesus Doran (Referring to M.I.D. "Patricia Case") Alleged Violation Sec-
     tion 2 Espionage Act," December 11, 1918, NARA, M1085, Investigating
     Case Files of the Bureau of Investigation 1908–1922, Roll 757, Roll boi_ger-
     man_257-850_0172, Case No. 334656, 47–48; Testimony of Paul B. Altendorf,
     NARA, RG76, MCC, United States and Germany 1922–1939, Printed United
     States Exhibits, Exhibit 321, 963.

47   **Major Robert Madison Campbell:** George W. Cullum, *Biographical Reg-
     ister of the Officers and Graduates of the United States Military Academy at
     West Point, New York, Supplement Vol. VI-A 1910–1920* (Saginaw, MI: Sher-
     man & Peters Printers, 1920), 1086–87.

47   **William Neunhoffer, supposedly a "slacker":** Unsigned letter to Robert
     L. Barnes, Special Agent in Charge, September 1917, NARA, M1085, Inves-

tigating Case Files of the Bureau of Investigation 1908–1922, Roll boi_german_257-850_0002, Case No. 54263, 68.

47   **William Neunhoffer was a special agent:** Testimony of William Neunhoffer, August 17, 1918, NARA, RG76, MCC, United States and Germany 1922–1939, Printed United States Exhibits, Exhibit 321, 1100–1; Landau, *The Enemy Within*, 112.

48   **I must report that my efforts:** Report from William Neunhoffer to A. Bruce Bielaski, "Number 30, August 24–29, 1917," NARA, M1085, Investigating Case Files of the Bureau of Investigation 1908–1922, Roll boi_german_257-850_0002, Case No. 54263, 83.

48   **During this period the writer:** Report from William Neunhoffer to A. Bruce Bielaski, "Number 30, September 12–19, 1917," NARA, M1085, Investigating Case Files of the Bureau of Investigation 1908–1922, Roll boi_german_257-850_0002, Case No. 54263, 75.

48   **Richard Walter "Ricardo" Schwierz:** Jamie Bisher, *The Intelligence War in Latin America, 1914–1922* (Jefferson, NC: McFarland, 2016), 133.

48   **"he escaped from a deputy marshal":** "German Secret Agents Trunk Is Seized by U.S.," *San Francisco Examiner*, March 2, 1917, 2.

48   **Once in Mexico:** Altendorf, "On Secret Service in Mexico," *El Paso Herald*, November 6, 1919, 1, 10.

49   **In conversation with Dr. Altendorf:** Report from William Neunhoffer to A. Bruce Bielaski, "Number 30, for Week Ending October 2, 1917," NARA, M1085, Investigating Case Files of the Bureau of Investigation 1908–1922, Roll boi_german_257-850_0002, Case No. 54263, 65–66.

50   **During the course of the night:** Report from William Neunhoffer to A. Bruce Bielaski, "Number 30, September 21, 1917," NARA, M1085, Investigating Case Files of the Bureau of Investigation 1908–1922, Roll boi_german_257-850_0002, Case No. 54263, 74.

50   **On October 3, Major Schwierz:** Letter from William Neunhoffer to A. Bruce Bielaski, "Supplementing My Previous Reports," January 9, 1918," NARA, M1085, Investigating Case Files of the Bureau of Investigation 1908–1922, Roll boi_german_257-850_0002, Case No. 54263, 45.

50   **With little to show:** Testimony of William Neunhoffer, NARA, RG76, MCC, United States and Germany 1922–1939, Printed United States Exhibits, Exhibit 321, 1100.

51   Information on the meeting between Altendorf and von Eckhardt is found in: Paul Bernardo Altendorf, "U.S. Secret Agent Fools German Envoy and Gets in His Clutches Mexico's Most Dangerous Foe Spy," *El Paso Herald*, November 20, 1919, 1, 7; Testimony of Paul B. Altendorf, NARA, RG76, MCC, United States and Germany 1922–1939, Printed United States Exhibits, Exhibit 321, 968–69; Paul B. Altendorf, "My Trip to Mexico," NARA, MID 10541-268, 1–2.

53 Information on Altendorf's meeting with Jahnke and his subsequent stay in Jahnke's home is found in: Paul Bernardo Altendorf, "U.S. Agent in Mexico Invades German Spy Files; El Paso Letter Writer Reveals Plot to Blow Up Canal," *El Paso Herald*, November 21, 1919, 1, 7; Testimony of Paul B. Altendorf, NARA, RG76, MCC, United States and Germany 1922–1939, Printed United States Exhibits, Exhibit 321, 969–70; Altendorf, "My Trip to Mexico," NARA, MID 10541-268, 2–3; "Summary for Captain Keppel," unsigned, undated, NARA, MID 10541-268, 2.

54 Information on Jahnke's return from: Veracruz and briefing on Witzke's mission to the United States from: Altendorf, "U.S. Agent Is Ordered to Join Mission to Border to Arrange Mexican-German Invasion of U.S.," *El Paso Herald*, November 22, 1919, 1, 12; Testimony of Paul B. Altendorf, NARA, RG76, MCC, United States and Germany 1922–1939, Printed United States Exhibits, Exhibit 321, 972–75; Altendorf, "My Trip to Mexico," NARA, MID 10541-268, 3, 5–6.

55 **"das groesterindsfich":** Altendorf, "U.S. Agent Is Ordered to Join Mission to Border to Arrange Mexican-German Invasion of U.S.," *El Paso Herald*, November 22, 1919, 1.

56 **On the afternoon of September 13, 1914:** Ronald Atkin, *Revolution! Mexico, 1910–20* (New York: John Day, 1970), 217–20; Friedrich Katz, *The Life and Times of Pancho Villa* (Stanford, CA: Stanford University Press, 1998), 369–70.

56 **"It is likely that":** Álvaro Obregón, *Ocho Mil Kilómetros en Campaña* (Mexico City: Libreria de la Vda. De CH. Bouret, 1917), 318.

56 **Being handed a suitcase:** Obregón, *Ocho Mil Kilómetros en Campaña*, 318.

57 **Byron Samuel Butcher was born:** "Byron S. Butcher," NARA, RG29, "Thirteenth Census of U.S. 1910," Douglas Arizona, Ward 1, District 0018, Records of the Bureau of Census, Roll T624_38, 19; "Byron Samuel Butcher," draft registration card, NARA, WW1 Selective Service System Registration Cards 1917–1918, M1509, Arizona, Santa Cruz County, 168; "Byron Samuel Butcher Death Certificate," Texas Department of State Health Services, Austin, Texas, Texas Death Certificates 1903–1982; Byron S. Butcher Passport Application, April 28, 1923, NARA, Passport Applications January 2, 1906–March 31, 1925, Roll 255, Certificates 284850–285349, 11 May 1922–11 May 1923, 540–41; Byron Samuel Butcher Passport Application, June 24, 1918, NARA, U.S. Passport Applications 1795–1925, Roll 547, Certificates 25000–25299, 8 July 1918–8 July 1919, 1–2; "Newspaperman Resigns to Join Hearst Service," *Tombstone Weekly Epitaph*, July 16, 1916, 4; "Border Journalist Here," *Arizona Daily Star*, April 1, 1917, 3.

57 **In July 1916, Butcher's experience:** "Border Journalist Here," *Arizona Daily Star*, April 1, 1917, 4; Testimony of Byron S. Butcher, NARA, RG76,

MCC, United States and Germany 1922–1939, Printed United States Exhibits, Exhibit 321, 1045.

58 **The results of Butcher's efforts:** "German Secret Agent's Trunk Is Seized by U.S.," *San Francisco Examiner*, March 2, 1917, 2; "It Failed But German Mexican Plot Was Deep," *Henry County Democrat* (Clinton, Missouri), March 8, 1917, 7.

58 **"I have just made an appointment":** Altendorf's visit with President Carranza is detailed in Paul Bernardo Altendorf, "Carranza Lets Spies Use Wires to Send German Code Messages; Seizes Wells Giving Allies Oil," *El Paso Herald*, November 24, 1919, 1–2.

59 **As he exited the official residence:** Altendorf, "Carranza Lets Spies Use Wires," 2.

CHAPTER 4

61 **In December 1914, the German foreign office:** Landau, *The Enemy Within*, 30–33; Bisher, *The Intelligence War in Latin America*, 60.

62 **Another German stratagem:** Information on the German plot to incite a holy war in India from: Peter Hopkirk, *Hidden Fire* (New York: Kodansha America, 1994).

62 **"rise as one and smite":** Hopkirk, *Hidden Fire*, 60.

62 **Ireland had been a British colony:** Reinhard R. Doerries, *Prelude to the Easter Rising* (Portland, OR: Frank Cass, 2000), 1–25.

63 **Imperial Russia's "Achilles' heel":** Catherine Merridale, *Lenin on the Train* (New York: Henry Holt, 2017), 6–7, 42–43, 136–40.

63 **"Since it is in our interests":** Merridale, *Lenin on the Train*, 139.

63 **In a secret operation, a "sealed train":** Merridale, *Lenin on the Train*, 143, 146–49.

64 **"Whether in the grain fields":** Mills, *The League*, 62.

64 **The most radical labor union of the time:** Mills, *The League*, 62–63.

64 **As a revolutionary the Industrial Workers:** Vincent St. John, *The IWW: Its History, Structure and Methods* (New Castle, PA: IWW Publishing Bureau, 1917), 17–18.

65 **"We will resent with all of the power":** William Preston, *Aliens and Dissenters: Federal Suppression of Radicals, 1903–1933* (Chicago: University of Illinois Press, 1994), 88–89.

65 **"During the spring and summer of 1917":** Mills, *The League*, 71.

65 **The response from government authorities:** "Nationwide Raid Is Made on All IWW Rendezvous," *Eau Claire (WI) Leader*, September 6, 1917, 1–2; "I.W.W Offices Raided by U.S., Haywood Taken," *Daily Free Press* (Carbondale, IL), September 6, 1917, 1.

66 **"branded as absolutely false":** "Haywood Files Bitter Protest," *Fort Wayne Journal-Gazette*, July 13, 1917, 8.

66 **One of the cities that experienced:** "Murder-Arson Orgy Over in East St. Louis; Blacks Are in Flight," *Atlanta Constitution*, July 4, 1917, 1–2; "East St. Louis Riot Smolders as Troops Take Control of City," *San Francisco Chronicle*, July 4, 1917, 2.

66 **"protesting the importation":** "6 Are Shot in East St. Louis Race Riot," *Washington Post*, May 30, 1917, 1.

66 **"two white men had been held up":** "6 Are Shot in East St. Louis Race Riot," 1.

66 **East St. Louis was quiet:** "Rioters Slaughter 100 Negroes and Put East St. Louis to Torch," *San Francisco Chronicle*, July 3, 1917, 1–2; "White Mobs Shoot Scores of Negroes as Hapless Blacks Flee Blazing Homes," *Atlanta Constitution*, July 3, 1917, 1–2; "Murder-Arson Orgy Over in East St. Louis," 1–2.

67 **"As three negroes were trying to escape":** "Rioters Slaughter 100 Negroes and Put East St. Louis to Torch," 2.

67 **"Hundreds of negro women":** "Rioters Slaughter 100 Negroes and Put East St. Louis to Torch," 2.

67 **"to maintain justice for colored native":** "Murder-Arson Orgy Over in East St. Louis," 2.

67 **"The situation in Chester is akin":** "Two Die as Race Rioting Is Renewed at Chester; Many Youngstown Negroes Beaten," *Washington Post*, July 27, 1917, 1.

68 **The Chester race riot began:** "Troops Stop Race Riot at Chester, Pa," *Chicago Daily Tribune*, July 26, 1917, 1; "Three Slain in New Race Riot at Chester, Pa," *Chicago Daily Tribune*, July 27, 1917, 1; "Two Die as Race Rioting Is Renewed at Chester," 1; "Race Riot Starts Anew at Chester; Many Youngstown Negroes Beaten," *Washington Post*, July 28, 1917, 1; "2 More Die in Chester," *Washington Post*, July 29, 1917, 1.

68 **"Hundreds of men armed with rifles":** "Two Die as Race Rioting Is Renewed at Chester," 1.

68 **Three weeks passed:** Information on the Camp Logan mutiny and riot from: Jaime Salazar, *Mutiny of Rage: The 1917 Camp Logan Riots and Buffalo Soldiers in Houston* (Lanham, MD: Prometheus, 2021), 54–55, 72–75, 84–114, 156, 158; "Negro Soldiers Out of Houston," *Fort Wayne News*, August 24, 1917, 1, 22; "Disarm Troops Who Shot Up Houston, Tex.," *Chicago Daily Tribune*, August 25, 1917, 1–2.

69 **Concerned about the effect:** Roy Talbert Jr., *Negative Intelligence* (Jackson: University Press of Mississippi, 1991), 113–17; Ann Hagedorn, *Savage Peace* (New York: Simon & Shuster, 2007), 40–43; Letter from Van Deman to Major Nicholas Biddle, March 18, 1918, NARA, RG165, Military Intelligence Division—Negro Subversion, M1440, Roll 0002, 1.

69 **"colored agent that we have":** Talbert, *Negative Intelligence*, 114.
69 **"Not since the East St. Louis riot":** Memorandum from Major Loving to Director, Military Intelligence, "Subject: Spirit of Unrest among Negroes," December 23, 1918, NARA, RG165, Military Intelligence Division—Negro Subversion, M1440, Roll 0004, 1.
69 **William "Guillermo" Gleaves had been born:** Testimony of William Gleaves, August 17, 1918, NARA, RG76, MCC, United States and Germany 1922–1939, Printed United States Exhibits, Exhibit 321, 1008, 1013; Landau, *The Enemy Within*, 114–15; Affidavit of William H. Gleaves, January 31, 1927, NARA, RG76, MCC, United States and Germany 1922–1939, Printed United States Exhibits, Exhibit 329, 1254–55.
69 **"a man of great physical strength":** Affidavit of Alfred Edward Woodley Mason, February 15, 1929, NARA, RG76, MCC, United States and Germany 1922–1939, Printed United States Exhibits, Exhibit 625, 2756.
70 **Consul Rieloff next instructed:** Affidavit of William H. Gleaves, January 31, 1927, NARA, RG76, MCC, United States and Germany 1922–1939, Printed United States Exhibits, Exhibit 329, 1255.
70 **"thought he could accomplish something":** Affidavit of William H. Gleaves, January 31, 1927, NARA, RG76, MCC, United States and Germany 1922–1939, Printed United States Exhibits, Exhibit 329, 1255.
70 **While biding his time:** Affidavit of William H. Gleaves, January 31, 1927, NARA, RG76, MCC, United States and Germany 1922–1939, Printed United States Exhibits, Exhibit 329, 1255–66.
70 **"The black traitor":** "German Spies in America," *Liberty Magazine*, May 2, 1931, 70.
70 **Consul Rieloff told Gleaves:** Details of Gleaves's meeting with the "Revolutionary Association" in Mexico City from: Testimony of William Gleaves, NARA, RG76, MCC, United States and Germany 1922–1939, Printed United States Exhibits, Exhibit 321, 1008–15, 1020–27.
72 **It had been a beautiful afternoon:** Details of Dr. Altendorf's meeting with Major Campbell from: Testimony of Major R. M. Campbell, NARA, RG76, MCC, United States and Germany 1922–1939, Printed United States Exhibits, Exhibit 321, 1029–31; Memorandum from Major R. M. Campbell to Van Deman, "Subject: Revolutionary Group," March 18, 1918, NARA, MID 10541-367, 1–2.
74 **Paul Bernardo Altendorf was born:** Background information on Paul Bernardo Altendorf is from: Paul Bernardo Altendorf, Questionnaire for Applicant for the Corps of Interpreters, May 1, 1919, NARA, RG165, Records of the War Department and Special Staffs, Military Intelligence Division, File 51-45; Captain Henry G. Pratt, Memorandum for Colonel Martin, April 10, 1919, NARA, RG165, Records of the War Department and Special Staffs, Military Intelligence Division, File 51-45.

74   **"deserted the country to avoid service":** Altendorf, Questionnaire for Applicant for the Corps of Interpreters, May 1, 1919, NARA, RG165, File 51-45.

74   **"When the world war began":** Altendorf, "On Secret Service in Mexico," *El Paso Herald*, November 3, 1919, 4; *Investigation of Mexican Affairs: Preliminary Report and Hearings of the Committee on Foreign Relations United States Senate Pursuant to S. Res. 106* (Washington, DC: Government Printing Office, 1920), 1229–30.

75   **"As the train pulled into the station":** Altendorf, "On Secret Service in Mexico," *El Paso Herald*, November 5, 1919, 1.

75   **"We had a little conversation":** Testimony of Paul B. Altendorf, NARA, RG76, MCC, United States and Germany 1922–1939, Printed United States Exhibits, Exhibit 321, 963.

75   **After a few days spent:** Details of the meeting between Altendorf and Jahnke from: Altendorf, "On Secret Service in Mexico," *El Paso Herald*, November 5, 1919, 10.

76   **Fate intervened and Altendorf awoke:** Altendorf, "My Trip to Mexico," NARA, MID 10541-268, 3.

76   **"He called on Ambassador von Eckhardt":** Altendorf, "On Secret Service in Mexico," *El Paso Herald*, November 5, 1919, 10.

76   **On September 13, 1917, Altendorf was discharged:** Altendorf, "On Secret Service in Mexico," *El Paso Herald*, November 6, 1919, 1; Altendorf, "My Trip to Mexico," NARA, MID 10541-268, 2; Testimony of Paul B. Altendorf, NARA, RG76, MCC, United States and Germany 1922–1939, Printed United States Exhibits, Exhibit 321, 963.

76   **From October into November:** Testimony of Paul B. Altendorf, NARA, RG76, MCC, United States and Germany 1922–1939, Printed United States Exhibits, Exhibit 321, 968.

77   **Weeks later, in a turbulent meeting:** Details of the meeting between Altendorf, Schwierz, and Calles from: Paul Bernardo Altendorf, "American Spy Has German Banished into United States against Which He Has Been Plotting from Mexico," *El Paso Herald*, November 13, 1919, 1, 5.

77   **While he was scheming to discredit Major Schwierz:** Paul Bernardo Altendorf, "German Spy Agents Get Warm Welcome from Mexicans as They Travel across Country Plotting against U.S.," *El Paso Herald*, November 7, 1919, 10.

77   **"A Turk who could speak perfect English":** Paul Bernardo Altendorf, "Calles Admits to American Agent That Invasion of United States from Mexico Secretly Planned," *El Paso Herald*, November 10, 1919, 5.

77   **Butcher sent a communiqué:** Memorandum from Major S. W. Anding, 25th Infantry Intelligence Officer, to War Department Intelligence Officer, Fort Sam Houston, Texas, "Subject: Report of German Activity," December

4, 1917, NARA, RG165, Records of the War Department and Special Staffs, Military Intelligence Division, File 51-45.

78 **This man [Altendorf, A-1] has been:** Memorandum from Major S. W. Anding, 25th Infantry Intelligence Officer, to Department Intelligence Officer, Fort Sam Houston, Texas, "Subject: Informant A-1," December 16, 1917, NARA, RG165, Records of the War Department and Special Staffs, Military Intelligence Division, File 51-45.

78 **I forwarded a copy of your letter:** Letter from Major Robert L. Barnes, Department Intelligence Officer, Fort Sam Houston, Texas, to Major S. W. Anding, December 10, 1917, NARA, RG165, Records of the War Department and Special Staffs, Military Intelligence Division, File 51-45.

78 **On December 13, 1917:** Paul Bernardo Altendorf, "American Secret Agent Discovers a German Plot in Mexico to Bomb El Paso and Other Cities on Border," *El Paso Herald*, November 17, 1919, 3; Testimony of Byron S. Butcher, NARA, RG76, MCC, United States and Germany 1922–1939, Printed United States Exhibits, Exhibit 321, 1074.

78 **The Austrian doctor was in an ideal:** Altendorf, "U.S. Agent in Mexico Invades German Spy Files; El Paso Letter Reveals Plot to Blow Up Canal," *El Paso Herald*, November 21, 1919, 1, 7; Testimony of Paul B. Altendorf, NARA, RG76, MCC, United States and Germany 1922–1939, Printed United States Exhibits, Exhibit 321, 969; Paul B. Altendorf, "My Trip to Mexico," NARA, MID 10541-268, 3–4.

79 **A dinner party had been organized:** Information on the dinner party of German agents from: Altendorf, "U.S. Agent Is Ordered to Join Mission to Border to Arrange Mexican-German Invasion of U.S.," *El Paso Herald*, November 22, 1919, 12; Testimony of Paul B. Altendorf, NARA, RG76, MCC, United States and Germany 1922–1939, Printed United States Exhibits, Exhibit 321, 976–77.

CHAPTER 5

81 **The house at Calle Colonia No. 4:** Paul Bernardo Altendorf, "U.S. Agent Gets German Spy Drunk Making Copies of Secret Papers; Finds British Agent Trailing Spy," *El Paso Herald*, November 25, 1919, 1; Altendorf, "My Trip to Mexico," NARA, MID 10541-268, 6; Testimony of Paul B. Altendorf, NARA, RG76, MCC, United States and Germany 1922–1939, Printed United States Exhibits, Exhibit 321, 978–79, 991–92.

82 **Arriving at the station on time:** Altendorf, "U.S. Agent Gets German Spy Drunk Making Copies of Secret Papers," 1; Testimony of Paul B. Altendorf, NARA, RG76, MCC, United States and Germany 1922–1939, Printed United States Exhibits, Exhibit 321, 979–80.

83 **The region around Guadalajara is famed:** Altendorf's and Witzke's experience in Guadalajara from: Altendorf, "U.S. Agent Gets German Spy Drunk Making Copies of Secret Papers," 1; Altendorf, "My Trip to Mexico," NARA, MID 10541-268, 6–7; Testimony of Paul B. Altendorf, NARA, RG76, MCC, United States and Germany 1922–1939, Printed United States Exhibits, Exhibit 321, 980–81.

84 **"I spent a large part of the night":** Altendorf, "U.S. Agent Gets German Spy Drunk Making Copies of Secret Papers," 1.

84 **"Doctor, has the door been closed":** Testimony of Paul B. Altendorf, NARA, RG76, MCC, United States and Germany 1922–1939, Printed United States Exhibits, Exhibit 321, 981.

84 **"He said that wine and women":** Affidavit of Alfred Edward Woodley Mason, February 15, 1929, NARA, RG76, MCC, United States and Germany 1922–1939, Printed United States Exhibits, Exhibit 625, 2760.

85 **Witzke returned to their room:** Altendorf, "U.S. Agent Gets German Spy Drunk Making Copies of Secret Papers," 1.

85 **When they called at the company:** Altendorf, "U.S. Agent Gets German Spy Drunk Making Copies of Secret Papers," 1, 10; Testimony of Paul B. Altendorf, NARA, RG76, MCC, United States and Germany 1922–1939, Printed United States Exhibits, Exhibit 321, 637.

85 **After the fruitless meeting:** Altendorf, "U.S. Agent Gets German Spy Drunk Making Copies of Secret Papers," 10.

85 **The extended stopover in Guadalajara:** Information on the train ride from Guadalajara to Manzanillo from: Altendorf, "U.S. Agent Gets German Spy Drunk Making Copies of Secret Papers," 10; Testimony of Paul B. Altendorf, NARA, RG76, MCC, United States and Germany 1922–1939, Printed United States Exhibits, Exhibit 321, 981–82, 1015–16; Altendorf, "My Trip to Mexico," NARA, MID 10541-268, 7.

85 **"I must leave . . . I've got to meet":** Testimony of Paul B. Altendorf, NARA, RG76, MCC, United States and Germany 1922–1939, Printed United States Exhibits, Exhibit 321, 981.

86 **"I don't mind the amount of money":** Testimony of Paul B. Altendorf, NARA, RG76, MCC, United States and Germany 1922–1939, Printed United States Exhibits, Exhibit 321, 981.

86 **The locomotive only traveled:** Altendorf, "U.S. Agent Gets German Spy Drunk Making Copies of Secret Papers," 10; Testimony of Paul B. Altendorf, NARA, RG76, MCC, United States and Germany 1922–1939, Printed United States Exhibits, Exhibit 321, 982.

86 **"There is a negro on the pilot":** Altendorf, "U.S. Agent Gets German Spy Drunk Making Copies of Secret Papers," 10; Altendorf, "My Trip to Mexico," NARA, MID 10541-268, 7; Testimony of Paul B. Altendorf, NARA, RG76, MCC, United States and Germany 1922–1939, Printed United States Exhibits, Exhibit 321, 982.

86 **"Now, G-d damn you"**: Altendorf, "My Trip to Mexico," NARA, MID 10541-268, 7.

86 **"I know everything else"**: Testimony of Paul B. Altendorf, NARA, RG76, MCC, United States and Germany 1922–1939, Printed United States Exhibits, Exhibit 321, 982.

86 **When the locomotive reached a point:** Altendorf, "U.S. Agent Gets German Spy Drunk Making Copies of Secret Papers," 10.

87 **They reached Manzanillo:** Altendorf, "My Trip to Mexico," NARA, MID 10541-268, 7.

87 **"Is the doctor also in this case?":** Testimony of Paul B. Altendorf, NARA, RG76, MCC, United States and Germany 1922–1939, Printed United States Exhibits, Exhibit 321, 982.

87 **"Yes, he will help us at the border":** Testimony of Paul B. Altendorf, NARA, RG76, MCC, United States and Germany 1922–1939, Printed United States Exhibits, Exhibit 321, 982; Altendorf, "My Trip to Mexico," NARA, MID 10541-268, 8.

87 **"By Jove, 'Waberski'":** Testimony of Paul B. Altendorf, NARA, RG76, MCC, United States and Germany 1922–1939, Printed United States Exhibits, Exhibit 321, 982–83.

87 **"The Minister is our friend":** Testimony of Paul B. Altendorf, NARA, RG76, MCC, United States and Germany 1922–1939, Printed United States Exhibits, Exhibit 321, 983.

87 **In reality the agent had:** "Spy," *American Foreign Service Journal* 11, no. 11 (November 1934): 583, 627.

87 **"Russia was giving signs":** "Spy," *American Foreign Service Journal* 11, no. 11 (November 1934): 627.

88 **Witzke tore open the envelope:** Information on Witzke receiving and interpreting Jahnke's letter from: Testimony of Paul B. Altendorf, NARA, RG76, MCC, United States and Germany 1922–1939, Printed United States Exhibits, Exhibit 321, 983; Altendorf, "My Trip to Mexico," NARA, MID 10541-268, 8.

88 **"This letter is from Jahnke":** Altendorf, "My Trip to Mexico," NARA, MID 10541-268, 8–9.

88 **The next day Witzke departed:** Information on Altendorf's meeting with Gleaves in the Manzanillo city plaza from: Altendorf, "My Trip to Mexico," NARA, MID 10541-268, 8; "Special Border Report from Captain Joel A. Lipscomb," February 4, 1918, NARA, RG76, MCC, United States and Germany 1922–1939, Printed United States Exhibits, Exhibit 226, 610; "Special Border Report from Captain Joel A. Lipscomb," February 2, 1918, NARA, RG76, MCC, United States and Germany 1922–1939, Printed United States Exhibits, Exhibit 228, 633.

89 **Later that afternoon, when Witzke learned:** Witzke's discussion with Altendorf regarding Gleaves is found in: Altendorf, "My Trip to Mexico,"

NARA, MID 10541-268, 8; "Special Border Report from Captain Joel A. Lipscomb," February 4, 1918, NARA, RG76, MCC, United States and Germany 1922–1939, Printed United States Exhibits, Exhibit 226, 610; "Special Border Report from Captain Joel A. Lipscomb," February 2, 1918, NARA, RG76, MCC, United States and Germany 1922–1939, Printed United States Exhibits, Exhibit 228, 633.

89   **That afternoon Witzke and Altendorf:** The story of Witzke's and Altendorf's encounter with the three U.S. naval officers is related in: Altendorf, "My Trip to Mexico," NARA, MID 10541-268, 9.

90   **"What do you think about blowing up":** Altendorf, "My Trip to Mexico," NARA, MID 10541-268, 9–10.

90   **The next morning, Altendorf and Witzke:** Altendorf, "U.S. Agent Gets German Spy Drunk Making Copies of Secret Papers," 10; "Special Border Report from Captain Joel A. Lipscomb," February 4, 1918, NARA, RG76, MCC, United States and Germany 1922–1939, Printed United States Exhibits, Exhibit 226, 610; "Special Border Report from Captain Joel A. Lipscomb," February 2, 1918, NARA, RG76, MCC, United States and Germany 1922–1939, Printed United States Exhibits, Exhibit 228, 633.

CHAPTER 6

93   **On January 24, 1918:** "The West Coast of Mexico," *Journal of Electricity*, January 15, 1917, 393.

93   **Suggesting that they should not be seen:** Altendorf, "My Trip to Mexico," NARA, MID 10541-268, 10; "Special Border Report from Captain Joel A. Lipscomb," February 4, 1918, NARA, RG76, MCC, United States and Germany 1922–1939, Printed United States Exhibits, Exhibit 226, 610.

93   **Mazatlán's favorable location:** "Mazatlán," in *Annual Report of the Board of Harbor Commissioners of the City of Los Angeles* (Los Angeles: Board of Harbor Commissioners of the City of Los Angeles, California, 1917), 19.

94   **Although Mazatlán had suffered:** Bill Mills, *Treacherous Passage* (Lincoln: University of Nebraska Press, 2017), 22.

94   **Friedrich Heinrich "Fritz" Unger:** *Melchers Sucs Mazatlán 1846–1921* (corporate history published to commemorate the company's seventy-fifth anniversary) (Mazatlán: Casa Melchers Sucs, 1921), 7, 20, 21.

94   **"Always immaculately attired":** Mills, *Treacherous Passage*, 22–23.

95   **Unger responded by engaging:** Mills, *Treacherous Passage*, 23; Paul Bernardo Altendorf, "German Submarines as Effective in Commerce as in Murder at Sea; Carried Food Cargoes from Mexico," *El Paso Herald*, November 28, 1919, 1; Report by H. B. Mock, "In re: One Connors, Pro-German Subject and Espionage Act Investigation," September 28, 1917, NARA, M1085, In-

vestigating Case Files of the Bureau of Investigation 1908–1922, Roll boi_german_257-850_0069, Case No. 162413, 9.

95 **The German consul's schemes:** Background of William Edgar Chapman from: "Biographical Statement Respecting Persons Serving under Appointment of the Department of State," *Register of the Department of State 23 December 1918* (Washington, DC: Government Printing Office, 1919), 94.

96 **As late as December 19, 1917:** Memorandum from W. E. Chapman to Secretary of State, March 10, 1918, NARA, RG59, Records of the Department of State, Neutral Commerce, M367, Roll 0225, Document No. 763.72112/7770; Memorandum Commanding Officer U.S.S. Brutus to Commander Division Two, Pacific Fleet (State Department Copy), February 28, 1918, NARA, RG59, Neutrality, M367, Roll 0227, Document No. 763.72112/8566; Letter from W. E. Chapman to Secretary of State, September 7, 1917, NARA, RG59, Neutral Commerce, M367, Roll 0215, Document No. 763.72112/4679.

96 **Chapman's greatest coup:** Letter from Leland Harrison to A. Bruce Bielaski, May 18, 1918, NARA, M1085, BI Files, Old German Files, Roll boi_german_257-850_0103, Case No. 8000-233186, 11; Letter from W. E. Chapman to Secretary of State, April 27, 1918, NARA, M1085, BI Files, Old German Files, Roll boi_german_257-850_0103, Case No. 8000-233186, 3–4.

96 **In the days that followed:** Letter from W. E. Chapman to Secretary of State, April 27, 1918, NARA, M1085, BI Files, Old German Files, Roll boi_german_257-850_0103, Case No. 8000-233186, 4–5.

97 **He admitted further that:** Letter from W. E. Chapman to Secretary of State, April 27, 1918, NARA, M1085, BI Files, Old German Files, Roll boi_german_257-850_0103, Case No. 8000-233186, 5–6.

97 **Jacobsen left the consulate:** Letter from W. E. Chapman to Secretary of State, April 27, 1918, NARA, M1085, BI Files, Old German Files, Roll boi_german_257-850_0103, Case No. 8000-233186, 6–7.

97 **Altendorf rose early on the morning:** Altendorf, "My Trip to Mexico," NARA, MID 10541-268, 10; Testimony of Paul B. Altendorf, NARA, RG76, MCC, United States and Germany 1922–1939, Printed United States Exhibits, Exhibit 321, 984; Charles Harris III and Louis R. Sadler, *The Border and the Revolution* (Silver City, NM: High Lonesome Books, 1988), 113.

98 **"that he [Altendorf] was en route":** Harris and Sadler, *The Border and the Revolution*, 113.

98 **The doctor entered the fortresslike headquarters:** Altendorf's visit to the German embassy in Mazatlán from: Testimony of Paul B. Altendorf, NARA, RG76, MCC, United States and Germany 1922–1939, Printed United States Exhibits, Exhibit 321, 984–85, 1109–12.

98 **It was standard procedure for German agents:** Testimony of Paul B. Altendorf, NARA, RG76, MCC, United States and Germany 1922–1939, Printed United States Exhibits, Exhibit 321, 1109–12.

98   **"The Waberski cipher proved to be an immensely":** David Kahn, *The Reader of Gentlemen's Mail* (New Haven, CT: Yale University Press, 2004), 43.

98   **Witzke asked Unger about "some items":** Testimony of Paul B. Altendorf, NARA, RG76, MCC, United States and Germany 1922–1939, Printed United States Exhibits, Exhibit 321, 985.

99   **They returned to the administration building:** "Special Border Report from Captain Joel A. Lipscomb," February 4, 1918, NARA, RG76, MCC, United States and Germany 1922–1939, Printed United States Exhibits, Exhibit 226, 611.

99   **"That is Waberski's man":** "Special Border Report from Captain Joel A. Lipscomb," February 4, 1918, NARA, RG76, MCC, United States and Germany 1922–1939, Printed United States Exhibits, Exhibit 226, 611.

99   **Altendorf gave the "third man":** "Special Border Report from Captain Joel A. Lipscomb," February 4, 1918, NARA, RG76, MCC, United States and Germany 1922–1939, Printed United States Exhibits, Exhibit 226, 611.

99   **"You must have patience":** Testimony of Paul B. Altendorf, NARA, RG76, MCC, United States and Germany 1922–1939, Printed United States Exhibits, Exhibit 321, 985–86.

99   **Before leaving Mazatlán:** Altendorf, "U.S. Agent Gets German Spy Drunk Making Copies of Secret Papers," 10.

99   **An hour before sunrise:** Information on Altendorf's second visit to the U.S. consulate in Mazatlán from: Altendorf, "My Trip to Mexico," NARA, MID 10541-268, 10; Testimony of Paul B. Altendorf, NARA, RG76, MCC, United States and Germany 1922–1939, Printed United States Exhibits, Exhibit 321, 984; "Special Border Report from Captain Joel A. Lipscomb," February 4, 1918, NARA, RG76, MCC, United States and Germany 1922–1939, Printed United States Exhibits, Exhibit 226, 611; Landau, *The Enemy Within*, 118.

99   **Chapman advised that:** "Special Border Report from Captain Joel A. Lipscomb," February 4, 1918, NARA, RG76, MCC, United States and Germany 1922–1939, Printed United States Exhibits, Exhibit 226, 611.

100   **Altendorf's survival as a double agent:** "Special Border Report from Captain Joel A. Lipscomb," February 4, 1918, NARA, RG76, MCC, United States and Germany 1922–1939, Printed United States Exhibits, Exhibit 226, 617.

100   **JANUARY 26—TO BUTCHER FROM A-1:** "Special Border Report from Captain Joel A. Lipscomb," February 2, 1918, NARA, RG76, MCC, United States and Germany 1922–1939, Printed United States Exhibits, Exhibit 228, 629.

101   **Hours later, Witzke, Gleaves, and Altendorf:** Testimony of Paul B. Altendorf, NARA, RG76, MCC, United States and Germany 1922–1939, Printed United States Exhibits, Exhibit 321, 986; "Special Border Report from Captain Joel A. Lipscomb," February 2, 1918, NARA, RG76, MCC,

United States and Germany 1922–1939, Printed United States Exhibits, Exhibit 228, 633.

101 **Like Friedrich Unger in Mazatlán:** Letter from Consul Frederick Simpich to Secretary of State, September 23, 1917, NARA, M1085, BI Files, Old German Files, Roll boi_german_257-850_0068, Case No. 53592, 95–96.

101 **The visit to Guaymas:** Testimony of Paul B. Altendorf, NARA, RG76, MCC, United States and Germany 1922–1939, Printed United States Exhibits, Exhibit 321, 986–87.

101 **After a few hours of sleep:** "Special Border Report from Captain Joel A. Lipscomb," February 4, 1918, NARA, RG76, MCC, United States and Germany 1922–1939, Printed United States Exhibits, Exhibit 226, 611–12.

101 **When the train got underway:** "Special Border Report from Captain Joel A. Lipscomb," February 2, 1918, NARA, RG76, MCC, United States and Germany 1922–1939, Printed United States Exhibits, Exhibit 228, 633; "Special Border Report from Captain Joel A. Lipscomb," February 4, 1918, NARA, RG76, MCC, United States and Germany 1922–1939, Printed United States Exhibits, Exhibit 226, 612–13, 615; Testimony of Paul B. Altendorf, NARA, RG76, MCC, United States and Germany 1922–1939, Printed United States Exhibits, Exhibit 321, 987.

102 **"I have gotten rid of over one hundred":** Landau, *The Enemy Within*, 118; "Special Border Report from Captain Joel A. Lipscomb," February 2, 1918, NARA, RG76, MCC, United States and Germany 1922–1939, Printed United States Exhibits, Exhibit 228, 633; Testimony of Paul B. Altendorf, NARA, RG76, MCC, United States and Germany 1922–1939, Printed United States Exhibits, Exhibit 321, 987; "Special Border Report from Captain Joel A. Lipscomb," February 4, 1918, NARA, RG76, MCC, United States and Germany 1922–1939, Printed United States Exhibits, Exhibit 226, 612.

102 **The train pulled into:** "Special Border Report from Captain Joel A. Lipscomb," February 4, 1918, NARA, RG76, MCC, United States and Germany 1922–1939, Printed United States Exhibits, Exhibit 226, 612.

102 **"thorough dressing down":** Harris and Sadler, *The Border and the Revolution*, 120.

102 **Since he was traveling:** "Special Border Report from Captain Joel A. Lipscomb," February 2, 1918, NARA, RG76, MCC, United States and Germany 1922–1939, Printed United States Exhibits, Exhibit 228, 634.

103 **Altendorf checked into the Cohen:** Testimony of Paul B. Altendorf, NARA, RG76, MCC, United States and Germany 1922–1939, Printed United States Exhibits, Exhibit 321, 987.

103 **The two agents arrived:** Description of Calles's Hermosillo Palacio de Gobierno from: "Calles Admits to American Agent That Invasion of United States From Mexico Secretly Planned," *El Paso Herald*, November 10, 1919, 1, 5.

103 **Calles was a big man:** Details of the meeting between Altendorf, Witzke, and Calles are found in: Altendorf, "U.S. Agent Gets German Spy Drunk

Making Copies of Secret Papers," 10; "Special Border Report from Captain Joel A. Lipscomb," February 2, 1918, NARA, RG76, MCC, United States and Germany 1922–1939, Printed United States Exhibits, Exhibit 228, 634–35, 637; Testimony of Paul B. Altendorf, NARA, RG76, MCC, United States and Germany 1922–1939, Printed United States Exhibits, Exhibit 321, 987–88; Landau, *The Enemy Within*, 118.

103   **"Witzke, with Altendorf acting as interpreter":** "Special Border Report from Captain Joel A. Lipscomb," February 2, 1918, NARA, RG76, MCC, United States and Germany 1922–1939, Printed United States Exhibits, Exhibit 228, 634–35.

104   **Recently a German agent:** "Special Border Report from Captain Joel A. Lipscomb," February 2, 1918, NARA, RG76, MCC, United States and Germany 1922–1939, Printed United States Exhibits, Exhibit 228, 637.

104   **Republica Mexicana. Ayuntamiento de Hermosillo:** Testimony of Paul B. Altendorf, NARA, RG76, MCC, United States and Germany 1922–1939, Printed United States Exhibits, Exhibit 321, 993–94.

105   **"I can say now, doctor":** Testimony of Paul B. Altendorf, NARA, RG76, MCC, United States and Germany 1922–1939, Printed United States Exhibits, Exhibit 321, 988.

105   **Witzke assured Altendorf:** Testimony of Paul B. Altendorf, NARA, RG76, MCC, United States and Germany 1922–1939, Printed United States Exhibits, Exhibit 321, 988.

105   **"The ambassador and Jahnke think very highly":** "Special Border Report from Captain Joel A. Lipscomb," February 2, 1918, NARA, RG76, MCC, United States and Germany 1922–1939, Printed United States Exhibits, Exhibit 228, 632.

CHAPTER 7

107   **Gleaves arrived in Nogales:** "Special Border Report from Captain Joel A. Lipscomb," February 4, 1918, NARA, RG76, MCC, United States and Germany 1922–1939, Printed United States Exhibits, Exhibit 226, 614–15.

108   **Witzke also directed Gleaves:** Testimony of William Gleaves, NARA, RG76, MCC, United States and Germany 1922–1939, Printed United States Exhibits, Exhibit 321, 1017–18, 1026.

108   **On the third day after arriving:** Testimony of William Gleaves, NARA, RG76, MCC, United States and Germany 1922–1939, Printed United States Exhibits, Exhibit 321, 1018–19.

108   **"Get some good colored men":** Testimony of William Gleaves, NARA, RG76, MCC, United States and Germany 1922–1939, Printed United States Exhibits, Exhibit 321, 1019.

108 **They parted company:** Details of Witzke meeting the army deserter are found in: Testimony of William Gleaves, NARA, RG76, MCC, United States and Germany 1922–1939, Printed United States Exhibits, Exhibit 321, 1019, 1026.

108 **Gleaves asked the ex-soldier to wait:** Details of Witzke meeting the army deserter are found in: Testimony of William Gleaves, NARA, RG76, MCC, United States and Germany 1922–1939, Printed United States Exhibits, Exhibit 321, 1019; "Special Border Report from Captain Joel A. Lipscomb," February 4, 1918, NARA, RG76, MCC, United States and Germany 1922–1939, Printed United States Exhibits, Exhibit 226, 615.

109 **In the afternoon, Witzke presided:** Affidavit of Oskar Sholars, February 6, 1927, NARA, RG76, MCC, United States and Germany 1922–1939, Printed United States Exhibits, Exhibit 349, 1310–12; Affidavit of William Colton, known as "Big Hat," February 11, 1927, NARA, RG76, MCC, United States and Germany 1922–1939, Printed United States Exhibits, Exhibit 350, 1313–15.

109 **In the discussion that followed:** Affidavit of William Colton, known as "Big Hat," February 11, 1927, NARA, RG76, MCC, United States and Germany 1922–1939, Printed United States Exhibits, Exhibit 350, 1313–15.

109 **That evening Gleaves reported:** Testimony of William Gleaves, NARA, RG76, MCC, United States and Germany 1922–1939, Printed United States Exhibits, Exhibit 321, 1020.

109 **"I have a considerable amount of money":** Testimony of William Gleaves, NARA, RG76, MCC, United States and Germany 1922–1939, Printed United States Exhibits, Exhibit 321, 1020.

109 **In two days (on February 2):** Testimony of William Gleaves, NARA, RG76, MCC, United States and Germany 1922–1939, Printed United States Exhibits, Exhibit 321, 1010–11; "Special Border Report from Captain Joel A. Lipscomb," February 4, 1918, NARA, RG76, MCC, United States and Germany 1922–1939, Printed United States Exhibits, Exhibit 226, 617.

110 **"Aren't you scared to cross":** Testimony of William Gleaves, NARA, RG76, MCC, United States and Germany 1922–1939, Printed United States Exhibits, Exhibit 321, 1021.

110 **After Altendorf finished shaving:** Altendorf, "U.S. Agent Gets German Spy Drunk Making Copies of Secret Papers; Finds British Agent Trailing Spy," *El Paso Herald*, November 25, 1919, 10.

110 **Altendorf rushed to the station:** Altendorf, "U.S. Agent Gets German Spy Drunk Making Copies of Secret Papers," 10; Testimony of Paul B. Altendorf, NARA, RG76, MCC, United States and Germany 1922–1939, Printed United States Exhibits, Exhibit 321, 989.

110 **At that moment Special Agent:** Testimony of Byron S. Butcher, NARA, RG76, MCC, United States and Germany 1922–1939, Printed United States Exhibits, Exhibit 321, 1048.

110 **"that he was on his way to the line":** Testimony of Byron S. Butcher, NARA, RG76, MCC, United States and Germany 1922–1939, Printed United States Exhibits, Exhibit 321, 1048.

110 **Based on past surveillance:** Testimony of Byron S. Butcher, NARA, RG76, MCC, United States and Germany 1922–1939, Printed United States Exhibits, Exhibit 321, 1048.

111 **The leading newspaper in Nogales:** *Border Vidette* (Nogales, AZ), January 26, 1918, 1.

111 TO WIN THIS WAR GERMAN SPIES: "To Win This War German Spies Must Be Jailed" (advertising coupon), *Border Vidette* (Nogales, AZ), January 26, 1918, 2.

112 **"The reports of all members":** "One Hundred Percent American Club," *Daily Morning Oasis* (Nogales, AZ), January 3, 1918, 2.

112 **On the night of January 30:** "Special Border Report from Captain Joel A. Lipscomb," February 2, 1918, NARA, RG76, MCC, United States and Germany 1922–1939, Printed United States Exhibits, Exhibit 228, 635.

112 **The next morning Consul Ezra Lawton:** Information on Witzke's arrival at the U.S. consulate at Nogales, Sonora, from: Testimony of Ezra M. Lawton, August 17, 1918, NARA, RG76, MCC, United States and Germany 1922–1939, Printed United States Exhibits, Exhibit 321, 1081–86.

112 **The consul also advised Witzke:** Testimony of Ezra M. Lawton, NARA, RG76, MCC, United States and Germany 1922–1939, Printed United States Exhibits, Exhibit 321, 1085.

113 **Lawton went to the telephone:** Testimony of Ezra M. Lawton, NARA, RG76, MCC, United States and Germany 1922–1939, Printed United States Exhibits, Exhibit 321, 1084–85; Testimony of Byron S. Butcher, NARA, RG76, MCC, United States and Germany 1922–1939, Printed United States Exhibits, Exhibit 321, 1048–49.

113 **His business in Mexico was:** Testimony of Charles L. Beatty, August, 17, 1918, NARA, RG76, MCC, United States and Germany 1922–1939, Printed United States Exhibits, Exhibit 321, 1040.

113 **"Going to join friend":** Testimony of Charles L. Beatty, NARA, RG76, MCC, United States and Germany 1922–1939, Printed United States Exhibits, Exhibit 321, 1037.

113 **Witzke made two trips over the border:** Testimony of Ezra M. Lawton, NARA, RG76, MCC, United States and Germany 1922–1939, Printed United States Exhibits, Exhibit 321, 1085; Testimony of Byron S. Butcher, NARA, RG76, MCC, United States and Germany 1922–1939, Printed United States Exhibits, Exhibit 321, 1049; Testimony of Lothar Witzke (Pablo Waberski), August 17, 1918, NARA, RG76, MCC, United States and Germany 1922–1939, Printed United States Exhibits, Exhibit 321, 1137–39.

114 **With each crossing:** "Special Border Report from Captain Joel A. Lipscomb," February 2, 1918, NARA, RG76, MCC, United States and Germany 1922–1939, Printed United States Exhibits, Exhibit 228, 636; Testimony of Byron S. Butcher, NARA, RG76, MCC, United States and Germany 1922–1939, Printed United States Exhibits, Exhibit 321, 1049.

114 **Butcher knew that he would need:** Testimony of Byron S. Butcher, NARA, RG76, MCC, United States and Germany 1922–1939, Printed United States Exhibits, Exhibit 321, 1049.

114 **After Witzke was taken:** Testimony of Byron S. Butcher, NARA, RG76, MCC, United States and Germany 1922–1939, Printed United States Exhibits, Exhibit 321, 1049.

114 **W. G. "Wirt" Bowman was the proverbial:** Report of Alfred S. Northrup, "Wirt G. Bowman, Alleged Violation of Neutrality Laws," July 30, 1918, NARA, M1085, Investigating Case Files of the Bureau of Investigation 1908–1922, Roll boi_german_257-850_0088, Case No. 8000-18765, 130–32.

115 **"stands for the extermination":** Untitled news brief, *Santa Cruz Patagonian,* January 4, 1918, 1.

115 **"That's what Wirt Bowman likes":** Report of Alfred S. Northrup, "Wirt G. Bowman, Alleged Violation of Neutrality Laws," 132.

115 **At nine o'clock that night:** Testimony of Paul B. Altendorf, NARA, RG76, MCC, United States and Germany 1922–1939, Printed United States Exhibits, Exhibit 321, 989–90; "Special Border Report from Captain Joel A. Lipscomb," February 2, 1918, NARA, RG76, MCC, United States and Germany 1922–1939, Printed United States Exhibits, Exhibit 228, 636.

115 **"the German always carried his papers":** "Special Border Report from Captain Joel A. Lipscomb," February 2, 1918, NARA, RG76, MCC, United States and Germany 1922–1939, Printed United States Exhibits, Exhibit 228, 636.

115 **Witzke checked the gold coins:** Testimony of Byron S. Butcher, NARA, RG76, MCC, United States and Germany 1922–1939, Printed United States Exhibits, Exhibit 321, 1050–51.

116 **I had a very real premonition of danger:** "Spy," *American Foreign Service Journal* 11, no. 11 (November 1934): 627.

116 **Shortly before nine o'clock:** Testimony of Byron S. Butcher, NARA, RG76, MCC, United States and Germany 1922–1939, Printed United States Exhibits, Exhibit 321, 1049.

116 **For nearly an hour:** "Special Border Report from Captain Joel A. Lipscomb," February 2, 1918, NARA, RG76, MCC, United States and Germany 1922–1939, Printed United States Exhibits, Exhibit 228, 636.

116 **The intelligence officer directed Smart:** Testimony of Byron S. Butcher, NARA, RG76, MCC, United States and Germany 1922–1939, Printed United States Exhibits, Exhibit 321, 1049.

116   **"Halt! Hands up!":** Altendorf, "U.S. Agent Gets German Spy Drunk Making Copies of Secret Papers," 10.

116   **"I suppose you think":** Paul Bernardo Altendorf, "U.S. Agent's Work Traps at Border German Spy on Mission of Murder; Captured Papers Bare Secret Code," *El Paso Herald*, November 26, 1919, 1.

117   **The enemy agent was spun:** Testimony of Byron S. Butcher, NARA, RG76, MCC, United States and Germany 1922–1939, Printed United States Exhibits, Exhibit 321, 1049; Testimony of Paul B. Altendorf, NARA, RG76, MCC, United States and Germany 1922–1939, Printed United States Exhibits, Exhibit 321, 990.

117   **At the base intelligence office:** Testimony of Byron S. Butcher, NARA, RG76, MCC, United States and Germany 1922–1939, Printed United States Exhibits, Exhibit 321, 1050–67; Testimony of Captain Joel A. Lipscomb, August 17, 1918, NARA, RG76, MCC, United States and Germany 1922–1939, Printed United States Exhibits, Exhibit 321, 1089–94.

117   **Witzke refused to answer any questions:** "Special Border Report from Captain Joel A. Lipscomb," February 2, 1918, NARA, RG76, MCC, United States and Germany 1922–1939, Printed United States Exhibits, Exhibit 228, 636.

117   **"If he makes a wrong move":** Altendorf, "U.S. Agent's Work Traps at Border German Spy on Mission of Murder; Captured Papers Bare Secret Code," *El Paso Herald*, November 26, 1919, 10.

117   **Within hours Butcher and Lipscomb:** Landau, *The Enemy Within*, 121; Testimony of Byron S. Butcher, NARA, RG76, MCC, United States and Germany 1922–1939, Printed United States Exhibits, Exhibit 321, 1050, 1080.

118   **The Americans were successful:** "Spy," *American Foreign Service Journal* 11, no. 11 (November 1934): 627.

118   **Butcher's satisfaction at obtaining:** Landau, *The Enemy Within*, 121.

118   **Over the next two days:** Testimony of Captain Joel A. Lipscomb, NARA, RG76, MCC, United States and Germany 1922–1939, Printed United States Exhibits, Exhibit 321, 1094; Testimony of Major Robert L. Barnes, August 17, 1918, NARA, RG76, MCC, United States and Germany 1922–1939, Printed United States Exhibits, Exhibit 321, 1098–99.

118   **In Sonora, Pablo's sudden disappearance:** "Special Border Report from Captain Joel A. Lipscomb," February 4, 1918, NARA, RG76, MCC, United States and Germany 1922–1939, Printed United States Exhibits, Exhibit 226, 609, 617.

119   **William H. Gleaves had been born:** "German Spies in America," *Liberty Magazine*, May 2, 1931, 70; Landau, *The Enemy Within*, 114–15; Testimony of William Gleaves, NARA, RG76, MCC, United States and Germany 1922–1939, Printed United States Exhibits, Exhibit 321, 1007–8, 1012–13; Testi-

mony of William Gleaves, NARA, RG76, MCC, United States and Germany 1922–1939, Printed United States Exhibits, Exhibit 339, 1254–56; Affidavit of Alfred Edward Woodley Mason, February 15, 1929, NARA, RG76, MCC, United States and Germany 1922–1939, Printed United States Exhibits, Exhibit 625, 1259.

119 **After being debriefed:** "Special Border Report from Captain Joel A. Lipscomb," February 4, 1918, NARA, RG76, MCC, United States and Germany 1922–1939, Printed United States Exhibits, Exhibit 226, 617.

119 **On the night of February 1:** "Special Border Report from Captain Joel A. Lipscomb," February 4, 1918, NARA, RG76, MCC, United States and Germany 1922–1939, Printed United States Exhibits, Exhibit 226, 615, 617–18.

120 **Captain Lipscomb advanced the British operative:** Major R. L. Barnes to Chief Military Intelligence Division, February 18, 1918, NARA, MID 10541-546, 1.

120 **"It was impressed upon him":** Major R. L. Barnes to Chief Military Intelligence Division, February 18, 1918, NARA, MID 10541-546, 1.

120 **In the weeks that followed:** Testimony of Captain Joel A. Lipscomb, NARA, RG76, MCC, United States and Germany 1922–1939, Printed United States Exhibits, Exhibit 321, 1091.

120 **Although the prisoner initially refused:** Testimony of Captain Joel A. Lipscomb, NARA, RG76, MCC, United States and Germany 1922–1939, Printed United States Exhibits, Exhibit 321, 1095.

120 **"He was afraid that his possession":** Testimony of Captain Joel A. Lipscomb, NARA, RG76, MCC, United States and Germany 1922–1939, Printed United States Exhibits, Exhibit 321, 1095.

120 **Witzke told Lipscomb that he had entered:** Testimony of Captain Joel A. Lipscomb, NARA, RG76, MCC, United States and Germany 1922–1939, Printed United States Exhibits, Exhibit 321, 1095–96.

121 **On February 14, Witzke was transferred:** Report of William Neunhoffer, "In Re: Pablo Waberski Alias Lathar Witcke, German Matter," February 10, 1918, NARA, MID 10541-268, 34.

121 **"Well, I am in a pretty hard position":** Conversation between Butcher and Witzke from: Report of William Neunhoffer, "In Re: Pablo Waberski Alias Lathar Witcke, German Matter," February 10, 1918, NARA, MID 10541-268, 34; also found in: Testimony of Byron S. Butcher, NARA, RG76, MCC, United States and Germany 1922–1939, Printed United States Exhibits, Exhibit 321, 1077–79.

122 **These would be the last words:** Altendorf, "U.S. Agent's Work Traps at Border German Spy on Mission of Murder; Captured Papers Bare Secret Code," *El Paso Herald*, November 26, 1919, 10.

CHAPTER 8

125   **Shortly after midnight:** Barbara Tuchman, *The Zimmerman Telegram* (New York: Ballantine, 1958), 10–11; David Kahn, *The Code-Breakers* (New York: Macmillan, 1967), 266.

125   **The secret cable-cutting operation:** Tuchman, *The Zimmerman Telegram*, 11.

126   **The French War Ministry created:** Kahn, *The Code-Breakers*, 255–56, 304–5.

126   **Besieged by a flood of coded:** Kahn, *The Code-Breakers*, 266–70; Lt. Commander James T. Westwood, USN, "Electronic Warfare and Signals Intelligence at the Outbreak of World War I," *Cryptologic Spectrum* (National Security Agency, Fort Meade, MD) 2, no. 2 (Spring 1981): 25.

126   **"university dons, barristers, linguists":** Tuchman, *The Zimmerman Telegram*, 13, 14–22; Kahn, *The Code-Breakers*, 269–74.

127   **On a routine morning in January:** Tuchman, *The Zimmerman Telegram*, 3–7.

127   **"to be handed to the Imperial Minister":** Tuchman, *The Zimmerman Telegram*, 6.

127   **Zimmerman's telegram notified:** Tuchman, *The Zimmerman Telegram*, 146–47.

128   **When Captain William Reginald "Blinker" Hall:** Tuchman, *The Zimmerman Telegram*, 9–10.

128   **Captain Hall devised a brilliant subterfuge:** Tuchman, *The Zimmerman Telegram*, 188–92; Kahn, *The Code-Breakers*, 288–93.

128   **Three months after the United States:** Kahn, *The Reader of Gentlemen's Mail*, 13, 20–21; Herbert O. Yardley, *The American Black Chamber* (Indianapolis: Bobbs-Merrill, 1931), 12–13.

129   **"This is a pretty big job":** Yardley, *The American Black Chamber*, 13.

129   **The military intelligence director:** Yardley, *The American Black Chamber*, 13–15; Kahn, *The Reader of Gentlemen's Mail*, 29–31.

129   **The first person that Yardley hired:** "John Matthews Manly 1865–1940," *Modern Philology* 38, no. 1 (August 1940): 1–2; Testimony of Captain John Matthews Manly, August 17, 1918, NARA, RG76, MCC, United States and Germany 1922–1939, Printed United States Exhibits, Exhibit 321, 1114.

129   **As a teenager Manly:** Kahn, *The Reader of Gentlemen's Mail*, 29.

129   **"if they could be of any value to him":** Testimony of Captain John Matthews Manly, NARA, RG76, MCC, United States and Germany 1922–1939, Printed United States Exhibits, Exhibit 321, 1113.

130   **"One trait of his [Manly's] that is known":** "Tribute to Manly," *University of Chicago Magazine*, November 1940, 17–18.

130   **"He was destined to develop":** Yardley, *The American Black Chamber*, 15.

130   **Once established in his new position:** "A Woman Medievalist Much-Maligned: A Note in Defense of Edith Rickert (1871–1938)," *PhiN-Beiheft*, Supplement 4/2009, 41–45; Elizabeth Scala, "Scandalous Assumptions: Edith Rickert and the Chicago Chaucer Project," *Medieval Feminist Forum* 30, no. 1 (2000): 28, 32.

130   **"With no more love than usual":** Scala, "Scandalous Assumptions: Edith Rickert and the Chicago Chaucer Project," 33.

130   **The dispatch from Major Barnes:** John Matthews Manly, "Waberski," undated, narrative report on the decipherment of the "Waberski Cipher," 811.1, William F. Friedman Papers, George C. Marshall Foundation Research Library & Archives. Lexington, VA, 1.

130   **For the first time:** Manly, "Waberski," 2, 10; Kahn, *The Reader of Gentlemen's Mail*, 43; Yardley, *The American Black Chamber*, 84–85; Testimony of Captain John Matthews Manly, NARA, RG76, MCC, United States and Germany 1922–1939, Printed United States Exhibits, Exhibit 321, 1116.

131   **The encrypted identification sheet:** Yardley, *The American Black Chamber*, 84.

131   **The first step in deciphering:** Manly, "Waberski," 2–3.

132   **To determine whether the Waberski message:** Yardley, *The American Black Chamber*, 86–89; Manly, "Waberski," 15–16; Testimony of Captain John Matthews Manly, NARA, RG76, MCC, United States and Germany 1922–1939, Printed United States Exhibits, Exhibit 321, 1118.

132   **The frequency table comparison:** Manly, "Waberski," 5–6.

132   **After establishing that the cipher:** Manly, "Waberski," 6, 17.

132   **Manly knew that in German:** Manly, "Waberski," 6.

133   **[It was found] that the interval:** Manly, "Waberski," 6–7.

134   **It was quite clear that:** Manly, "Waberski," 17.

134   **After achieving this breakthrough:** Manly, "Waberski," 18.

134   **Scanning through the letter groups:** Yardley, *The American Black Chamber*, 100–101; Manly, "Waberski," 19.

134   **Based on this apparently positive:** Manly, "Waberski," 8–9.

135   **After a good many groups:** Manly, "Waberski," 8, 18.

136   **The outcome of long hours:** Manly, "Waberski," 10.

136   **They discovered that the group:** Manly, "Waberski," 8.

137   **In the combination that formed:** Manly, "Waberski," 8–9.

137   **Following the same rules:** Manly, "Waberski," 9.

137   **Manly and Rickert continued working:** Kahn, *The Reader of Gentlemen's Mail*, 43.

137   **By examining the groups:** Manly, "Waberski," 9.

138   **An die Kaiserlichen Konsular-Behoerden:** Testimony of Captain John Matthews Manly, NARA, RG76, MCC, United States and Germany 1922–1939, Printed United States Exhibits, Exhibit 321, 1116–17.

139   **To The Imperial Consular Authorities:** Testimony of Captain John Matthews Manly, NARA, RG76, MCC, United States and Germany 1922–1939, Printed United States Exhibits, Exhibit 321, 1117.

139   **"with its multiple horizontal shiftings":** Kahn, *The Code-Breakers*, 354.

139   **The triumphant professors:** Manly, "Waberski," 11.

139   **When Major Van Deman arrived:** Yardley, *The American Black Chamber*, 106.

139   **"Please offer my sincere congratulations":** Yardley, *The American Black Chamber*, 106.

139   **"point to a well-organized, smoothly working division":** Manly, "Waberski," 11.

139   **In August, Captain Manly:** Manly, "Waberski," 12–13.

CHAPTER 9

141   **The court-martial of the alleged spy:** "German Spies in America," *Liberty Magazine*, May 9, 1931, 52, 54; Manly, "Waberski," 12–13; "Detail for the Commission," NARA, RG76, MCC, United States and Germany 1922–1939, Printed United States Exhibits, Exhibit 24, 957–58; U.S. War Department, *A Manual for Courts-Martial, Courts of Inquiry, and of Other Procedure under Military Law* (Washington, DC: Government Printing Office, 1917), 44.

141   **almost invariably open to the public:** U.S. War Department, *A Manual for Courts-Martial, Courts of Inquiry, and of Other Procedure under Military Law*, 47.

142   **"death by hanging is considered more ignominious":** U.S. War Department, *A Manual for Courts-Martial, Courts of Inquiry, and of Other Procedure under Military Law*, 160.

142   **"pale and nervous, but quiet as a stone":** Manly, "Waberski," 14.

142   **The army order designating:** Witzke court-martial arraignment, NARA, RG76, MCC, United States and Germany 1922–1939, Printed United States Exhibits, Exhibit 24, 958.

142   **In that Lothar Witzke, alias Pablo Waberski:** Witzke court-martial arraignment, NARA, RG76, MCC, United States and Germany 1922–1939, Printed United States Exhibits, Exhibit 24, 958–59.

142   **The commission asked:** Witzke court-martial arraignment, NARA, RG76, MCC, United States and Germany 1922–1939, Printed United States Exhibits, Exhibit 24, 959.

142   **As the only person to testify:** Examination and cross-examination of Dr. Paul Altendorf from: Testimony of Paul B. Altendorf, NARA, RG76, MCC, United States and Germany 1922–1939, Printed United States Exhibits, Exhibit 321, 961–1007, 1105–12.

144 **The next witness to be called was William Gleaves:** Examination and cross-examination of William Gleaves from: Testimony of William Gleaves, NARA, RG76, MCC, United States and Germany 1922–1939, Printed United States Exhibits, Exhibit 321, 1007–27.

146 **Major R. M. Campbell:** Examination and cross-examination of Major Campbell from: Testimony of Major R. M. Campbell, NARA, RG76, MCC, United States and Germany 1922–1939, Printed United States Exhibits, Exhibit 321, 1027–34.

146 **The next witness called by the prosecution:** Examination and cross-examination of immigrant inspector Charles Beatty from: Testimony of Charles L. Beatty, NARA, RG76, MCC, United States and Germany 1922–1939, Printed United States Exhibits, Exhibit 321, 1034–44.

146 **After Beatty was excused, Byron S. Butcher:** Examination and cross-examination of Byron S. Butcher from: Testimony of Byron S. Butcher, NARA, RG76, MCC, United States and Germany 1922–1939, Printed United States Exhibits, Exhibit 321, 1044–80.

147 **U.S. consul Ezra Lawton was the next witness:** Examination of Consul Ezra Lawton from: Testimony of E. M. Lawton, NARA, RG76, MCC, United States and Germany 1922–1939, Printed United States Exhibits, Exhibit 321, 1081–86.

147 **Captain Joel Lipscomb was called:** Examination of Captain Lipscomb from: Testimony of Captain Joel A. Lipscomb, NARA, RG76, MCC, United States and Germany 1922–1939, Printed United States Exhibits, Exhibit 321, 1086–97.

148 **Major Robert L. Barnes:** Examination of Major Barnes from: Testimony of Major Robert L. Barnes, NARA, RG76, MCC, United States and Germany 1922–1939, Printed United States Exhibits, Exhibit 321, 1097–100.

148 **Special Agent William Neunhoffer testified:** Examination and cross-examination of William Neunhoffer from: Testimony of William Neunhoffer, NARA, RG76, MCC, United States and Germany 1922–1939, Printed United States Exhibits, Exhibit 321, 1100–5.

148 **The final witness to be called:** Examination and cross-examination of John Matthews Manly from: Testimony of Captain John Matthews Manly, NARA, RG76, MCC, United States and Germany 1922–1939, Printed United States Exhibits, Exhibit 321, 1112–24.

149 **I was born in Winski:** Examination and cross-examination of Lothar Witzke from: Testimony of Lothar Witzke (Pablo Waberski), NARA, RG76, MCC, United States and Germany 1922–1939, Printed United States Exhibits, Exhibit 321, 1125–39.

155 **"we cannot get any witnesses":** Closing arguments of the court-martial of Pablo Waberski (Lothar Witzke), NARA, RG76, MCC, United States and Germany 1922–1939, Printed United States Exhibits, Exhibit 321, 1155.

155 **"Now you take Dr. Altendorf":** Closing arguments of the court-martial of Pablo Waberski (Lothar Witzke), NARA, RG76, MCC, United States and Germany 1922–1939, Printed United States Exhibits, Exhibit 321, 1155.

155 **"What did the possession":** Closing arguments of the court-martial of Pablo Waberski (Lothar Witzke), NARA, RG76, MCC, United States and Germany 1922–1939, Printed United States Exhibits, Exhibit 321, 1158.

156 **"act as a spy in and about":** Closing arguments of the court-martial of Pablo Waberski (Lothar Witzke), NARA, RG76, MCC, United States and Germany 1922–1939, Printed United States Exhibits, Exhibit 321, 1159.

156 **"The man himself says":** Closing arguments of the court-martial of Pablo Waberski (Lothar Witzke), NARA, RG76, MCC, United States and Germany 1922–1939, Printed United States Exhibits, Exhibit 321, 1159–60.

156 **"In the Manual for Courts-Martial":** Closing arguments of the court-martial of Pablo Waberski (Lothar Witzke), NARA, RG76, MCC, United States and Germany 1922–1939, Printed United States Exhibits, Exhibit 321, 1161.

156 **"We have no desire to reply":** Closing arguments of the court-martial of Pablo Waberski (Lothar Witzke), NARA, RG76, MCC, United States and Germany 1922–1939, Printed United States Exhibits, Exhibit 321, 1165.

156 **After seven hours and twenty minutes:** U.S. War Department, *A Manual for Courts-Martial, Courts of Inquiry, and of Other Procedure under Military Law* (Washington, DC: Government Printing Office, 1917), xiii, 46, 145.

156 **"The commission sentence the accused":** Closing arguments of the court-martial of Pablo Waberski (Lothar Witzke), NARA, RG76, MCC, United States and Germany 1922–1939, Printed United States Exhibits, Exhibit 321, 1165–66.

CHAPTER 10

157 **This seemed a likely possibility:** "German Spies in America," *Liberty Magazine*, May 9, 1931, 55; Affidavit of Sergeant George D. Haslam, April 14, 1926, NARA, RG76, MCC, United States and Germany 1922–1939, Printed United States Exhibits, Exhibit 334, 1230.

157 **Late one night:** "German Spies in America," *Liberty Magazine*, May 9, 1931, 55.

157 **The prisoner was escorted back:** "German Spies in America," *Liberty Magazine*, May 9, 1931, 55; Landau, *The Enemy Within*, 127.

158 **My name is Lothar Witzke:** "German Spies in America," *Liberty Magazine*, May 9, 1931, 55.

158 **It appeared to his jailers:** "German Spies in America," *Liberty Magazine*, May 9, 1931, 55.

158 **The days slowly passed:** Affidavit of Amos J. Peaslee, February 7, 1927, NARA, RG76, MCC, United States and Germany 1922–1939, Printed United States Exhibits, Exhibit 322, 1168.

158 **Languishing in his prison cell:** Affidavit of Sergeant George D. Haslam, April 14, 1926, NARA, RG76, MCC, United States and Germany 1922–1939, Printed United States Exhibits, Exhibit 334, 1230; Affidavit of Corporal John Shores, March 21, 1926, NARA, RG76, MCC, United States and Germany 1922–1939, Printed United States Exhibits, Exhibit 333, 1227–28.

158 **"every American has his price":** Affidavit of Sergeant George D. Haslam, April 14, 1926, NARA, RG76, MCC, United States and Germany 1922–1939, Printed United States Exhibits, Exhibit 334, 1230.

159 **The military prison at Fort Sam Houston:** Another affidavit of Sergeant George D. Haslam, April 14, 1926, NARA, RG76, MCC, United States and Germany 1922–1939, Printed United States Exhibits, Exhibit 335, 1232–33.

159 **The ceiling at the top of each cage:** Another affidavit of Sergeant George D. Haslam, April 14, 1926, NARA, RG76, MCC, United States and Germany 1922–1939, Printed United States Exhibits, Exhibit 335, 1233–34.

159 **At midnight on that particular:** Another affidavit of Sergeant George D. Haslam, April 14, 1926, NARA, RG76, MCC, United States and Germany 1922–1939, Printed United States Exhibits, Exhibit 335, 1234.

160 **In an anteroom on the third story:** Another affidavit of Sergeant George D. Haslam, April 14, 1926, NARA, RG76, MCC, United States and Germany 1922–1939, Printed United States Exhibits, Exhibit 335, 1235.

160 **The moon was a thin crescent:** Another affidavit of Sergeant George D. Haslam, April 14, 1926, NARA, RG76, MCC, United States and Germany 1922–1939, Printed United States Exhibits, Exhibit 335, 1235.

160 **Meanwhile, inside the prison:** Another affidavit of Sergeant George D. Haslam, April 14, 1926, NARA, RG76, MCC, United States and Germany 1922–1939, Printed United States Exhibits, Exhibit 335, 1235.

160 **The telephone soon began:** Another affidavit of Sergeant George D. Haslam, April 14, 1926, NARA, RG76, MCC, United States and Germany 1922–1939, Printed United States Exhibits, Exhibit 335, 1235.

160 **Stumbling through the dark night:** Another affidavit of Sergeant George D. Haslam, April 14, 1926, NARA, RG76, MCC, United States and Germany 1922–1939, Printed United States Exhibits, Exhibit 335, 1235–36.

161 **The directive that Witzke:** Another affidavit of Sergeant George D. Haslam, April 14, 1926, NARA, RG76, MCC, United States and Germany 1922–1939, Printed United States Exhibits, Exhibit 335, 1235–36.

161 **Tunney's interrogation:** Thomas Tunney's interrogation of Lothar Witzke found in: "Statement of Lothar Witzke of September 16, 1919, in His Examination by Capt. Thomas J. Tunney," NARA, RG76, MCC, United States and Germany 1922–1939, Printed United States Exhibits, Exhibit 24, 55–97.

162 **"around September 1916":** "Statement of Lothar Witzke of September 16, 1919, in His Examination by Capt. Thomas J. Tunney," NARA, RG76, MCC, United States and Germany 1922–1939, Printed United States Exhibits, Exhibit 24, 84.

162 **Arriving at the Criminal Court police:** Norman Thwaites, *Velvet and Vinegar* (London: Grayson & Grayson, 1932), 146–48.

163 **"Voluntary statement of Lothar Witzke, alias Pablo Waberski":** "Statement of Lothar Witzke of September 16, 1919, in His Examination by Capt. Thomas J. Tunney," NARA, RG76, MCC, United States and Germany 1922–1939, Printed United States Exhibits, Exhibit 24, 92.

163 **"Voluntary statement by Lothar Witzke, alias Waberski":** "Statement of Lothar Witzke of September 16, 1919, in His Examination by Capt. Thomas J. Tunney," NARA, RG76, MCC, United States and Germany 1922–1939, Printed United States Exhibits, Exhibit 24, 94.

163 **"MEMORANDUM: Waberski is going":** "Statement of Lothar Witzke of September 16, 1919, in His Examination by Capt. Thomas J. Tunney," NARA, RG76, MCC, United States and Germany 1922–1939, Printed United States Exhibits, Exhibit 24, 97.

163 **"President Woodrow Wilson gave orders":** "German Spies in America," *Liberty Magazine*, May 9, 1931, 55.

164 **On November 2, 1918, Wilson received:** Harris and Sadler, *The Border and the Revolution*, 124; Affidavit of Amos J. Peaslee, February 7, 1927, NARA, RG76, MCC, United States and Germany 1922–1939, Printed United States Exhibits, Exhibit 322, 1168–69.

164 **"it was most strenuously urged":** "Court-Martial Proceedings over Non-Military Persons under the Articles of War," *Minnesota Law Review* 6, no. 2 (January 1920): 80.

164 **"Waberski is not a spy in the sense":** Letter from Attorney General T. W. Lansing to the President, November 25, 1918, NARA, MID 10541-268, 9.

164 **In the foregoing case of Lothar Witzke:** Sentence commutation in the court-martial of Pablo Waberski (Lothar Witzke), NARA, RG76, MCC, United States and Germany 1922–1939, Printed United States Exhibits, Exhibit 321, 1166.

164 **On June 16, Lothar Witzke:** Inmate file of Lothar Witzke, NARA, RG129, Records of the Bureau of Prisons 1870–2009, Series Inmate Case Files 7/3/1895–11/5/1957, 178.

CHAPTER 11

165 **By late February 1918:** Memorandum from Major R. M. Campbell to Chief, Military Intelligence Branch, September 4, 1918, NARA, MID 10541-367.

165 **Aside from worries:** From Madrid to Berlin 27.12.17 No. 409, "German Cablegrams, Wireless and Other Messages Intercepted by the British Government during the War," NARA, RG76, MCC, United States and Germany 1922–1939, Printed United States Exhibits, Exhibit 320, 883–84; From Madrid to Berlin 4.1.18 For Delmar, "German Cablegrams, Wireless and Other Messages Intercepted by the British Government during the War," NARA, RG76, MCC, United States and Germany 1922–1939, Printed United States Exhibits, Exhibit 320, 884; From Madrid to Berlin 27.3.18 No. 1073 of March 26th, "German Cablegrams, Wireless and Other Messages Intercepted by the British Government during the War," NARA, RG76, MCC, United States and Germany 1922–1939, Printed United States Exhibits, Exhibit 320, 902–3; From Madrid to Berlin 3.4.18 Nos. 367, 368, 369, 370, "German Cablegrams, Wireless and Other Messages Intercepted by the British Government during the War," NARA, RG76, MCC, United States and Germany 1922–1939, Printed United States Exhibits, Exhibit 320, 905–7.

166 **"Jahnke's work must not be interrupted":** From Madrid to Berlin 28.3.18 No. 178 of March 26th, "Our Minister in Mexico Has Sent the Following Telegram for the Foreign Office," "German Cablegrams, Wireless and Other Messages Intercepted by the British Government during the War," NARA, RG76, MCC, United States and Germany 1922–1939, Printed United States Exhibits, Exhibit 320, 903–4.

166 **"Please inform Delmar":** From Madrid to Berlin 29.4.18 No. 25935, "German Cablegrams, Wireless and Other Messages Intercepted by the British Government during the War," NARA, RG76, MCC, United States and Germany 1922–1939, Printed United States Exhibits, Exhibit 320, 915.

166 **His status as *Bevollmächtigter Geheimagent*:** From Berlin Admiralty Staff to Madrid Naval Attaché 28.4.18 No. 203, "In Reply to Your Telegrams of April 3rd, April 7th, and April 9th about Jahnke," "German Cablegrams, Wireless and Other Messages Intercepted by the British Government during the War," NARA, RG76, MCC, United States and Germany 1922–1939, Printed United States Exhibits, Exhibit 320, 913–14.

166 **In his directive:** From Berlin Admiralty Staff to Madrid Naval Attaché 28.4.18 No. 203, "In Reply to Your Telegrams of April 3rd, April 7th, and April 9th about Jahnke," "German Cablegrams, Wireless and Other Messages Intercepted by the British Government during the War," NARA, RG76, MCC, United States and Germany 1922–1939, Printed United States Exhibits, Exhibit 320, 913–14.

166 **Throughout the spring and summer:** From Nauen to Mexico No. 7th of 8th June, MOST SECRET, "German Cablegrams, Wireless and Other messages Intercepted by the British Government during the War," NARA, RG76, MCC, United States and Germany 1922–1939, Printed United States Exhibits, Exhibit 320, 923–24; From Madrid to Berlin 3.7.18 No. 850, "German

Cablegrams, Wireless and Other Messages Intercepted by the British Government during the War," NARA, RG76, MCC, United States and Germany 1922–1939, Printed United States Exhibits, Exhibit 320, 928; From Madrid to Berlin 8.10.18 No. 1220, "German Cablegrams, Wireless and Other Messages Intercepted by the British Government during the War," NARA, RG76, MCC, United States and Germany 1922–1939, Printed United States Exhibits, Exhibit 320, 943.

166   **"giving close attention to all":** From Nauen to Mexico No. 7th of 8th June, MOST SECRET, "German Cablegrams, Wireless and Other Messages Intercepted by the British Government during the War," NARA, RG76, MCC, United States and Germany 1922–1939, Printed United States Exhibits, Exhibit 320, 923.

167   **"not to continue relations":** From Nauen to Mexico 21.8.18 No. 10 of 19th August, "To the Legation Mexico," "German Cablegrams, Wireless and Other Messages Intercepted by the British Government during the War," NARA, RG76, MCC, United States and Germany 1922–1939, Printed United States Exhibits, Exhibit 320, 936.

167   **FOR JAHNKE: EVERY ACTIVITY IS:** From Nauen to Mexico transmitted 2nd November No. 14, "German Cablegrams, Wireless and Other Messages Intercepted by the British Government during the War," NARA, RG76, MCC, United States and Germany 1922–1939, Printed United States Exhibits, Exhibit 320, 946.

167   **After the armistice was signed:** Report of 1952 interrogation of Lothar Witzke, "Lothar Witzke / Kurt Jahnke, Witzke's Appreciation of Jahnke," undated, National Archives (UK) Kew, Richmond, MI6 Security Service (PF Series) Files, 23 Aug 1918–01 Oct 1945, Witzke, Lothar, Reference KV2/2296, 3.

167   **In 1921 Jahnke returned:** "Kurt Jahnke Personal Particulars (30.7.41)," National Archives (UK) Kew, Richmond, MI6 Security Service (PF Series) Files, 23 Aug 1918–01 Oct 1945, Jahnke, Kurt, Reference KV2/755, 1; "SECRET Counter-Bolshevism OX/7435 1V.B., London," January 17, 1921, National Archives (UK) Kew, Richmond, MI6 Security Service (PF Series) Files, 23 Aug 1918–01 Oct 1945, Jahnke, Kurt, Reference KV2/755, 1.

167   **During the 1920s, Jahnke:** "Kurt Jahnke Personal Particulars (30.7.41)," National Archives (UK) Kew, Richmond, MI6 Security Service (PF Series) Files, 23 Aug 1918–01 Oct 1945, Jahnke, Kurt, Reference KV2/755, 1; "For p.a. in PF.37,755 Original filed in PF.600, 900 5a Kurt Jahnke," National Archives (UK) Kew, Richmond, MI6 Security Service (PF Series) Files, 23 Aug 1918–01 Oct 1945, Jahnke, Kurt, Reference KV2/755, 1.

168   **In 1927, during a period of close:** "Extract for File No. PF 37755 Jahnke C. A., Jahnke 4th double agent, July 1940," National Archives (UK) Kew, Richmond, MI6 Security Service (PF Series) Files, 23 Aug 1918–01 Oct 1945, Jahnke, Kurt, Reference KV2/755, 1; Unsigned letter addressed "Dear

Cowgill," February 16, 1940, National Archives (UK) Kew, Richmond, MI6 Security Service (PF Series) Files, 23 Aug 1918–01 Oct 1945, Jahnke, Kurt, Reference KV2/755, 1.

168   **Jahnke's life was devoted to sabotage:** Unsigned letter addressed "Dear Cowgill," February 16, 1940, National Archives (UK) Kew, Richmond, MI6 Security Service (PF Series) Files, 23 Aug 1918–01 Oct 1945, Jahnke, Kurt, Reference KV2/755, 1; "Kurt Jahnke Personal Particulars (30.7.41)," National Archives (UK) Kew, Richmond, MI6 Security Service (PF Series) Files, 23 Aug 1918–01 Oct 1945, Jahnke, Kurt, Reference KV2/755, 2.

168   **With the death of Weimar statesman:** "Kurt Jahnke Personal Particulars (30.7.41)," National Archives (UK) Kew, Richmond, MI6 Security Service (PF Series) Files, 23 Aug 1918–01 Oct 1945, Jahnke, Kurt, Reference KV2/755, 1–2; "For p.a. in PF.37,755 Original Filed in PF.600, 900 5a Kurt Jahnke," National Archives (UK) Kew, Richmond, MI6 Security Service (PF Series) Files, 23 Aug 1918–01 Oct 1945, Jahnke, Kurt, Reference KV2/755, 1–2; "Dictionary (Code Name) Information about the UK and Eire Interrogation No. 25," April 5, 1945, National Archives (UK) Kew, Richmond, MI6 Security Service (PF Series) Files, 23 Aug 1918–01 Oct 1945, Jahnke, Kurt, Reference KV2/755, 1.

168   **"were high-level foreign politicians":** Report of 1952 interrogation of Lothar Witzke, "Lothar Witzke / Kurt Jahnke, 3. Jahnke's Sources," undated, National Archives (UK) Kew, Richmond, MI6 Security Service (PF Series) Files, 23 Aug 1918–01 Oct 1945, Witzke, Lothar, Reference KV2/2296, 2.

168   **The official location of Jahnke's:** "Kurt Jahnke," "HQ," undated, National Archives (UK) Kew, Richmond, MI6 Security Service (PF Series) Files, 23 Aug 1918–01 Oct 1945, Jahnke, Kurt, Reference KV2/755, 2; Copy of translation of report by Walter Schellenberg, Head of Amt VI of the RSHA, on Herr Jahnke and his activities (Nr. 95a), August 23, 1945, National Archives (UK) Kew, Richmond, MI6 Security Service (PF Series) Files, 23 Aug 1918–01 Oct 1945, Jahnke, Kurt, Reference KV2/755, 1; Doerries, *Diplomaten und Agenten*, 92.

169   **In September 1939, a consolidation:** "Kurt Jahnke Personal Particulars (30.7.41)," National Archives (UK) Kew, Richmond, MI6 Security Service (PF Series) Files, 23 Aug 1918–01 Oct 1945, Jahnke, Kurt, Reference KV2/755, 2; Schellenberg, *The Labyrinth*, xii.

169   **Schellenberg relied on Jahnke:** Copy of translation of report by Walter Schellenberg, Head of Amt VI of the RSHA, on Herr Jahnke and his activities (Nr. 95a), August 23, 1945, National Archives (UK) Kew, Richmond, MI6 Security Service (PF Series) Files, 23 Aug 1918–01 Oct 1945, Jahnke, Kurt, Reference KV2/755, 1–2.

169   **"the full value of a secret service":** Copy of translation of report by Walter Schellenberg, Head of Amt VI of the RSHA, on Herr Jahnke and his activities (Nr. 95a), August 23, 1945, National Archives (UK) Kew, Richmond,

MI6 Security Service (PF Series) Files, 23 Aug 1918–01 Oct 1945, Jahnke, Kurt, Reference KV2/755, 2.

169　**"Politically he was interested":** Schellenberg, *The Labyrinth*, 24.

169　**Jahnke became a senior adviser:** Schellenberg, *The Labyrinth*, 25–26, 237.

170　**In late 1941, German secret service:** Schellenberg, *The Labyrinth*, 236–37.

170　**"Jahnke was persona non grata with Hitler":** Schellenberg, *The Labyrinth*, 238.

170　**At the end of October, Jahnke delivered:** Schellenberg, *The Labyrinth*, 243.

170　**Hitler at first remained skeptical:** Schellenberg, *The Labyrinth*, 243–44.

170　**As the war progressed, Jahnke's star:** Schellenberg, *The Labyrinth*, 253–60; Copy of translation of report by Walter Schellenberg, Head of Amt VI of the RSHA, on Herr Jahnke and his activities (Nr. 95a), August 23, 1945, National Archives (UK) Kew, Richmond, MI6 Security Service (PF Series) Files, 23 Aug 1918–01 Oct 1945, Jahnke, Kurt, Reference KV2/755, 1.

171　**"he intended to let himself be overrun":** Report of 1952 interrogation of Lothar Witzke, "Lothar Witzke / Kurt Jahnke, 5. Jahnke's Attitude to Russia and His R.I.S. Connections," undated, National Archives (UK) Kew, Richmond, MI6 Security Service (PF Series) Files, 23 Aug 1918–01 Oct 1945, Witzke, Lothar, Reference KV2/2296, 2.

171　**After the Soviet occupation:** Copy of translation of report by Walter Schellenberg, Head of Amt VI of the RSHA, on Herr Jahnke and his activities (Nr. 95a), August 23, 1945, National Archives (UK) Kew, Richmond, MI6 Security Service (PF Series) Files, 23 Aug 1918–01 Oct 1945, Jahnke, Kurt, Reference KV2/755, 2. Recently discovered evidence suggests that Kurt Jahnke may have been executed by firing squad in Moscow on April 22, 1950, for past espionage against the U.S.S.R. See *Saxon Memorials Foundation in Memory of Victims of Political Tyranny* posting: https://stsg.rz-wisys.de/PersData/ShowDokument/1B78F80F1A4F922EBB2B33DCF457C8EF511 B5C5E4970302D28A79B152DA70585.

171　**For almost three years:** "Letter from Warden William I. Biddle addressed 'To Whom It May Concern,'" January 31, 1922, NARA, Inmate File of Lothar Witzke (aka Luther Witzke, aka Lather Witcke), RG129, Records of the Bureau of Prisons 1870–2009, Series Inmate Case Files, 7/31/1895–11/5/1957, 102.

171　**This man never shows:** "United States Penitentiary Leavenworth Kansas, Record of Lothar Witzke, No. 15309," April 14, 1923, NARA, Inmate File of Lothar Witzke (aka Luther Witzke, aka Lather Witcke), RG129, Records of the Bureau of Prisons 1870–2009, Series Inmate Case Files, 7/31/1895–11/5/1957, 9.

171　**The German government had not forgotten:** Affidavit of Amos J. Peaslee, February 7, 1927, NARA, RG76, MCC, United States and Germany 1922–1939, Printed United States Exhibits, Exhibit 322, 1168–69.

172 **Other countries, including Germany:** Affidavit of Amos J. Peaslee, February 7, 1927, NARA, RG76, MCC, United States and Germany 1922–1939, Printed United States Exhibits, Exhibit 322, 1169.

172 **On September 26, the judge advocate general:** "German Spies in America," *Liberty Magazine*, May 9, 1931, 56.

172 **On the day before Thanksgiving:** "Witzke, the Spy, Is Free," *Kansas City Star*, November 21, 1923, 1.

172 **"Prison life would not be so bad":** "Witzke, the Spy, Is Free," *Kansas City Star*, November 21, 1923, 1; "German Spy Released," *Battle Creek Enquirer*, November 30, 1923, 22.

172 **The consul provided Witzke:** "German Spies in America," *Liberty Magazine*, May 9, 1931, 56–57.

173 **"As he [Witzke] described it":** "Unofficial Memorandum of Additional Facts Disclosed by Lothar Witzke," January 13, 1929, NARA, RG76, MCC, United States and Germany 1922–1939, Printed United States Exhibits, Annex A to Exhibit 630, 2818.

173 **For a time the ex–naval officer:** "German Spies in America," *Liberty Magazine*, May 9, 1931, 57; "Unofficial Memorandum of Additional Facts Disclosed by Lothar Witzke," January 13, 1929, NARA, RG76, MCC, United States and Germany 1922–1939, Printed United States Exhibits, Annex A to Exhibit 630, 2820.

173 **By 1934 Witzke was in Hankow, China:** "Spy," *American Foreign Service Journal* 11, no. 11 (November 1934): 581.

173 **When the Second World War began:** "Personal Characteristics of Lieutenant Lothar Witzke, File No. PF, 601, 803," undated, National Archives (UK) Kew, Richmond, MI6 Security Service (PF Series) Files, 23 Aug 1918–01 Oct 1945, Witzke, Lothar, Reference KV2/2296, 1–4.

174 **When the war ended, Witzke:** Report of 1952 interrogation of Lothar Witzke, "3. Jahnke's Previous Collaborators," May 15, 1952, National Archives (UK) Kew, Richmond, MI6 Security Service (PF Series) Files, 23 Aug 1918–01 Oct 1945, Witzke, Lothar, Reference KV2/2296, 1; Richard R. Doerries, "Tracing Kurt Jahnke: Aspects of the Study of German Intelligence," in *Historians and Archivists*, ed. George O. Kent (Fairfax, VA: George Mason University Press, 1991), 41.

174 **In an effort to answer this question:** Report of 1952 interrogation of Lothar Witzke, May 15, 1952, National Archives (UK) Kew, Richmond, MI6 Security Service (PF Series) Files, 23 Aug 1918–01 Oct 1945, Witzke, Lothar, Reference KV2/2296, 1–3.

174 **"No success was achieved":** Report of 1952 interrogation of Lothar Witzke, "Lothar Witzke / Kurt Jahnke," May 15, 1952, National Archives (UK) Kew, Richmond, MI6 Security Service (PF Series) Files, 23 Aug 1918–01 Oct 1945, Witzke, Lothar, Reference KV2/2296, 1.

174 **"Jahnke never made any secret":** Report of 1952 interrogation of Lothar Witzke, "Lothar Witzke / Kurt Jahnke, 5. Jahnke's Attitude to Russia and His

R.I.S. Connections," May 15, 1952, National Archives (UK) Kew, Richmond, MI6 Security Service (PF Series) Files, 23 Aug 1918–01 Oct 1945, Witzke, Lothar, Reference KV2/2296, 2.

174   **Witzke stated that he succeeded:** "Unofficial Memorandum of Additional Facts Disclosed by Lothar Witzke," January 13, 1929, NARA, RG76, MCC, Printed United States Exhibits, Annex A to Exhibit 630, 2819.

175   **William Gleaves left British naval intelligence:** Affidavit of William H. Gleaves, January 31, 1927, NARA, RG76, MCC, United States and Germany 1922–1939, Printed United States Exhibits, Exhibit 329, 1254.

175   **Dr. Paul Bernardo Altendorf:** Altendorf, "U.S. Agent's Work Traps at Border German Spy on Mission of Murder; Captured papers Bare German Code," *El Paso Herald*, November 26, 1919, 10; Paul Bernardo Altendorf, "U.S. Agent Disguised as Doctor, Returns to Mexico to Trail Spies Knowing Mission May Mean Death," *El Paso Herald*, November 27, 1919, 5.

175   **"put in the cemetery":** Altendorf, "U.S. Agent Is Ordered to Join Mission to Border to Arrange Mexican-German Invasion of U.S.," *El Paso Herald*, November 22, 1919, 12.

175   **In the months that followed:** Mills, *Treacherous Passage*, 129–33, 135–39.

175   **But soon the double agent's cover:** Mills, *Treacherous Passage*, 139–45.

175   **"the Germans are after you":** Paul Bernardo Altendorf, "U.S. Agent in Mexico, with Reward on His Head, Eludes His Pursuers; Finds Himself Betrayed at Border," *El Paso Herald*, December 5, 1919, 1.

176   **"look around San Antonio":** Paul Bernardo Altendorf, "U.S. Agent in San Antonio Traps Austrian with Scheme to Destroy Whole Armies with Disease Germs," *El Paso Herald*, December 6, 1919, 1.

176   **Among these was Dr. Ludwig Heinrich Reuter:** Information on Dr. Altendorf's part in uncovering German agent Dr. Ludwig Reuter from: Altendorf, "U.S. Agent in San Antonio Traps Austrian with Scheme to Destroy Whole Armies with Disease Germs," *El Paso Herald*, December 6, 1919, 1, 19; Report by William Neunhoffer, "In Re: Ludwig Reuter, Suspected German Agent," October 31, 1918, NARA, M1085, Investigating Case Files of the Bureau of Investigation 1908–1922, Roll boi_german_257-850_0069, Case No. 92604, 43, 49; Report by W. A. Wiseman, "In Re: Dr. Ludwig Heinrich, German Activities," August 3, 1918, NARA, M1085, Investigating Case Files of the Bureau of Investigation 1908–1922, Roll boi_german_257-850_0069, Case No. 92604, 25.

176   **In early October:** Report by William Neunhoffer, "In Re: Ludwig Reuter, Pro-German," October 8, 1918, NARA, M1085, Investigating Case Files of the Bureau of Investigation 1908–1922, Roll boi_german_257-850_0069, Case No. 92604, 39.

176   **A short time later, Dr. Altendorf knocked:** Report by William Neunhoffer, "In Re: Ludwig Reuter Alias Paul Reuter Alias Louis Reuter Alias Neuman Alias Mason Alias Louis Caballeros, German Agent," October 17,

1918, NARA, M1085, Investigating Case Files of the Bureau of Investigation 1908–1922, Roll boi_german_257-850_0069, Case No. 92604, 88.

176 **"My name is Dr. Amagini":** Report by William Neunhoffer, "In Re: Ludwig Reuter, Pro-German," October 8, 1918, NARA, M1085, Investigating Case Files of the Bureau of Investigation 1908–1922, Roll boi_german_257-850_0069, Case No. 92604, 39–40.

177 **Following this initial encounter:** Report by William Neunhoffer, "In Re: Ludwig Reuter Alias Louis Reuter Alias Paul Reuter Alias Neuman," October 15, 1918, NARA, M1085, Investigating Case Files of the Bureau of Investigation 1908–1922, Roll boi_german_257-850_0069, Case No. 92604, 30–34.

177 **"the seriousness of such a course":** Report by William Neunhoffer, "In Re: Ludwig Reuter Alias Louis Reuter Alias Paul Reuter Alias Neuman," October 15, 1918, NARA, M1085, Investigating Case Files of the Bureau of Investigation 1908–1922, Roll boi_german_257-850_0069, Case No. 92604, 31.

177 **"he did not fear detectives":** Report by William Neunhoffer, "In Re: Ludwig Reuter Alias Louis Reuter Alias Paul Reuter Alias Neuman," October 15, 1918, NARA, M1085, Investigating Case Files of the Bureau of Investigation 1908–1922, Roll boi_german_257-850_0069, Case No. 92604, 33.

178 **On the evening of October 8, 1918:** Report by William Neunhoffer, "In Re: Ludwig Reuter Alias Louis Reuter Alias Paul Reuter Alias Neuman," October 15, 1918, NARA, M1085, Investigating Case Files of the Bureau of Investigation 1908–1922, Roll boi_german_257-850_0069, Case No. 92604, 33–34.

178 **At 9 P.M. writer in company:** Report by William Neunhoffer, "In Re: Ludwig Reuter Alias Louis Reuter Alias Paul Reuter Alias Neuman," October 15, 1918, NARA, M1085, Investigating Case Files of the Bureau of Investigation 1908–1922, Roll boi_german_257-850_0069, Case No. 92604, 33–34.

178 **"could hardly control his laughter":** Altendorf, "U.S. Agent in San Antonio Traps Austrian with Scheme to Destroy Whole Armies with Disease Germs," *El Paso Herald*, December 6, 1919, 1, 19.

178 **Dr. Amagini next made the acquaintance:** Altendorf, "U.S. Agent in San Antonio Traps Austrian with Scheme to Destroy Whole Armies with Disease Germs," *El Paso Herald*, December 6, 1919, 19; Report by C. E. Breniman, "In Re: Saint Pierce Fremont Rodynke, Alien Enemy," November 15, 1918, NARA, M1085, BI Files, Old German Files, Roll boi_german_257-850_0090, Case No. 27926, 3–4; Report by Louis De Nette, "In Re: Saint Pierro Y Fremont Rodynke, Alien Enemy," November 27, 1918, NARA, M1085, BI Files, Old German Files, Roll boi_german_257-850_0090, Case No. 27926, 5; Report by W. A. Wiseman, "In Re: Saint Pierre De Rodynko, Interned Prisoner," May 21, 1919, NARA, M1085, BI Files, Old German Files, Roll boi_german_257-850_0090, Case No. 27926, 12; Report by C. E. Breniman,

"In Re: St. Pierce Fremont Rodynke," November 1, 1918, NARA, M1085, BI Files, Old German Files, Roll boi_german_257-850_0090, Case No. 27926, 26–31.

179 **"when he had been in the War School":** Altendorf, "U.S. Agent in San Antonio Traps Austrian with Scheme to Destroy Whole Armies with Disease Germs," *El Paso Herald*, December 6, 1919, 19; Report by E. T. Needham, "In Re: Saint Pierce Fremont Rodynko, German Suspect," October 26, 1918, NARA, M1085, BI Files, Old German Files, Roll boi_german_257-850_0090, Case No. 27926, 221.

179 **"in accordance with the present ruling":** Memorandum from Captain E. F. McCarron for Marlborough Churchill to Intelligence Officer, Southern Department, Fort Sam Houston, November 15, 1918, NARA, RG165, Records of the War Department and Special Staffs, Military Intelligence Division, File 51-45.

179 **Finding himself unemployed:** Letter from Marlborough Churchill to Alexander B. Coxe, September 9, 1920, NARA, RG165, Records of the War Department and Special Staffs, Military Intelligence Division, File 51-45.

180 **"I was hard up for money":** Information on Dr. Altendorf's return to Mexico in 1920 from: "Statement dictated by Dr. P. B. Altendorf at San Antonio, Texas, relative to his journey to the City of Mexico, his imprisonment while there, and his re-entry into the United States," undated, NARA, RG165, Records of the War Department and Special Staffs, Military Intelligence Division, File 51-45, 1–17.

180 **"Keep quiet and do not say":** "Statement dictated by Dr. P. B. Altendorf at San Antonio, Texas, relative to his journey to the City of Mexico, his imprisonment while there, and his re-entry into the United States," undated, NARA, RG165, Records of the War Department and Special Staffs, Military Intelligence Division, File 51-45, 7.

180 **"Bring Altendorf back to Mexico City":** "Statement dictated by Dr. P. B. Altendorf at San Antonio, Texas, relative to his journey to the City of Mexico, his imprisonment while there, and his re-entry into the United States," undated, NARA, RG165, Records of the War Department and Special Staffs, Military Intelligence Division, File 51-45, 16.

181 **On the morning of September 16, 1920:** "Wall Street Disaster Caused by Time Bomb According to Experts," *Dallas Morning News*, September 17, 1920, 1, 3; "31 Killed, 225 Injured in Wall Street Explosion," *Anaconda Standard* (MT), September 17, 1920, 1, 8; "'Reds' Responsible for Blast, First Tangible Clue Is Obtained in Metropolis Explosion which Caused 35 Deaths and Hurt 300," *Albuquerque Journal*, September 18, 1920, 1, 3.

181 **Investigations into the bombing:** Beverly Gage, *The Day Wall Street Exploded* (New York: Oxford University Press, 2009), 140–44; "Wall Street Disaster Caused by Time Bomb According to Experts," 1; "Big Reward for Solving Bomb Blast," *San Diego Evening Tribune*, November 23, 1920,

9; "Wall Street Bomb Plot Cleared with Arrest in Poland," *Evening Star* (Washington, DC), December 17, 1921, 1; "Capture of Wall Street Bomber Result of 15 Months Still Hunt by Burns' Men," *Duluth (MN) News-Tribune*, December 18, 1921, 1.

181 **To locate his missing informant:** Report by P. W. Lamb, Bureau of Investigation, "In Re; Paul Bernardo Altendorf—Information for the San Antonio Office," July 16, 1921, NARA, RG59, Records of the State Department 1910–1929, 811.08/1152 to 811.108 F11/1, 7370; Memorandum for file from J. Edgar Hoover, July 19, 1921, NARA, RG59, Records of the State Department, central decimal file 1910–1929, decimal 811.108 A1 72/2.

182 **After arriving in his homeland:** Memorandum for file from J. Edgar Hoover, July 19, 1921, NARA, RG59, Records of the State Department, central decimal file 1910–1929, decimal 811.108 A1 72/2; "Wall Street Bomb Plot Cleared with Arrest in Poland," 1; Letter from William J. Hurley to Richard E. Pennoyer, American Commission Berlin, October 6, 1921, NARA, RG59, Records of the State Department 1910–1929, 811.108/115 to 811.108 F11/1, 7370; "Capture of Wall Street Bomber Result of 15 Months Still Hunt by Burns' Men," 1; "Held for Hand on Wall Street Bomb Horror," *Boston Herald*, December 17, 1921, 1.

182 **With the capture of Wolfe Lindenfeld:** "U.S. Agent, Nemesis of German Plotters, Caught Wall Street Bombers," *New York Evening Telegram*, December 18, 1921, 7; "To Sift Linde's Story of Bomb," *Springfield Daily News* (MA), May 9, 1922, 10.

182 **In September 1928, a New York promoter:** "$46,875 Awaits Adventurer if Found at Once," *New York Daily News*, September 6, 1928, 494; Letter from Lieutenant Colonel Vaughn M. Cooper to Major James C. Schwenck, American Embassy, Havana Cuba, November 23, 1928, NARA, RG165, Records of the War Department and Special Staffs, Military Intelligence Division, File 51-45.

182 **"as a reward for services":** "$46,875 Awaits Adventurer if Found at Once," *New York Daily News*, September 6, 1928, 494.

183 **A conference was expected to be held:** Report by William Neunhoffer includes a memo from R. L. Barnes, National Army, "In Re: German and IWW Activities," March 16, 1918, NARA, M1085, Investigating Case Files of the Bureau of Investigation 1908–1922, Roll boi_german_257-850_0069, Case No. 345240, 137.

183 **At the end of March:** "Government Agents Visit in District," *Bisbee (AZ) Daily Review*, April 4, 1918, 3; Local update without title describing Obregón trip with Butcher, *Arizona Daily Star* (Tucson), April 3, 1918, 4; Local update without title describing Obregón's export of jute sacks, *Border Vidette* (Nogales, AZ), April 6, 1918, 3.

183 **The friendship between the two men:** Harris and Sadler, *The Border and the Revolution*, 125–26.

184   **The situation came to a head in June:** Letter from Sam B. Ratge to Con-
      fidential Investigator R. J. Lester, Bureau of War Trade Intelligence Wash-
      ington DC, July 1, 1918, NARA, M1085, BI Files, Old German Files, Roll
      boi_german_257-850_0088, Case No. 8000-18765, 91–92; Letter from A. M.
      Hardie, Manager Western Union Telegraph Co. Nogales to Special Investiga-
      tor R. J. Lester, War Trade Board Nogales AZ, July 2, 1918, NARA, M1085,
      BI Files, Old German Files, Roll boi_german_257-850_0088, Case No. 8000-
      18765, 85–86; Harris and Sadler, *The Border and the Revolution*, 126.

184   **"General Pershing was making a big mistake":** Letter from Sam B.
      Ratge to Confidential Investigator R. J. Lester, Bureau of War Trade Intel-
      ligence Washington DC, July 1, 1918, NARA, M1085, BI Files, Old German
      Files, Roll boi_german_257-850_0088, Case No. 8000-18765, 91.

184   **The senior intelligence officers:** Letter from Major Robert L. Barnes to
      Van Deman titled "Memorandum for the Director of Military Intelligence,"
      November 6, 1918, NARA, MID 9685-129, 1–3.

184   **"probably for the further purpose":** Letter from Major Robert L. Barnes
      to Van Deman titled "Memorandum for the Director of Military Intelli-
      gence," November 6, 1918, NARA, MID 9685-129, 1.

184   **Hoping to limit Butcher's contact:** "Dejó su puesto en el gobierno por
      servile a Obregón," *La Prensa* (San Antonio, TX), June 18, 1918, 1; "Butch
      with Obregón," *Arizona Daily Star* (Tucson), June 22, 1918, 5; Harris and
      Sadler, *The Border and the Revolution*, 126.

184   **Byron S. Butcher, the well-known:** "Local Items," *Border Vidette* (No-
      gales, AZ), June 15, 1918, 2.

185   **The job at the general's commission house:** Letter from Byron S.
      Butcher to General Álvaro Obregón, February 16, 1919, "Correspondence of
      Byron S. Butcher of the United States Graphite Company to General Álvaro
      Obregón," New Mexico Digital Collections, University of New Mexico Li-
      braries, Source: Archivo Fernando Torreblanca-Fondo Álvaro Obregón, 1–2.

185   **The only stipulation I have:** Letter from Byron S. Butcher to General
      Álvaro Obregón, February 16, 1919, "Correspondence of Byron S. Butcher
      of the United States Graphite Company to General Álvaro Obregón," New
      Mexico Digital Collections, University of New Mexico Libraries, Source:
      Archivo Fernando Torreblanca-Fondo Álvaro Obregón, 1.

185   **To present the Mexican position:** Kevin J. Fernlund, "Senator Holm O.
      Borsun and the Mexican Ring, 1921–1924," *New Mexico Historical Review*
      66, no. 4 (Oct 1991): 440–43, 446.

185   **In the late 1920s, Butcher:** "Obregón Was Big Grower of Mexico," *Press
      Democrat* (Santa Rosa, CA), July 29, 1928, 15; "Nogales to Be Home of Huge
      Export Firm," *Tucson Citizen*, January 24, 1929, 1, 4; "Cia. Distribuidora Del
      Yaqui, S.A. (Yaqui Distributing Co.), advertisement, *Tucson Citizen*, January
      27, 1929, 6.

186 **The former intelligence agent's path:** "Obregón Was Big Grower of Mexico," 15.

186 **On that day, Álvaro Obregón:** "President-Elect Obregón Assassinated at Luncheon Celebrating His Election," *New York Times*, July 18, 1921, 1; John W. F. Dulles, *Yesterday in Mexico: A Chronicle of the Revolution, 1919–1936* (Austin: University of Texas Press, 1961), 367, 169.

186 **The assassination of Álvaro Obregón:** "Nogales to Be Home of Huge Export Firm," *Tucson Citizen*, January 24, 1929, 4; "Local News—Byron S. Butcher Local Commission Broker Has Returned from Tucson," *Border Vidette* (Nogales, AZ), December 23, 1933, 1; "Local News—Byron S. Butcher Is on His Own; Shipped Several Carlots of Beans and Peas," *Border Vidette* (Nogales, AZ), February 3, 1934, 1; "Byron S. Butcher," Sixteenth Census of the United States 1940, Brownsville, Cameron, Texas, NARA, United States Bureau of the Census, Roll m-10627-03998, T-627, Sheet 7A.

186 **His situation improved:** Byron Samuel Butcher, April 27, 1942, United States Selective Service System, Selective Service Registration Cards, World War II Draft Cards: 4th Registration for the State of Texas, NARA, RG147, Records of the Selective Service System, 554.

187 **In 1950 Byron Butcher retired:** Byron S. Butcher, Social Security Application and Claims Index 1936–2007, Claim Date 22 November 1950; Byron Samuel Butcher death certificate, State File No. 51395, October 23, 1956, Texas Death Certificates 1903–1982, Texas Department of State Health Services, Austin, Texas.

187 **On the State of Texas death certificate:** Byron Samuel Butcher death certificate, State File No. 51395, October 23, 1956, Texas Death Certificates 1903–1982, Texas Department of State Health Services, Austin, Texas.

Bibliography

Atkin, Ronald. *Revolution! Mexico 1910–20*. New York: John Day, 1970.

Bisher, Jamie. *The Intelligence War in Latin America, 1914–1922*. Jefferson, NC: McFarland, 2016.

Christensen, C. P. *Letzte Kaperfahrt nach Quirinquina*. Berlin: Drei Masken Verlag, A.G., 1936.

Corson, William R. *The Armies of Ignorance*. New York: Dial Press, 1977.

Cullum, George W. *Biographical Register of the Officers and Graduates of the United States Military Academy at West Point, New York, Supplement Vol. VI-A 1910–1920*. Saginaw, MI: Sherman & Peters Printers, 1920.

Digby, Michael. *Burn, Bomb, Destroy*. Philadelphia: Casemate, 2021.

Doerries, Reinhard R. *Diplomaten und Agenten*. Heidelberg: Universitätverlag C. Winter, 2001.

———. *Hitler's Last Chief of Foreign Intelligence*. Oxon (UK): Routledge, 2003.

———. *Prelude to the Easter Rising*. Portland, OR: Frank Cass, 2000.

Dulles, John W. F. *Yesterday in Mexico: A Chronicle of the Revolution, 1919–1936*. Austin: University of Texas Press, 1961.

Eppinga, Jane. *Nogales: Life and Times on the Frontier*. Charleston, SC: Arcadia, 2002.

Farago, Ladislas. *The Game of the Foxes*. New York: Bantam, 1971.

Feilitzsch, Heribert von. *The Secret War Council*. Amissville: Henselstone Verlag, 2015.

———. *The Secret War on the United States in 1915*. Amissville, VA: Henselstone Verlag, 2015.

Gage, Beverly. *The Day Wall Street Exploded*. New York: Oxford University Press, 2009.

Green, Roger Lancelyn. *A. E. W. Mason: The Adventure of a Story-Teller*. London: Max Parrish & Company, 1952.

Hagedorn, Ann. *Savage Peace*. New York: Simon & Shuster, 2007.

Hall, Sir W. Reginald, and Amos J. Peaslee. *Three Wars with Germany*. New York: Putnam, 1944.

Harris, Charles H., III, and Louis R. Sadler. *The Border and the Revolution*. Silver City, NM: High Lonesome Books, 1988.

Hewitt, Nick. *The Kaiser's Pirates*. New York: Skyhorse, 2013.

Hopkirk, Peter. *Like Hidden Fire*. New York: Kodansha America, 1994.

Humphrey, John. *German Surface Raider Warfare*. London: Leonaur, 2017.

Jensen, Joan M. *The Price of Vigilance*. New York: Rand McNally, 1968.

Jones, John Price, and Paul Merrick Hollister. *The German Secret Service in America, 1914–1918*. Boston: Small, Maynard & Company, 1918.

Kahn, David. *The Code-Breakers*. New York: Macmillan, 1967.

———. *The Reader of Gentlemen's Mail*. New Haven, CT: Yale University Press, 2004.

Katz, Friedrich. *The Life and Times of Pancho Villa*. Stanford, CA: Stanford University Press, 1998.

———. *The Secret War in Mexico*. Chicago: University of Chicago Press, 1981.

Kent, George O. *Historians and Archivists*. Fairfax, VA: George Mason University Press, 1991. [Contains Richard R. Doerries, "Tracing Kurt Jahnke: Aspects of the Studies of German Intelligence."]

Koenig, Robert. *The Fourth Horseman*. New York: Public Affairs, 2006.

Landau, Captain Henry. *The Enemy Within*. New York: Putnam, 1937.

Merridale, Catherine. *Lenin on the Train*. New York: Henry Holt, 2017.

Millman, Chad. *The Detonators*. New York: Little, Brown, 2006.

Mills, Bill. *The Estrada Plot*. Lincoln: University of Nebraska Press, 2020.

———. *The League*. New York: Skyhorse, 2013.

———. *Treacherous Passage*. Lincoln: University of Nebraska Press, 2017.

Mueller, Michael. *Nazi Spymaster*. New York: Skyhorse, 2017.

Obregón, General Álvaro. *Ocho Mil Kilómetros en Campaña*. Mexico City: Libreria de la Vda. De CH. Bouret, 1917.

Pagels, Albert. *Mein Leben*. Berlin: Verlag Scherl, 1940.

Preston, William. *Aliens and Dissenters*. Chicago: University of Illinois Press, 1994.

Rintelen, Captain Franz von. *The Dark Invader*. New York: Macmillan, 1933.

Salazar, Jaime. *Mutiny of Rage*. Lanham, MD: Prometheus, 2021.

Sams, Chris. *German Raiders of the First World War*. Croydon (UK): Fonthill Media, 2015.

Schellenberg, Walter. *The Labyrinth*. New York: Harper and Brothers, 1956.

Søhr, Johan. *Spioner og bomber. Fra opdagelsespolitiets arbeide under verdenskrigen*. Oslo: Johan Grundt Tanum, 1938.

St. John, Vincent. *The IWW: Its History, Structure and Methods*. New Castle, PA: IWW Publishing Bureau, 1917.

Talbert, Roy, Jr. *Negative Intelligence*. Jackson: University Press of Mississippi, 1991.

Thwaites, Norman. *Velvet and Vinegar*. London: Grayson & Grayson, 1932.

Tuchman, Barbara. *The Zimmerman Telegram*. New York: Ballantine, 1958.

Tunney, Thomas J. *Throttled!* Boston: Small, Maynard & Company, 1919.

U.S. War Department. *A Manual for Courts-Martial, Courts of Inquiry, and of Other Procedure under Military Law*. Washington, DC: Government Printing Office, 1917.

Weber, Ralph E., ed. *The Final Memoranda*. Wilmington, DE: Scholarly Resources, 1988.

Witcover, Jules. *Sabotage at Black Tom*. Chapel Hill, NC: Algonquin Books of Chapel Hill, 1989.

Yardley, Herbert O. *The American Black Chamber*. Indianapolis: Bobbs-Merrill, 1931.

Index

Note: Photo spread images between pages 124 and 125 are indicated by *p1, p2, p3,* etc.

Abteilung II army (Germany), 173
Abteilung III B army (Germany), 34, 47, *p8*
ADS. *See* American Defense Society
Afghanistan, Muslim uprising against colonialism in, 62
African Americans: German intelligence agents' instigation of insurrection by, 61, 63–64; instigation of racial conflict among, 54; labor unions' response towards, 66–68; migration of, 66–68; Negro League for Afro-American Suffrage, 67; racial violence against, 66–69
Albert, Heinrich, 19
Albert Ballin (German passenger liner), 172
HTMS *Alert* (British warship), 125
Alfonso XIII (Spanish passenger liner), 52, 81
Altendorf, Joseph, 74

Altendorf, Paul Bernardo, 175, 187, *p9–10*; Carranza and, 58–59; early life of, 74; von Eckhardt and, 51; imprisonment of, 180; Jahnke and, 51–56; in Mexico, 74–76, 79, 81–91, 93–105, 110–23; Nuenhoffer and, 49–50; Paglasch and, 50–51; public notoriety of, 179–80; Reuter and, 176–79; Revolutionary Association and, 144; Schwierz and, 48–49; in South America, 74; in Tannhauser Halle, 176; as U.S. Army Agent, 78–79; in Witzke court-martial, 141–44
Alvarado, Salvador, 74
Amasis (German ship), 3–4
American Defense Society (ADS), 44
American Protective League (APL), 44
Anding, S. W., 77
Annie Larsen (schooner), 62
APL. *See* American Protective League

Baird, Alexander, 183
Baltimore, Charles, 68
SS *Bankdale* (U.S. warship), 21
Barnes, Robert L., 57, 77–78, 118, 183;
    in Witzke court-martial, 148
Barnes, William, 47
Beatty, Charles L., 113–14, 146
Behncke, Paul, 172
Bell, Edward, 128
von Bernstorff, Johann, 18–19, 55,
    128
Bielaski, A. Bruce, 29–30, 47–48, 50
Black Reichswehr, 167–68, 173
Black Tom, New Jersey, munitions site
    at, 32, *p4–5*; Jahnke at, 33–36, 80;
    Witzke at, 33–36, 80
Blanford, E. M., 30
Bode, Eno, 24
Boer War, 100
Bolsheviks, 63
Bonaparte, Charles J., 44
Bopp, Franz, 46; Jahnke and, 15, 25–
    26; as U.S. consular officer, 18–19,
    25; Witzke and, 12–13, 25–26
"Borden, Kort." *See* Jahnke, Kurt
Border Vidette, 111, 184–85
Bowman, Wirt G., 114–15
Boxer Rebellion, 2; Pagels and, 3;
    Schindlich and, 3
Boy-Ed, Karl, 19, 25, 48
von Brincken, Wilhelm, 13, 25
HMS *Bristol* (British cruiser), 5
Brown, T. H., 141
Bru, Joe, 77–78
Bucarelli Conference of 1923, 185
Burgwin, A.J., 141–56
Burns, William J., 181–82
Butcher, Byron, 56, 77, 83, 162, 182,
    p9, p12; at American Club, 116;
    German code ciphers and, 118; as
    journalist, 57; in Mexico, 57–58,
    110, 112–23; Obregón and, 183–85;
    retirement of, 187; Witzke court-
    martial and, 146–47; at Yaqui
    Distributing Company, 185–86

Cabell, DeRosey C., 164
Calles, Plutarco Elías, 50, 76, 79, 104–
    5, 180, *p11*
Campbell, Robert Madison, 47, 49,
    72–74, 146
Camp Logan, 71; racial violence at,
    68–69
Camp Steven Little, 117–18; Witzke at,
    120–21
Canaris, Wilhelm, 10; alternate
    identities for, 11; execution of, 11
capitalism, Industrial Workers of the
    World response to, 64–66
SS *Carlton* (U.S. warship), 21
HMS *Carnarvon* (British cruiser), 5
Carranza, Venustiano, 45, 56–57, 79,
    102, 127; Altendorf, P. B., and,
    58–59
Carroll, J. H., 29
Casement, Roger, 62–63
Castenberg, Bertha, 74
Chapman, William Edgar, 94–101, *p10*
Chaucer, Geoffrey, 123
Chiang Kai-shek (Madame), 16
China: Boxer Rebellion in, 2; Witzke
    in, 173
Churchill, Winston, 6
citizenship, U.S., for Witzke, 36
code-breaking operations: Butcher
    and, 118; by France, 126; frequency
    tables, 132; against Germany,
    126–27; by Great Britain, 126–27;
    during Great War, 126; Manley
    and, 129–30, 132–36; MI-8 and,
    129–31, 148; Rickert and, 130,
    132–36, *p13*; transposition ciphers,
    131; by U.S., 129; for Witzke coded
    messages, 130–40, *133, 135–36, 138*;
    Zimmerman Telegram and, 127
colonialism, by Great Britain, 62–63

Colton, William, 109

Conway Castle (British sailing ship), 9

Coolidge, Calvin, 172

Coppedge, Sam, 66–67

Cosgrove, Silvester, 182

court-martial, of Witzke: Altendorf, P. B., and, 141–44; Barnes, R. L., and, 148; Beatty and, 113–14, 146; Burgwin and, 141–56; Butcher and, 146–47; Campbell, R. M., and, 146; closing arguments in, 155; death penalty sentence after, 156; Glasgow and, 141–45, 156; Gleaves and, 144–45; Lawton and, 147; Lipscomb and, 147–48; mandatory punishments and, 141; Manley and, 148–49; *A Manual for Courts-Martial,* 141–42, 156; Wilson and, 164; Witzke on witness stand, 149–55

Crane, Arthur, 39

SS *Cressington Court* (U.S. warship), 21

Crowley, Charles, 25

cryptoanalysis: frequency tables, 132; Manley and, 129–30, 132–36; Rickert and, 130, 132–36, *p13*; transposition ciphers, 131; Yardley and, 128–31. *See also* code-breaking operations

Cummings, William, 119

Curtis, Van, 121

Curtze, Walter, 2

Customs Service, U.S., 16

Daly, Julia, 39

Damstedt, Nils, 39, 42

Daniels, Rufus, 68

SS *Devon City* (U.S. warship), 21

Dilger, Anton, 46–47, 165–66

Dodge, Phelps, 65

Dresden (German capital ship), 4–6, 8, 173, *p1*; attacks against, 10–11; as coal source, 9; Witzke escape from, 11–12

East Asia Squadron. *See* Kreuzergeschwader Ostasien

von Eckhardt, Heinrich, 45, 79, 128, 138–39, 166; Altendorf, P. B., and, 51

Eduardo (tugboat), 6

Edwards, Alonzo, 68

Edwards, Mena, 32

Elfriede (fishing boat), 1–3, 6–9

Elías, Francisco, 56

Emden (German cruiser), 2

Epstein, Hyman, 182

Espionage Act of 1917, U.S., 44, 158

Europe: during Great War, 17; munitions production during Great War, 17. *See also specific nations; specific topics*

Fabyan, George, 129

SS *Fairhaven* (U.S. warship), 96–97

Falkland Islands battle, 12

Fay, Robert, 23

Fischer, E., 18

Fletcher, Henry, 45

Fort Sam Houston, 118, 121–22; military prison at, 157–64

France: code-breaking bureau in, 126; during Great War, 126

George, Harry, 39

German armed and naval forces: Abteilung II army, 173; Abteilung III B army, 34, 47, *p8*; *Amasis,* 3; *Dresden,* 4–6, 8–12, 173, *p1*; *Emden,* 2; *Gneisenau,* 4–5; *Gotha,* 9–10; *Herzogin Cecilie,* 11; Kaiserliche Marine, 1–2; Kreuzergeschwader Ostasien, 2–3, 9; SMS *Magdeburg,* 126; *Nürnberg,* 4; *Scharnhorst,* 5

German intelligence agents: Indian nationalists and, 61; insurrection of African Americans instigated by,

61, 63–64; in Mexico, 61–80, 101–2, 110–11; "100% American Club" and, 111–12, 114–15; smuggling of arms and ammunition by, 61–62. *See also* code-breaking operations; Jahnke, Kurt; Witzke, Lothar; *specific topics*

Germany: Black Reichswehr and, 167–68; code-breaking operations against, 126–27; instigation of racial conflict in U.S. by, 54; loss of life during Great War, 127; Mazatlán, Mexico, and, 94; Mexican invasion of U.S. and, 61, 98; Trading with the Enemy Act and, 94; U.S. declaration of war against, 43. *See also* German armed and naval forces; Nazi Germany; Weimar Germany

Glasgow, W. J., 141–45, 156

HMS *Glasgow* (British cruiser), 5, 8, 10

Gleaves, William "Guillermo," 82, 187, *p10*; arrest of, 102; early years for, 119; in Mexico, 69–72, 107–10, 118–23; Paglasch and, 70; resignation from British naval intelligence, 175; Witzke and, 71–72, 86–87, 155; at Witzke court-martial, 144–45

Gneisenau (German cruiser), 4–5; sinking of, 5

Gobel, Karl, 53–54, 72–73, 79

Gotha (German collier ship), 9–10

Göttingen (German steamer ship), 11

Great American Steamship Company, 27–29, 31

Great Britain: Afghanistan and, 62; code-breaking operations during, 126–27; Great War and, 125–26; India and, 62; Muslim uprising against, 62; rejection of colonialism by, 62–63

Great Britain armed and naval forces: HMS *Bristol,* 5; HMS *Carnarvon,* 5; HMS *Glasgow,* 5, 8, 10; *Inflexible,* 3; *Invincible,* 3; HMS *Kent,* 5, 7, 10; SS *Kirkoswald,* 21–23; *Orama,* 10. *See also* code-breaking operations

Great War (World War I): American Defense Society, 44; American Protective League and, 44; armistice for, 158; beginning of, 17; Espionage Act of 1917 (U.S.) and, 44; France during, 126; German loss of life during, 127; Great Britain during, 125–26; munitions production in Europe, 17; munitions sabotage during, 19–20; "100% American Club" during, 111–12, 114–15; Sabotage Act (U.S.) and, 44; Trading with the Enemy Act during, 94; U.S. draft regulations for, 111; U.S. entry into, 43; U.S. Steel Corporation during, 17; Wilson and, 158. *See also specific topics*

Greece, Witzke in, 173

Gregory, Thomas W., 65, 164

Grey, Nigel de, 127

Guerrera (Mexican gunboat), 90

Haley, William, 183

Hall, William Reginald, 119, 128

Haslam, George, 158, 160

Haywood, Bill, 66

Held, Martha, 32

Helle, Carl zur, 2

Hermann, Fred, 163

Herzogin Cecilie (German training ship), 11

Hess, Rudolph, 168–69

Heydrich, Reinhard, 169–70

Hickstein, Otto, 40

Hideki Tojo, 170

Himmler, Heinrich, 169–70, 186

Hinsch, Frederick, 34, 47, 165; in Mexico, 43

Hitler, Adolf, 11; Nazi Germany and,
    169–71; in Weimar Germany, 168
Hornbrook, James J., 141
Hourwich, Isaac, 181–82
Howick, Tom, 30

von Igel, Wolf, 23
incendiary cigars, explosions from:
    damage costs from, 21; manufacture
    of, 21; Scheele and, 20–21, *p7–8*; in
    U.S., 21–23
India: nationalism in, 61; revolt against
    British rule in, 62
Industrial Workers of the World
    (IWW) ("Wobblies"), 54, 64–65;
    German financing of, 66
inequality, economic, in U.S., 63–65
Inflexible (British cruiser), 3
Invincible (British cruiser), 3
Ireland, British colonialism in, 62–63
Iron Cross (military award), for
    Pagels, 9
Isendahl, Walter, 25
"Iturbe, José," as alias. *See* Jahnke,
    Kurt
IWW. *See* Industrial Workers of the
    World

Jacobsen, Carl, 96–97, 175
Jahnke, Kurt, *p2*; as adviser to Nazi
    leadership, 169–71; Altendorf, P. B.,
    and, 51–56; alternate identities for,
    26, 37, 46, 102; Black Reichswehr
    and, 167–68, 173; Bopp and, 15,
    25–26; emigration to U.S., 15–16;
    explosion at Black Tom munitions
    site and, 33–36, 80; explosions
    arranged by, 26; Gleaves and,
    69–72; informants and, 41–42;
    Landau and, 27; Lawton and,
    112–13; on Mare Island, 40; in
    Mexico, 45–46, 79, 81–91, 93–105,
    107–23; as naturalized U.S. citizen,

15; in Nogales, Arizona, 107–23;
    in Nogales, Mexico, 107–23; in
    prison, 171; return to Mexico, 167;
    smuggling activities of, 36; in U.S.
    Customs Service, 16; in U.S. Marine
    Corps, 15–16; Waberski cipher and,
    p13; in Weimar Germany, 167–73;
    Witzke and, 16, 71–72
James, Jesse, 57
Japan, attack on Pearl Harbor, 170
Jebsen, Frederick, 62
Jim Crow segregation, 69
Johnson 17 (U.S. warship), 33–34, 36,
    p4; damage costs for, 35; explosion
    of, 35
Johnson Lighterage, executive arrests
    at, 36
Josefina (steamer ship), 88–90, 93

Kahn, David, 98
Kaiser Friedrich der Gross (German
    passenger liner), 20–21, 24
Kaiserliche Marine, Pagels in, 1–2
HMS *Kent* (British cruiser), 5, 7, 10
SS *Kirkoswald* (British warship), 21–23
von Kleist, Charles, 23–24
Koenig, Paul, 19, 33; arrest of, 25
Kreger, E. A., 171–72
Kreuzergeschwader Ostasien (East
    Asia Squadron), 2–3; warships of, 9
Kristoff, Michael, 34–36

labor strikes, racial violence as result
    of, 66–67
labor unions: African American
    migration and, 66–68; civil unrest
    by, 64–66; Industrial Workers of the
    World, 64–66; racial violence by,
    66–68; in U.S., 64–66
Landau, Henry, 27
Lawton, Ezra, 110–11; Jahnke and,
    112–13; Witzke court-martial and,
    147

Lehigh Railroad, executive arrests at, 36
Lenin, Vladimir, 63
Lindenfeld, Wolfe, 181–82
Lipscomb, Joel A., 117–18, 120–21; Witzke court-martial and, 147–48
Listas Negras, 95
Loving, Walter H., 69
Lowden, Frank, 67
Luce, John, 10
Lüdecke (Fregattenkapitän), 6, 8–10
Ludendorff, Erich, 63
lynching, of African Americans, 69

MacKenzie, Allen, 38, 41
MacKenzie, Dorothy, 38
MacKenzie, Mildred, 38
Macomb, Augustus C., 141, 156
SMS *Magdeburg* (German cruiser), 126
Manley, John Matthews, 139–40, *p13*; code-breaking by, 129–30, 132–36; Witzke court-martial and, 148–49
A Manual for Courts-Martial, 141–42, 156
Mare Island Naval Station, 37, *p6*; explosions at, 26–27, 38–39, 100; Jahnke at, 40; post-explosion investigation at, 39; Witzke at, 40–41
Marines Corps, U.S., Jahnke in, 15–16
Marseille, France, as port city, 22–23
Martin, W. D., 30
Martin, William A., 28–30
Mason, Alfred, 119
Mason, Alfred Edward Woodley, 119
Maverick (oil tanker), 62
Mazatlán, Mexico, 93, 96; German influences in, 94; *Listas Negras* in, 95; Melchers Sucesores in, 94–95, 98, *p10*; during Mexican Revolution, 94; U.S. consul in, 95
McIntyre, John R., 111

McKenna, George, 38
McKenna, James, 38
McKinney, William, 68
McMillian, W.G., 40
Melchers Sucesores, 94–95, 98, *p10*
Mexican Revolution, 94, 183–84
Mexico: Altendorf, P. B., in, 74–76, 79, 81–91, 93–105; Butcher in, 57–58, 110, 112–13; campaign against Yaqui Indians, 50, 120, 151, 180; cross-border invasion into U.S., 61, 98; German intelligence agents in, 61–80, 101–2, 110–11; German spies relocating to, 44–45; Gleaves in, 69–72; Hinsch in, 43; Jahnke in, 45–46, 79, 81–91, 93–105, 167; Nogales, *p11–12*; NOVIA plot in, 100–101; Revolutionary Association in, 71, 144, 145; Witzke in, 55, 79, 81–91, 93–105. *See also* Mazatlán; Nogales, Sonora
Military Intelligence Section 8 (MI-8), 129–31, 148
military training, for Witzke, 11. *See also* German armed and naval forces
Miller, Charles F., 157
SS *Minnehaha* (U.S. warship), 21
SS *Minnesota* (U.S. warship), 26, 30–32, 80, *p3*; damage to, 28–29; Great American Steamship Company and, 27–29, 31
Montgomery, William, 127
Morelos (Mexican gunboat), 175
Morse, Henry Nicholson "Harry," 16
Müller, Heinrich, 171
munitions production, during Great War: incendiary cigars by, 20–21; Mare Island Naval Station explosions, 26–27; sabotage of, 19–20, 24, 26–27; in U.S., 24

National Storage Warehouse Company, executive arrests at, 36

Nazi Germany, Jahnke as adviser in, 169–71
Negro League for Afro-American Suffrage, 67
Neunhoffer, William, 47, 148; Altendorf, P. B., and, 49–50; as U.S. investigator, 50
von Niedermayer, Oskar, 62
Nogales, Arizona (U.S.), *p11–12*; Ambos Nogales and, 107; *Border Vidette,* 111, 184–85; Jahnke in, 107–23; "100% American Club," 111–12, 114–15; Witzke in, 107–23
Nogales, Sonora (Mexico), *p11–12*; Altendorf, P. B., in, 110–23; Ambos Nogales and, 107; at American Club, 116; Butcher in, 110, 112–23; German intelligence agents in, 110–11; Gleaves in, 107–10, 118–23; Jahnke in, 107–23; Witzke in, 107–23
NOVIA plot, 100–101
Nuenhoffer, William, 176
Nürnberg (German cruiser), 4

Obregón, Álvaro, 56–57; assassination of, 186; Butcher and, 183–85; election to presidency, 185
O'Brien, Henry O., 161
"100% American Club," 111–12, 114–15
Orama (British warship), 10
Orange Bank, 7
SS *Orton* (U.S. warship), 21
Osborne, Jim, 38
Osborne, Roberta (nee MacKenzie), 38

Pagels, Albert, 5, *p1*; *Amasis* and, 4; Boxer Rebellion and, 3; capture of, 8; on *Elfriede,* 1–3, 6–9; in Kaiserliche Marine, 1–2; military awards for, 9; occupations of, 2; Schindlich and, 3; on *Sierra Cordoba,* 9

Paglasch, Otto, 46, 48; Altendorf, P. B., and, 50–51; Gleaves and, 70; on Schwierz, 51
Painvin, Georges, 126
von Papen, Franz, 19, 23–24, 48, 177; Scheele and, 20; Tauscher and, 61
Paschal, Harold A., 112
Pearl Harbor, Japanese attack on, 170
Perez, John, 176
von Pfeffer, Franz, 168
Phillips, Erwin J., 141
von Plessen, Hans George Hermann, 172
Pyett, Lon, 111

race riots: in Chester, Pennsylvania, 67–68; in East St. Louis, 66–67. *See also* African Americans
racial violence: against African Americans, 66–69; at Camp Logan, 68–69; by labor unions, 66–68; lynching of African Americans, 69; Negro League for Afro-American Suffrage, 67; in U.S. Army, 68–69; in U.S. media, *p9*
Rademacher, Otto, 101
Rathbun, Donald, 30–31
Reuter, Ludwig Heinrich, 176–77, 179; arrest of, 178
Revolutionary Association, 71, 144–45
Rickert, Edith, 130, 132–36, 139–40, *p13*
Rieloff, Friedrich, 69–70
von Rintelen, Franz, 19
Rodynko, Saint Pierre Fremonte, 179
Roosevelt, Theodore, 44
"Rosa, Reed." *See* Canaris, Wilhelm
Russia: Bolsheviks in, 63; social revolution in, 63
Ryan, James A., 141, 156

Sabotage Act, U.S., 44
Sailors' Union, 27

Sanchez, Theodora, 46
von Schack, E. H., 13, 25
Schaeffer, Heinrich, 7, 9
Scharnhorst (German cruiser), 5
Scheele, Walter T.: incendiary cigars
    by, 20–21, *p7–8*; von Papen and, 20
Schellenberg, Walter, 169–70
Schindlich, Karl: *Amasis* and, 4; Boxer
    Rebellion and, 3; Pagels and, 3
Schwierz, Richard Walter, 50, 79,
    101; arrest of, 48; Paglasch on, 51;
    training camp run by, 48
Scott, Barton, 35
Second World War (World War II),
    173, 186. *See also* Nazi Germany
Shakespeare, William, 123
Sholars, Oskar, 109
Siegel, Adam, 101, 163
Sierra Cordoba (German passenger
    ship), 7; as coal source, 8; Pagels
    on, 9
Skottsberg, Carl, 2
Smart, Harry, 114
Smith, Lewis J., 24–25
South America: Altendorf, P. B., in, 74;
    Witzke in, 12
Soviet Union, Weimar Germany
    cooperation with, 168
Spanish-American War, 95
Sparks, Lee, 68
Spence, E. V., 178
von Spree, Maximilian Graf,
    Kreuzergeschwader Ostasien under,
    2–3
spying, death penalty punishment for,
    141–42
Stalin, Josef, 169
Stanton, George, 38
Stephens, Roy, 157
Stevens, David, 130
St. John, Vincent, 64–65
Stoll, Adolfo, 87; Witzke and, 88–89
Stresemann, Gustave, 167–68

Stretton, F. P., 161
Stubenrauch, Rudolph, 2, 5; Pagels
    and, 3; Schaeffer, 7
Sturdee, Frederick, 4–5
Sun Yat-sen, 16

Tauscher, Hans, 61
Thwaites, Norman, 162–63
Tinto (German sailing ship), 11
Toral, León, 186
Tossen, Arthur, 83
SS *Touraine* (U.S. warship), 21
Trading with the Enemy Act, U.S., 94
Travers, Sara, 68
Treaty of Versailles, 167, 173
Tucuman (steamer), 6
Tunney, Thomas J., 22–23, 25, 161–
    62, *p7*
Turkey, 62

Unger, Friedrich, 94–101
United States (U.S.): American Defense
    Society, 44; American Protective
    League, 44; as "Colossus of the
    North," 45; Customs Service, 16;
    declaration of war against Germany,
    43; "destructive agents" in, 19; draft
    regulations for Great War, 111;
    economic inequality in, 63–65; entry
    into Great War, 43; Espionage Act
    of 1917, 44, 158; German agents in,
    43–44; German-Mexican invasion
    of, 61, 98; historical racial tensions
    in, 63–64; incendiary explosions
    in, 21–23; Jahnke emigration to,
    15–16; Japanese attack on Pearl
    Harbor, 170; labor unions in, 64–66;
    Marines Corps, 15–16; monitoring
    of German consular officials, 25;
    Sabotage Act, 44; Spanish-American
    War, 95; Trading with the Enemy
    Act, 94. *See also* African Americans;
    specific topics

U.S. armed and naval forces: SS *Bankdale*, 21; SS *Carlton*, 21; SS *Cressington Court*, 21; SS *Devon City*, 21; SS *Fairhaven*, 96–97; Japanese attack on Pearl Harbor, 170; *Johnson 17*, 33–36; Marines Corps, 15–16; SS *Minnehaha*, 21; SS *Minnesota*, 26–32, 80, *p3*; SS *Orton*, 21; SS *Touraine*, 21. *See also* code-breaking operations; Mare Island Naval Station

U.S. Army: Altendorf, P. B., as agent of, 78–79; Camp Logan, 68–69, 71; Camp Steven Little, 117–18, 120; Fort Sam Houston, 118, 121–22; racial violence in, 68–69

U.S. Steel Corporation, 17

Van Deman, Ralph, 69, 128–29, 139

Velvet and Vinegar (Thwaites), 162–63

Villa, Pancho, 45, 102

Volkmar, Walter, 42

"Waberski, Pablo," as alias. *See* Jahnke, Kurt

Waberski cipher, *p13*

Wasmuss, Wilhelm, 126

Watson, Theodore E. S., 99

Weimar Germany: Black Reichswehr in, 167–68, 173; Hess in, 168–69; Jahnke in, 167–73; rise of Hitler in, 168; Soviet Union cooperation with, 168

Wheeler, Harry C., 65

Wiedfeldt, Otto, 172

Wild, Gustave, 41

Wilde, Henry, 172

Wiley, C. W., 29

Wilhelm, Eugene, 46, 166

Wilson, Woodrow, 43; Espionage Act of 1917 and, 44, 158; Great War and, 158; Witzke court-martial and, 164

Witzke, Lothar, *p2, p10–12, p14*; arrest of, 114, 116–17; Bopp and, 12–13, 25–26; at Camp Steven Little, 120–21; capture of, 82; in China, 173; coded messages of, 130–40, *133, 135–36, 138*; court-martial of, 141–56; death penalty for, 156; on *Dresden*, 11–12; explosion at Black Tom munitions site and, 33–36, 80; in Falkland Islands battle, 12; at Fort Sam Houston, 121–22; Gleaves and, 71–72, 86–87, 155; in Greece, 173; imprisonment of, 174; interrogation of, 174; Jahnke and, 16, 71–72; jailbreak of, 157–64; Landau and, 27; Lipscomb and, 120; at Mare Island, 40–41; in Mexico, 55, 79, 81–91, 93–105; military training for, 11; on SS *Minnesota*, 27–28; in Nogales, Mexico, 107–23; registering for U.S. draft, 37; search for, 165–66; in South America, 12; Stoll and, 88–89; U.S. citizenship for, 36; in U.S. custody, 114; as U.S. enemy operative, 123–24

"Wobblies." *See* Industrial Workers of the World

Wodley, Frank, 67

Wolpert, Otto, 24

Woodruff, R. B., 161

Woods, Arthur, 22

World War I. *See* Great War

World War II. *See* Second World War

Yaqui Indians, Mexican campaign against, 50, 120, 151, 180

Yardley, Herbert O., 128–31

Yorck (German passenger liner), 10

Zimmerman, Arthur, 45, 127

Zimmerman Telegram, 127